Praise f
BOTTOM OF T.

"This season brings a bumper crop of b
the best of which concerns a team an
Michael Shapiro's *Bottom of the Ninth* . . . is one of the best tales of what
might have been, how baseball might have harnessed the power of television and how the sport might have staved off the rise of football."

—*Bloomberg News*

"Elegant and exhaustively researched . . . It's a testament to Shapiro's sharp
eye for detail that he keeps the story zipping along. . . . He captures the
sense of loss—not only for Rickey and Stengel, but for baseball and its fans."

—*The New York Times Book Review*

"Shapiro . . . is a terrific writer. His accounts of Branch Rickey's struggle
and eventual failure to create a third major league, the Continental, as well
as the last Yankee season of baseball's most successful manager, Casey Stengel (whose team lost the 1960 Series on Bill Mazeroski's home run in the
seventh game), makes for compelling reading."   —*San Francisco Chronicle*

"A compelling and thoroughly enjoyable trip back in time to a turning
point that never turned."   —*The Washington Times*

"[Shapiro] has once again hit it out of the literary park. . . . This retelling of
a little-known chapter in baseball history is exemplary sports reporting."

—*Tucson Citizen*

"Sharply researched . . . Exactly how the Continental League gathered
strength and then faltered, and exactly how its impact is felt today, are trea-
sures to be unearthed in [*Bottom of the Ninth*]."   —*Sports Illustrated*

"[An] engaging look at a significant, though often forgotten, chapter in the
game's history."   —*The Boston Globe*

"Shapiro is a marvelous storyteller with a keen ear and eye for the cadence
of the game."   —*Choice*

"If you like an untold story, and who of us does not, and if you are even a
little bit of a sports junky then *Bottom of the Ninth* belongs on your reading
list. . . . Shapiro, author of *The Last Good Season*, is in top form breaking
new ground and providing new awarenesses of a little reported on chapter
in American sports history. . . . A good read."

—*Harvey Frommer, author of* New York City Baseball, 1947–1957

BOTTOM OF THE NINTH

BOTTOM OF THE
NINTH

Branch Rickey, Casey Stengel,
and the Daring Scheme to
Save Baseball from Itself

MICHAEL SHAPIRO

A HOLT PAPERBACK

TIMES BOOKS   HENRY HOLT AND COMPANY   NEW YORK

For, *who else?*

Susan, Eliza, and Jake

Holt Paperbacks
Henry Holt and Company, LLC
Publishers since 1866
175 Fifth Avenue
New York, New York 10010
www.henryholt.com

A Holt Paperback® and ® are registered trademarks of
Henry Holt and Company, LLC.

Library of Congress Cataloging-in-Publication Data
Shapiro, Michael.
Bottom of the ninth : Branch Rickey, Casey Stengel, and the daring scheme to
save baseball from itself / Michael Shapiro.
        p.   cm.
Includes bibliographical references and index.
ISBN-13: 978-0-8050-9236-3
1. Baseball—United States—History—20th century.   2. Rickey, Branch,
1881–1965.   3. Stengel, Casey.   I. Title.
GV863.A1S53 2009
796.3570973—dc22   2008043582

Henry Holt books are available for special promotions and
premiums. For details contact: Director, Special Markets.

Originally published in hardcover in 2009 by Times Books

First Holt Paperbacks Edition 2010

Designed by Kelly Too

Printed in the United States of America
1 3 5 7 9 10 8 6 4 2

▪ CONTENTS ▪

BOTTOM OF THE NINTH

OCTOBER 13, 1960

Later, when people spoke about the game and how it was won and what it had been like to be in the ballpark that afternoon, they spoke of the silence that came just before the end. Odd, given how things had unfolded.

The New York Yankees had tied the game at nine in the top of the ninth, which came after the Pittsburgh Pirates had gone ahead with five runs in the bottom of the eighth, which came after the Yankees had extended their lead to 7–4 with two runs in the top of the inning, which came after they had gone ahead 5–4 on Yogi Berra's home run in the sixth, which came after Pittsburgh had gone up 4–0 in the second. Now, in the bottom of the ninth inning of the seventh game of the 1960 World Series, Ralph Terry returned to the mound. He was the fifth Yankees pitcher of the day. He had spent the afternoon in the bullpen warming up, sitting down, warming up again, waiting to see what use, if any, his manager, Casey Stengel, might make of him. He had entered the game with two out in the eighth to face the Pirates' third baseman, Don Hoak, his arm a little weary from so much throwing and with the sinking discovery that the bullpen mound to which he had grown accustomed was several inches lower than the mound in the center of the diamond at Forbes Field. Terry took his warm-ups and could not seem to get the ball down in the strike zone. He managed to retire Hoak on a fly ball to left. But now, as he waited for the Pittsburgh second baseman, Bill Mazeroski, to lead off the home ninth, his fastball remained perilously high. He started Mazeroski with a ball, too high. His catcher, Johnny Blanchard, ran out to the mound to tell him to get his pitches down. Terry went into his windup and the great park fell curiously silent, as if, at once, everyone was too drained and too anxious to cheer.

What happened next would be recalled and celebrated in the years to come as arguably the most dramatic moment in the history of the World Series, if not of the game itself. Bottom of the ninth, World Series tied, game tied, a child's dream carried across a nation that now boasted fifty-two million homes with television sets—eighty-five homes out of every hundred. At 3:43 in the afternoon on October 13, 1960, baseball achieved a moment too sublime to invent, an event that, given all the many people who witnessed it—in black and white and in *color*—might well have sealed baseball's standing as the nation's game. *Were you watching? Did you see . . . ?*

But that did not happen. Instead, the remarkable conclusion of the 1960 World Series marked the end of almost one hundred years when baseball stood atop all sports. Other games soon began passing baseball by. When the Gallup Organization asked Americans in 1960 to name their favorite spectator sport, 34 percent chose baseball, 21 percent football, and 10 percent basketball. Twelve years later, the numbers had all but reversed: 32 percent chose football, 21 percent baseball. For the next thirty years, baseball would continue to decline in popularity, so much so that by 2007, football was the choice of 43 percent of those Gallup surveyed, with baseball slipping to third place at 11 percent, a point below basketball. The conventional wisdom had it that baseball's decline in the public's heart and imagination was inevitable, the price to be paid by an old game in a nation that wanted only what was new. But that was not the case.

In 1960, baseball had the chance to transform itself from a tired remnant of a bygone age and become a sport that reflected the desires and needs of a nation that was not looking to the past with longing. The game was in a position to use the growing power, influence, and wealth of television for its own common purpose. America's booming cities were clamoring for teams of their own. Baseball had a vision for the future and a plan to make it happen. The blueprint was devised by perhaps the most respected—and in some circles, revered—figure in the game, Branch Rickey. It had a name, the Continental League.

Rickey had witnessed the changes to the game and saw in them possibilities and peril. The baseball map was being redrawn, dramatically. Fading teams in Boston, St. Louis, and Philadelphia—two-team towns that could barely support a single franchise—had moved. The relocated teams drew fans in numbers they had seldom if ever seen. The most successful of these teams was the Milwaukee Braves, who had abandoned Boston in 1953 to become winners on the field and the highest-drawing team in the game. The Braves' reversal of fortune was noted, with envy, by the owner of the Brooklyn Dodgers, Walter O'Malley. Despite owning the majors' most profitable team, O'Malley did not believe he could maintain his success if he remained in his tiny, aging ballpark, Ebbets Field. He, too, would move, heading west in 1957 with his crosstown rival, Horace Stoneham, the owner of the New York Giants. The city of New York, which had assumed it would always have three baseball teams, was suddenly reduced to one. The mayor, belatedly alarmed, sent an emissary in search of a replacement team; this man quickly learned that, despite the declining fortunes of so many National League franchises and despite the fact that the city was willing to build a modern ballpark for its new team, no club wanted to come to New York. Desperate, the emissary turned to Branch Rickey and soon fell under his spell.

For years, baseball had been talking vaguely of adding new franchises, but the only people who took this seriously were the representatives of cities that could not seem to lure an existing team. This was just as well, Rickey explained; adding a team or two would accomplish no more than saddling each league with losers that no one would pay to see. The answer, he believed, lay in a far more radical approach: a new league. Eight teams in seven cities that had never had ball clubs of their own and in New York—because New York, with its many people, newspapers, magazines, and television networks, was the key. The Continental League would be a third major league, not a rival circuit; Rickey had lived through two baseball wars and wanted no part of a third. The new league's teams would not play the established major leaguers, not yet. They would play one another for four years or maybe five, until they were ready, until they had developed their own players, their own stars. Rickey learned long ago from his idol, Ban Johnson, the founder of the American League, that competition was relative: it did not necessarily matter who a team played as long as the contest was fair and the outcome uncertain. People would pay to see their team play if they believed it had a chance of winning. To ensure this parity, Rickey took his bold proposal a step further and insisted that the teams of the Continental League pool the money the television networks would pay to carry their games, so that no team could dominate at the expense of the others. Rickey, the mighty cold warrior, was advocating a plan that he himself might once have dismissed as socialism.

If the approach sounds familiar, that is because it was soon adopted and, in time, proved to be a great success. But it was not baseball that followed Branch Rickey's blueprint. It was football.

As professional football in the 1960s and 1970s became ever more an enterprise whose priority was the collective needs of the league (rather than the individual needs of its dominant teams), baseball fought off every attempt to recast itself for a different time in a changing country. Baseball, of course, did expand in the fall of 1960, not happily, not willingly, not without threat of congressional action, and not well. Instead, the major-league owners battled Rickey and the men who represented the cities that had joined the Continental League. They battled Congress when critics of the sport introduced legislation limiting baseball's historic exemption from antitrust laws. They enlisted their allies on Capitol Hill and their important friends in the press to help ensure that the old order endured, even as evidence mounted that the old ways no longer worked and that change—in particular the change that Branch Rickey was advocating—might well be good for everyone. Good for everyone, that is, except for the Yankees and, with the riches that awaited them in Southern California, the Dodgers.

If there is a metaphor for the story of baseball in the final years of its dominance it is the New York Yankees. No team, before or since, has held sway over a sport as did the Yankees. It was as if their success provided the game with its rhythm—predictable, relentless, and in the view of everyone but their fans, rather dull. The Yankees won with such numbing frequency that by the late 1950s, thousands of seats for World Series games at Yankee Stadium would go wanting. Watching the Yankees win another championship was like a New Yorker's visit to the Statue of Liberty: a trip always put off because it could always be made. But the Yankees were more than the game's inevitable champions; they were, especially in the American League, essential to everyone else's financial stability. Teams that barely drew a thousand fans to their home games could rely on a three-day sold-out visit by the Yankees to avoid having to sell players to meet the payroll. So it was that the Yankees were able to impose themselves and their needs upon the game.

The face of that team was not a player, even though the Yankees did feature the most popular player in the game, its first great television star—Mickey Mantle. No, the Yankees were Casey Stengel's team. He had come to New York in 1949, a baseball lifer with little to show for his prior nine years as a major-league manager—eight losing seasons, two dismissals, and a reputation as something of a clown. But with the Yankees, Stengel became a baseball genius. His Yankees were pennant winners every year but two, and world champions in each of his first five seasons. But Stengel, like the game, like the dominance of his team, was growing old. He was not, however, inclined to change; he did not believe it necessary.

Casey Stengel, the face of baseball: familiar, lined, and sagging.

Casey Stengel and Branch Rickey had never been part of the same team, remarkably, given all their years as baseball men. Rickey was nine years older, and he arrived first, beginning a brief and unexceptional playing career as a catcher with the 1904 St. Louis Browns. Casey Stengel followed in 1913, his first full season with Brooklyn. That was the year Rickey moved to the front office, running the Browns, his true calling.

They crossed paths only once, in New York, as adversaries in 1949 when Rickey's Dodgers fell to the Yankees in the first of Stengel's seven world championships. The Yankees were back in the World Series the following year but Brooklyn was not, and by the time the Dodgers won their next pennant, Rickey was running the Pittsburgh Pirates, for whom Stengel had played thirty years before.

They were not friends, nor, it seems, did Rickey ever consider signing Stengel as a player or hiring him as a manager. In truth, they would have made a dreadful pair. Each was too big, too much himself, too insistent upon being the man at the center of things. Each considered himself smarter and more daring than the men around him, and in many ways this was true, if hard to swallow. The game has never known another executive whose intelligence and cunning were matched by his soaring dreams for what the game could and should be, if people were prudent enough to follow his counsel. Nor was there ever a manager who so skillfully and successfully manipulated his players while at the same time crafting himself into a legend, a genius in the guise of a wizened, outsized imp. No telling of the story of baseball is complete without the stories of Branch Rickey and Casey Stengel. This, however, is about the end of their stories, about the end of the long era when each man, in his way, dominated the game.

This tale of the turning point in baseball's place in America takes place both on the field and off. It begins in the fall of 1958 and ends two years later, in the fall of 1960, autumn not winter, not just yet. Autumn was to have been the season for redemption, or so the two old men hoped. For Stengel, it was to have been the time to show that he stood alone among managers, that he was so bold, and understood the game so deeply that he could master it. For Rickey it was more, but then Rickey was always the one who could see beyond himself and his own considerable self-regard.

They both came close. And when the end came, it came suddenly: for Stengel, in the bottom of the ninth inning of the seventh game of the 1960 World Series; for Rickey, just weeks earlier, surrounded by seemingly adoring men at a Chicago hotel. Just like that, they were advised that their services, though much appreciated, would no longer be required.

If the game suffered from Stengel's absence at Yankee Stadium, it did not suffer nearly so deeply as it did by the crushing of Rickey's dream of an equal chance for everyone on the field of play. Because to this day baseball still pays for its refusal to heed him. To have done so, however, would have required the sport to do what it has never been capable of doing, which is to see beyond the moment and beyond itself.

Baseball has always lived in the present, which is fitting for a game that measures time by the pitch and by the inning. When confronted with change or challenge, it has looked not to the future but to the past, and there has found the best and reassuring reflection of itself in the sepia images of the men and the teams that came before. Yet, even at those moments when it shows signs of flourishing, baseball manages, time and again, to act with self-destructive myopia. Confronted with evidence of a looming crisis, baseball behaves like a man with a toothache who believes that if he ignores the pain it will somehow go away. It has always been so—from the baseball wars of the nineteenth century, to the nearly ruinous throwing of the 1919 World Series, to the decades-long shame of the color line, to the resistance to expansion, to the collusion among owners against free agency, to the greed for television dollars, to the disastrous player strikes of 1972, 1981, and 1994, and, most recently, to the scandalous pervasiveness of performance-enhancing drugs. In each instance, baseball somehow believed that it could get away with things, that people might not notice—or even if they did, that they would not care. To a certain extent, this was so. Through it all, the game rumbles along, not because of the men who run it but because of the singular mystery and majesty of the game itself.

Casey Stengel loved the game so deeply that he allowed himself to believe that he and baseball would go on forever together and never grow old. Branch Rickey loved baseball with equal devotion but could not ignore the game's decline. Perhaps, he reasoned, others had seen it, too, and would welcome him back to be the agent of the great game's salvation.

CHAPTER ONE

FALL 1958

OCTOBER: Lamentations

Warren Spahn was shutting out the Yankees, and all Casey Stengel could do by the bottom of the eighth inning of Game Four of the World Series was march up and down his dugout barking, "Let's go. Let's go." He might just as well have saved himself the exertion. The Yankees were going quietly, as they had all afternoon—strikeout, pop to second, strikeout, the last by Norm Siebern, who had lost four fly balls in the sun in left field, making gifts of two of Milwaukee's three runs. Mickey Mantle's grounder to short an inning later brought the day to a close and the Braves to within a victory of repeating as world champions.

Nothing had gone right for Stengel all week, with the exception of Game Three at Yankee Stadium, his team's only victory, when all the cruel things that had happened in Games One and Two in Milwaukee seemed forgotten, and Stengel was back in chatty form. "Now let me ask ya why I shouldn't be glad," he said. He spoke as he studied himself in front of a mirror, adjusting his ten-gallon hat. "We win a game and I'm glad, which is what I'd rather be than nervous, which is what I was after they win the first two games."

He had not helped himself strategically, and his players knew it—and for once said so. Hank Bauer had opened Game One by singling against Spahn, and Stengel, never one to leave things solely to the discretion and talents of his men, promptly called for a hit-and-run. Spahn possessed one of the finest pickoff moves in the game and caught Bauer leaning. "When they gave me the sign I had to go," Bauer later said, "even though I didn't agree with the old man." The writers picked up where Bauer left off, questioning Stengel's decision in the eighth to pitch to a power hitter, Wes Covington, with a man on third and one out, rather than walking him and setting up a potential double play. Covington's fly ball scored Eddie Matthews, tying the game, which Milwaukee won in the tenth. Game Two was a 13–5 drubbing in which Stengel's primary function was to make six trips to the mound to change pitchers. "This could be a shambles," said the former Dodgers and Giants manager Leo Durocher, who stopped by the press box after the rout to offer his views. Durocher may have been between teams but was never shy about his opinions. "You can see the signs."

What do you see, Leo? someone asked.

"It's not just the two defeats," he replied. "The Yankees are playing lousy baseball."

A writer shared Durocher's diagnosis with Stengel, who snapped, "Hell, you're telling me? Ain't I been saying that for a month and a half?"

He'd been saying that, and more. He had berated his players publicly. After losing three out of four at Fenway Park in mid-August he first locked his men in their clubhouse for a heated forty-five-minute lecture and then docked them a rare off-day by holding a two-hour practice, even though they were in first place by eleven and a half games. He was seeing too many mistakes and insisted that his men needed drilling on the fundamentals rather than a day of rest after playing thirty games in twenty-eight days. His players rebelled, cautiously, grousing to the beat reporters but insisting that their names not appear: "He just wants to flaunt his authority" and "Is he going to give his brain a workout, too?" and "I never seen him get on guys as bad as he's been lately." Stengel did not much care. "If they don't like it they can read their contracts," he said. "I'm the manager and as long as I'm here they'll do what I tell them to do."

But Stengel had been unable to roust the Yankees from their torpor; they finished the season by going 17–18 in their last thirty-five games, and their rowdiness off the field had prompted management to hire private detectives to tail them. Even clinching the American League pennant came with a cloud: on the train back from Kansas City, Ralph Houk, a coach, and reliever Ryne Duren got into a nasty fistfight. The game had gone late and the players had already begun to celebrate by the time they arrived at the station. Duren, who could be a mean drunk, smashed Houk's unlit cigar into his mouth and ended up kicking another pitcher, Don Larsen, in the mouth when his teammates tried to get him into his berth. "You get whiskey drunk and then you fight with your own," snapped Stengel as he stormed into the car. Houk, ten years Duren's senior, was judged the winner, leaving Duren with a gash over his right eye.

Still, the oddsmakers favored the Yankees to win the World Series against the Braves, a choice that reflected the powerful tug of nostalgia rather than a cool assessment of the prospects: never mind that Milwaukee had dethroned the Yankees in the 1957 series; New York owned so many other Octobers. Then came the first two games, which brought a change of heart among the bookmakers. The Yankees returned to the Bronx from Milwaukee talking comeback, as they had done in 1956, when they dropped the first two games in Brooklyn, only to win in seven. But Stengel seemed oblivious to good omens and silver linings. A television crew approached as the Yankees took their warm-ups, and the reporter, apparently unschooled in the lexicon of the game, made the grievous mistake of asking Stengel to assess his players' mettle by invoking the word most damning to an athlete's soul.

"Is your team choking?" he asked.

"Do you choke on the fucking microphone?" said Stengel. He turned and scratched his behind for the camera.

Game Three's 4–0 Yankees victory brought a day's respite. But Spahn held the Yankees to two hits in Game Four, and afterward Jimmy Cannon of the *New York Post* wrote as if he were preparing the earth to receive the remains for the team he used to know: "They have lost what they once had alone and they won't be the Yankees until they get it back. It will take a long time because this team has to be torn apart and put together again."

Cannon had known and admired the Yankees of Charlie Keller, Tommy Henrich, Bill Dickey, and above all, Joe DiMaggio. "They were the greatest hitting teams in all the seasons of baseball," he wrote. And then he offered his grim conclusion. "This is the end of something all right. And you have the feeling it isn't temporary."

It was fitting that the first drafting of the Yankees' obituary should fall to Cannon; of all the men then writing sports columns in New York, he was the most romantic, especially about his town and the way it used to be. The world, he suggested none too subtly, had been a better place when it was defined by certain immutable truths: the best song ever recorded was Bing Crosby's rendition of "Stardust"; the best strawberry cake could be found at Sid Allen's; and the best baseball in the world was played in the Bronx.

Cannon had been a protégé of Damon Runyon, though the two parted on the question of drink—Runyon was a legendary boozer and Cannon saw the wisdom in not trying to keep up; he drank coffee to excess. Nor did Cannon subscribe to Runyon's ordering of the universe: greatest fighter, Jack Dempsey; greatest ballplayer, Christy Mathewson. He had found his own favorites—Joe Louis in the prize ring and, on the ball field, his pal DiMaggio. But now Louis had been bludgeoned into retirement by Rocky Marciano, and DiMaggio, divorced and lonely, was no longer available to spend his nights driving around town with Cannon and the gossip columnist Walter Winchell. Runyon was gone, and Ring Lardner, too, and, as if overnight, the press box was filling up with young men whom Cannon dismissed as "the chipmunks" for all their annoying chatter. Everywhere Cannon looked he saw a New York filled ever more with cynics and clever men who did not appreciate his city as it had been when he was young.

"People in this town seemed to be enjoying what happened to the Yankees in the first two games of the World Series," Cannon wrote before Game Three. "Their embarrassment of the Yankees in the second game entertained them. . . . It is as if nothing can impress them anymore and they have lost their faith in the old traditions. . . . Their snide comments followed me across town as though they had collaborated to declaim a nasty monologue."

He was angry at the Yankees, too, for taking their pennant for granted. The players now found themselves in a hole from which there was, in his view, only one escape that mattered. "The prize this year isn't only the winner's end of the take," Cannon concluded. "They must fight to get their town back. . . . It is not enough for the Yankees to win a pennant. They must also be champions of baseball if they hope to perpetuate their myth. This is expected of them."

What was unexpected was what came next. Milwaukee's Lew Burdette, hero of the '57 series—three victories, two by shutouts—would be on the mound to pitch the clincher in Game Five. The Yankees were underdogs. They were about to become something even Jimmy Cannon had never witnessed: lovable.

It started with pity, for the team and for Casey. It appeared in, of all places, the *New York Times* and under the byline of its august Washington correspondent James Reston. It came in the form of parody, "a plea for the relief of poor Casey," addressed to Dag Hammarskjöld, the secretary-general of the United Nations. Dreadful acts, Reston wrote, had been perpetrated upon the New Yorkers by the cruel legions from the west. "I have been instructed by the leader of the defenders, Prime Minister Charles Dillon Stengel, to bring these alarming events to the attention of the United Nations." And so on, for laughs, for everyone but Casey, who alone understood that it was not merely the series at stake, but perhaps his job as well.

Stengel called on Bob Turley to face Burdette in Game Five. Turley had enjoyed his best season in the big leagues, winning twenty-one games and losing only seven. He typically threw very hard and with little artistry, and so it was especially surprising for the Milwaukee batters to watch him work. He struck out eight through the first six innings, punching most of them out on his big sweeping curve. Gil McDougald, the Yankees' second baseman, staked Turley to a 1–0 lead with a homer in the third, a cheap one, 301 feet down the right-field line, where it caught the foul-pole netting. Hardly an omen for what was about to happen in the bottom of the sixth.

With the top of the order up for the Yankees, Hank Bauer opened with a single. Jerry Lumpe muffed on his first two attempts to sacrifice and Stengel, eager to score any way he could, ordered him to try again. Lumpe bunted foul—one out. But Mickey Mantle was up, and he promptly singled. Yogi Berra doubled, scoring Bauer, and Braves manager Fred Haney ordered Elston Howard walked, loading the bases for Bill Skowron, who singled in the second run. The bases were still loaded when Haney emerged from the dugout to inform Burdette that his day was over. Juan Pizzaro came on to face McDougald, who lofted a drive to left.

It was generally acknowledged that there was no worse place to play left field in the major leagues than at Yankee Stadium on a sunny afternoon. The "sun field," as it was known, had made a goat of poor Norm Siebern in Game Four, and was now playing havoc on the eyesight and self-esteem of the Braves' Wes Covington, who was trying very hard to locate the ball in the bright sky. He turned. And then he turned again. He appeared to spot it, only to lose it. The ball, meanwhile, was sinking fast and caught the earth at Covington's feet with enough bounce to send it hopping over the bullpen fence, a ground-rule double that scored two. Turley, a feeble hitter even by pitchers' standards, completed the scoring with a single to left.

Turley would strike out ten that afternoon and would limit the Braves to five singles. The Yankees were alive, barely.

Stengel could not decide on a pitcher for Game Six in Milwaukee and shared his ruminations with the press. He could go with Don Larsen but suspected that he needed more rest given the parlous state of his arm. Art Ditmar was a possibility, and so was Johnny Kucks. And then there was Whitey Ford, who had been Stengel's best and most reliable pitcher and who had started Games One and Four. But Ford had spent much of the season nursing a sore arm, and Stengel was not inclined to use him on a mere two days' rest. But Ford wanted in, and Stengel, operating without a net, had no man better in a big game.

Haney had no such worries. He would go with Spahn, the great left-hander. It did not much matter that Spahn was thirty-seven years old and had had only two days to recover from the nine innings he had thrown in Game Four. Haney, unlike Stengel, did not like playing an unfamiliar hand. He had Burdette and he had Spahn and he was a game away from another championship.

Spahn spent the afternoon making his manager look like a sage. Bauer nicked him for a run on a homer in the first, but Milwaukee evened things in the bottom of the inning on a run-scoring single by Henry Aaron. Spahn was not as sharp as he had been in Game Four, but even when he missed he didn't miss by much. Ford, meanwhile, was not nearly so fortunate. In the bottom of the second he was facing the sixth-, seventh-, and eighth-place hitters, quick work for Ford on a good day. But with one out, Covington singled, as did Andy Pafko. Spahn was next, and Ford lost his chance to escape untouched when he surrendered yet another single and a run. He walked Johnny Logan to load the bases, and Stengel called for Ditmar.

Johnny Logan drove Ditmar's first pitch to left, and as the ball sailed over the infield it appeared that two more runs would score, which could well give the Braves the series. Elston Howard, a catcher by trade but playing left field today, drew a quick bead on the ball and set off in a sprint. Still, it was unclear whether he would arrive before the ball hit the turf. He made the catch at full extension, and the Braves' third-base coach, Billy Herman, sent Pafko home.

The prudent call would have been to have Pafko tag up, then hold up and return to third, drawing the throw and leaving matters to the next batter, Eddie Matthews. But Matthews was having a dreadful series, striking out with alarming frequency. Besides, Howard had had a similar chance to throw a man out at home in Game Two and had lofted a throw so off the mark it appeared headed for Green Bay.

Off went Pafko. Berra waited for him at home. He took Howard's throw and could have had a coffee and a Danish, given all the time he had to station himself in front of the plate, ball in hand. Pafko arrived headfirst, a dead duck. Double play, side retired, and the bases-loaded threat a memory.

Ditmar kept Milwaukee at bay through the sixth inning, when the Yankees tied things at two apiece on a couple of singles and a sacrifice fly. Duren relieved him and was flawless but for a single by Covington. The teams remained tied at the end of nine, and though Spahn's pitch count was rising, Haney sent him back out for the tenth. McDougald led off, and Spahn threw him a fastball that looked like a good pitch when it left his hand, only to become something altogether different as it approached the plate. McDougald caught it flush and drove it over the wall in left center, and the crowd at County Stadium suddenly got very quiet. Spahn dispatched Bauer on a fly to center and Mantle on a grounder to second, but he surrendered singles to Howard and Berra. Haney, feeling terrible for what he was about to do, finally came to fetch him. Don McMahon arrived from the bullpen to surrender another run on a single by Skowron. New York now led 4–2.

Milwaukee would bat last, and Duren applied his foot to the Braves' throats, retiring Red Schoendienst and Eddie Matthews. But in between he sandwiched a walk to Logan, who took second and then scored on a single by Aaron. Joe Adcock followed with another single, putting the Braves a base hit away from tying the game. Stengel trudged to the mound and, in his customary defiance of conventional wisdom, called for Bob Turley, who had pitched a complete game two days before. Haney countered by sending Frank Torre in to bat for Del Crandell. He appeared to be the wiser man when Torre looped a soft liner over second base. But as the ball drifted over the infield it assumed the sorry aspect of a deflating balloon, losing altitude and speed and falling not to the ground but into the outstretched mitt of Gil McDougald. The series was tied.

Bill McCorry, the Yankees' road secretary, pushed through the crowd to call the team's hotel and advise the front desk that the team would be staying for one more night and that the bags left on the veranda should stay where they were and not be loaded onto a van and taken to the airport for the return trip to New York. Not yet.

Jimmy Cannon worked for an afternoon newspaper, which meant the news he was hearing could not break until Game Seven had begun. A pity, because he was onto a good one.

Stengel was out. Cannon had it on good authority that the Yankees' owners, Del Webb and Dan Topping, had run out of patience with Stengel's ways—his strategies and his self-absorption and self-promotion. Cannon had heard that Webb, in particular, had been on Stengel's back for months, challenging his approach to the game as the Yankees slumbered their way to the pennant. George Weiss, the team's general manager, had also wearied of Stengel's endless substitutions and had concluded that the strategy was merely a way for Stengel to draw attention to himself. Weiss wanted to see his new players in the lineup, but Stengel ignored him.

"They think he has gotten too big and is overshadowing the Yankee organization," one source told Cannon. "They can't handle him."

It did not take a baseball man of Stengel's sagacity to recognize just how fortunate he was to have his team in Game Seven. Milwaukee had played sloppy ball ever since Game Four. They had had their chances to win and had muffed each one. Stengel now alternated between dyspepsia and caution, fretting about whom he would send out to pitch the deciding game. Meanwhile, the city of New York now found itself in the grip of a fever the likes of which had not been felt in a very long time: the Yankees, back from the dead, were attracting a following. In the bars near Times Square, the patrons were packed three deep as they stared up at the televisions, waiting to see if the Yankees could complete their improbable comeback.

Stengel had weighed starting Turley—he had thrown only three pitches to Torre to end Game Six—or Ditmar, and he even contemplated going with Duren, a reliever. The morning brought clouds and a threatening sky. An overnight rain of biblical proportions had soaked Milwaukee, but the field was playable, leaving Stengel without the benefit of a much-needed rainout. An hour before game time Stengel announced that Don Larsen, two years removed from his singularly heroic moment—his perfect game against the Dodgers in the 1956 World Series—was his choice to face Lew Burdette, who would be pitching on two days' rest.

Larsen did little to justify Stengel's last-minute faith. He spotted the Braves a run in the first—three walks and a single—and escaped with the bases loaded. His teammates scored two in the second through more self-destructive behavior by the Braves—two throwing errors by Torre on tosses that Burdette could not handle covering first. But in the third Larsen surrendered singles to Bill Bruton and Henry Aaron, and Stengel had seen enough. He called, once again, for Bob Turley, who did not appear to suffer from overwork. He surrendered only a walk until the sixth when, with two out, Del Crandell homered to tie the score at 2–2.

Stengel had won with the last of the mighty DiMaggio teams and with Mickey Mantle at his best and with a demonstratively judicious use of the many role players George Weiss had been sending his way for ten years. His teams had won with good pitching, and fine defense and also with a confidence that comes with having performed well in so many big games. The Yankees were good, but more important, they were powerful in a way that could make opponents doubt themselves at crucial moments. Home runs may lack the artistry of the well-executed hit-and-run. But they can make the knees go weak.

These Yankees, however, had so far displayed little of that muscle, and Stengel had been left to tinker, maneuver, and pray. Burdette opened the eighth by getting McDougald on a fly ball to left and Mantle on strikes. Then came Berra, who had been at this longer than anyone else on the team.

He doubled off the wall in right. Howard followed. He had been having an awful series at bat. But now he singled, sending Berra home and giving the Yankees a lead. Andy Carey, who'd come on to play third in the sixth for Jerry Lumpe, bounced a ball off Eddie Matthews's glove and beat his throw to first. Two men on for Bill Skowron, who was batting barely .250 for the series.

His home run landed in the bleachers in left center. New York led 6–2, and had, in one moment, restored a reputation that had only days earlier appeared on the verge of evaporating. Milwaukee went quietly in the eighth, save for a man in a brown suit who jumped the railing and made it as far as second base, where he shook McDougald's hand before the police escorted him off the field. And when Red Schoendienst flied to Mantle for the final out, the crowd dispersed quietly; on Wisconsin Avenue the hawkers were giving away Braves pennants to anyone who'd buy a Yankees souvenir.

Stengel's men were jubilant in the clubhouse, a marked contrast to the formality with which they accepted the seventeen championships that had come before. There was no champagne, but Johnny Kucks and Tom Sturdivant doused each other with water, and Berra and Mantle agreed that they had never played in a better World Series.

Jimmy Cannon, who had had the Yankees all but buried, now praised their persistence and grit. "There were instances in this series when the Yankees seemed to disgrace their myth," he wrote. "They were as ineffectual as love in the old folks home." But these Yankees, a lesser team in his estimation than the clubs that had come before, had nonetheless proved themselves worthy of the affection that grew with each victory. They had become so likable, in fact, that Cannon did not think it a stretch to compare them to that most beloved of teams—Brooklyn's recently departed Dodgers. "They were being admired for a new trait," he went on. "They were scuffling, shoving and pushing, holding on and fighting back when it looked as if they couldn't win but were giving it a loser's shuffle.

"This," he concluded, "could be the biggest they ever won."

His column ran inside the paper, alongside the jump from his dispatch about Stengel's fate. Stengel's friends from California, he reported, insisted that the manager now had the victory he not only wanted but needed. "Casey," said one, "would never think of quitting if he lost. He wants to quit a winner. I wouldn't be surprised if he quits, but this was the sweetest victory he ever won. He figures that he beat his bosses. He did it his way and won."

Stengel had little to say worthy of quoting that afternoon. He talked about the pleasure of the championship and joked about his team proving they could play in the National League. He was stripping off his shirt when a photographer stopped to snap his picture. "Don't take me undressed," he said. "Our club don't do that."

Webb and Topping scheduled a steak dinner for the team at the Savoy Hotel. And Weiss announced that contrary to published reports, Stengel was not about to be fired.

"If Casey doesn't want to come back, it is because he wants to quit," he said. "We're not firing him. We expect him to be with us again. He is a great manager."

But if Weiss was hoping that Stengel would depart of his own volition, he would be disappointed. "That's just plain rubbish," Stengel declared. "There's too much work for me to think about quitting."

A week later he signed a new two-year contract. It would take him through the end of the 1960 World Series.

NOVEMBER: Dawn

It was only right that the Yankees win the 1958 World Series and that Casey Stengel be rehired and then named manager of the year. It was only right that the order that defined baseball be restored, so that on the morning of November 12, the commissioner of baseball, Ford Frick, could rise and look out his window and know that the world over which he presided had been set correctly back upon its axis. One last comforting sunrise. Because by the end of the day, life as he had come to know it would never again be the same.

Ford Frick may not have been a wise man, but neither was he a fool. He was sixty-four years old and midway through his second five-year term as commissioner. He was a pleasant man with a grand title that, in truth, meant very little. He served at the pleasure of the owners and always made sure to please. The writers especially liked him, given that before he became a baseball executive he had been one of them. He had been particularly close to Babe Ruth, and in fact had served as the Babe's ghostwriter, effectively keeping America blissfully unaware that the great Ruthian appetites extended beyond hot dogs and cigars. Ford Frick did not like to cause trouble, nor did he welcome it.

Frick presided over a domain that for decades had managed to endure as the nation's game, despite the absence of a prevailing organizational logic, a vision for the future, a governing voice, or a conscience. It was an enterprise run as a patchwork of fiefdoms, divided between two leagues that had very little to do with each other. Team owners operated with impunity; long ago they had drained virtually all authority from the office of commissioner, a position they had grudgingly accepted in the wake of the scandal that erupted after the fixing of the 1919 World Series. Frick did mete out fines for infractions on the field, but he left the owners alone, lest he find himself looking for work. Better not to speak loudly, if at all, about the worries facing his game.

Baseball attendance had peaked at 21 million in 1948, but in 1958 that number now stood at just over 17 million, a decline of nearly 20 percent. As bad as things were in the National League—where the average team drew 16,500 customers a game—they were worse still in the American League, where each game averaged 4,700 fewer spectators and where the suspense of the pennant race typically was limited to seeing who would finish second to the Yankees. The game's distribution of wealth and power had always been lopsided: the rich teams stayed rich and the poorer teams struggled to minimize their losses on the strength of their share of the gate when they played their wealthy counterparts. In the ten seasons from 1949 to 1958, that wealth was concentrated in the city of New York, which had hosted every World Series in that span, six of them exclusively in New York—five between the Yankees and the Dodgers, one between the Yankees and the Giants. What in years to come would be recalled as the golden age of New York baseball only served to alienate fans everyplace else.

Ballparks, which had been models of steel and brick construction when they were built forty years earlier, were now regarded by owners and fans alike as cramped arenas in decaying neighborhoods where there was never enough parking. The ballparks were like the game itself, vestiges of another time, one that held ever less appeal for a nation moving to new split-level homes in the suburbs. The game was old and America was not interested in old. Baseball trundled along, seemingly oblivious to the rise of new games that people in growing numbers were paying to see: harness racing, professional basketball, roller derby, wrestling, automobile racing, and the sport that had not yet captured the glamour of its college equivalent—professional football.

In fairness, baseball had made some accommodations. In 1953, the National League permitted Lou Perini to move his benighted Boston Braves to Milwaukee, the first franchise relocation in fifty years. In 1952, the Braves had drawn a paltry 280,000 spectators, and Perini had had enough. The unanimous vote spurred Walter O'Malley, the owner of the Brooklyn Dodgers, to say, prophetically, "This is bound to start a chain reaction." The American League allowed the St. Louis Browns to move to Baltimore in 1954 and the Philadelphia Athletics to Kansas City in 1955. But it was Milwaukee that showed everyone who cared to notice the good things that change could bring.

The city embraced the Braves with all the innocent enthusiasm of a high school sophomore asked to the senior prom. Ten thousand people and a brass band playing "On Wisconsin" descended on the railroad depot to welcome the team in April 1953. As the first home opener neared, the Milwaukee Meat Council asked the mayor to declare a half-day holiday, and the county board adopted a resolution urging children to be given a half day off school.

The fever did not abate once play began. The city changed its postal stamp to read "Home of the Braves." Birth announcements came bearing news of the arrival of "Milwaukee's newest Brave." Those who did not make it to the games were left to listen on the radio; Perini was not televising games. No matter; so enraptured was Milwaukee with its new team that on the night of a doubleheader against the Phillies the police blotter was all but empty—seven domestic disputes, seven car accidents, and thirty-eight minor arrests. Department stores, fearful of losing customers, brought in radios so their shoppers could follow the games, rather than listen at home. In their first twenty-seven home games, the Braves drew 692,130 fans—two and a half times what they had drawn all season in Boston.

"A whole reservoir of interest has been dammed up and here is the release for it," said the mayor. "Here, a man's world is his church, his tavern, his lodge. In those, no program can be new enough or fresh enough to make for an emotional release of this kind." The rise of the Braves in Milwaukee was not lost on Walter O'Malley, who saw in Milwaukee the potential for wealth, which he envied and with which he could not compete if he could not extricate himself from tiny, aging Ebbets Field.

But O'Malley was not prepared to leave Brooklyn. In fact, for years, he had lobbied New York City officials for permission to build a new Dodgers ballpark in downtown Brooklyn. But for all his gifts and cunning, O'Malley could not sway the one man who mattered, the city's master of all that fell and rose, park commissioner Robert Moses. Moses refused to condemn the land where O'Malley hoped to build. If the Dodgers wanted to move, he would be happy to rent them space in a new ballpark he envisioned rising in the Flushing Meadows section of Queens. O'Malley, who wanted to own and not to rent, turned to Los Angeles, a city he had once spurned, and which was prepared to offer him all that any businessman could want. In 1957, the league granted him permission to move, so long as he could persuade the equally restless owner of the New York Giants, Horace Stoneham, to move west, too.

Contingency plans were drawn up in New York, lest the city find itself without a National League club. The task was undertaken by George V. McLaughlin, a man of considerable reputation and clout. McLaughlin was seventy years old, a tall and sometimes imperious figure known as George the Fifth. He had been the city's police commissioner in the 1920s until he began organizing one too many gambling raids on the clubhouses of Tammany Hall, the political machine that ran New York. A Dodgers fan, a banker, and a presence and power in Brooklyn political circles, he later became the head of the Brooklyn Trust Company, which counted among its many holdings the estate of Charles Ebbets and the then-moribund ball club that came with it. One day during the Great Depression, a young, ambitious bankruptcy lawyer called on McLaughlin and began suggesting ways to turn a profit on his seemingly worthless holdings. The lawyer's name was Walter O'Malley, and it was through the good offices of George V. McLaughlin that O'Malley came to the Dodgers, first as a lawyer and then as vice president, before finally making the club his own in 1950.

By the spring of 1957, McLaughlin was not prepared to wait to act until the teams were gone. In June, he offered to broker a deal to buy the Giants for $2.75 million. Stoneham turned him down. He then proposed creating a nonprofit organization that would invest $5 million to bring a new National League team to New York. He even suggested the heresy of sharing some of the earnings with the players. He took his proposal to the National League owners, hoping to lure a troubled franchise to Queens or perhaps even convince the league to add a team or two. The league spurned him, swiftly. The Dodgers and Giants, explained Warren Giles, the National League president, were still in New York, and adding another franchise was out of the question. So McLaughlin was left to wait, along with everyone else, to see whether his protégé would take away the team he loved.

The Giants were first to go. In August, Horace Stoneham announced his plan to relocate to San Francisco and wisely was not present at his team's final game at the Polo Grounds. The looting began at the last out of the last inning, a Giants loss, their eighty-fifth of the season. Eleven thousand people had come to see the Giants play that afternoon and, with the shadows stretching across the infield and the temperature beginning to drop, many in attendance vaulted the walls and streaked across the outfield, grabbing what someone else had not grabbed before them. They unearthed home plate, the bullpen plates, two bases, the rubber sheeting on the outfield wall, divots of outfield grass, and the wooden base to which home plate had been attached. They could not remove the bullpen sun shelter and so were left to smash it. The players fled across the outfield, where they hurried up the ladder to their clubhouse, shutting the door behind them. The crowd's blood was up. They chanted, "We want Stoneham." And then, "We want Stoneham with a rope around his neck."

O'Malley allowed his team to close its season unsure of where it would be playing in the spring. Perhaps in Los Angeles. Perhaps in Jersey City, waiting while O'Malley built his new Brooklyn stadium. But Ebbets Field had been sold and there would be no more baseball on the corner of McKeever Place and Sullivan Place. On the team's last night at Ebbets Field, Danny McDevitt pitched a shutout for the Dodgers and Gladys Gooding, the organist, played a farewell recital. She opened with "Am I Blue?" and "After You're Gone" in the bottom of the first. In the third she played "Don't Ask Me Why I'm Leaving," after the Dodgers scored their second run on singles by Gino Cimoli and Gil Hodges. In the scoreless later innings she chose "Que Sera, Sera," "Thanks for the Memories," "How Can You Say We're Through?" and "When I Grow Too Old to Dream." The end came just after nine o'clock. Someone thought it would be a good idea to put on a recording of "Follow the Dodgers," the team's anthem, because this was, after all, a Dodgers win. But a sentimental head prevailed. The song was switched off, and it was left to Gooding to conclude the evening with "Auld Lang Syne." The groundskeepers emerged. They raked the infield and pulled tarpaulins over the mound and home plate, as if there would be another game tomorrow.

On October 8, 1957, the Dodgers announced that they were moving to Los Angeles. Two weeks later, O'Malley set off on a transcontinental journey to his team's new home aboard the plane now emblazoned with the words *Los Angeles Dodgers*. He arrived just after six o'clock in the evening on October 23 and was greeted by a thousand cheering people. He and his entourage descended onto the tarmac wearing blue caps with the letters L and A interwoven. "There was a headwind," O'Malley announced, "or we would have been here sooner."

In the Bronx, the Yankees had troubles of their own, having lost the 1957 World Series to the upstart Milwaukee Braves. But Del Webb and Dan Topping were looking forward to 1958. They had assumed that with the departure of the Dodgers and Giants the city, and all its many baseball fans, would belong to them alone. Topping had said as much in July. "We consider that our American League franchise is for the City of New York, and that includes Brooklyn and Manhattan," he said. As for the National League, he went on, "We've got the right to veto any application for a major league franchise in New York."

Meanwhile, George McLaughlin's efforts to find a new team had come to naught. So he turned to Branch Rickey for help. Rickey had been the president and general manager of the Pittsburgh Pirates until 1955, and McLaughlin hoped he might still have some sway with the team's owner, John Galbreath. In 1957, the Pirates had finished seventh for the second straight year (a modest improvement over their last-place finish in 1955) and attendance was slipping—the 850,000 fans they drew to Forbes Field represented a drop of 100,000 from 1956. McLaughlin had calculated that the Pirates were losing $500,000 a year, and he thought that Rickey might be able to convince Galbreath to sell the team to a New York buyer. The Pirates could play at Ebbets Field until the city built the ballpark that Robert Moses had long envisioned rising in Flushing Meadows.

The Brooklyn Pirates, if only for a season or two.

Meanwhile, Moses, who regarded baseball as a base form of entertainment performed by men of questionable social standing, was suddenly showing an interest in the game. He wanted his stadium built, and he knew that for all his considerable political muscle, the city council would be reluctant to assume the cost if the park did not have a tenant. Moses was now sending hectoring notes to McLaughlin: "What happened to the Pittsburgh option? Did you see the Mayor? Anything new about Flushing Meadows?"

Unfortunately, Rickey had not been encouraging about the Pittsburgh ploy. "George," he told McLaughlin, "money can't buy a franchise." Indeed, the dream of Roberto Clemente in Brooklyn's right field, playing where Carl Furillo had, died quickly. John Galbreath kept his team in Pittsburgh. Flushing Meadows was still only an artist's rendering. But McLaughlin had seen the mayor, and in November 1957 they drew up a list of men to form a committee charged with finding a team to play in Moses's park: Bernard Gimbel, who owned one of the city's biggest department stores; James A. Farley, the former postmaster general and a friend of the powerful; and Clinton Blume, a prominent real estate agent who had pitched briefly for the Giants in the era of John McGraw.

The committee would be chaired by the least-known member of the group, a Brooklyn lawyer whom McLaughlin liked, William A. Shea.

Bill Shea was fifty years old, tall, broad, gregarious, and quick to appreciate where power resided. He had grown up in Manhattan, a handsome boy and a good enough athlete to win a scholarship to New York University. He did not play baseball but did play lacrosse, football, and freshman basketball before transferring to Georgetown University. He hoped to study law. The Depression, however, cost his father, a real estate and insurance agent, his business. Luckily, Shea's sister Gloria had gone to Hollywood to become an actress. She was cast in many movies, among them *23-Skidoo*, *Dancing Around*, and *Big City Blues*, and she helped pay his way through law school.

Shea found legal work in government, first as counsel to the New York State Insurance Fund and then as assistant general counsel to the state's superintendent of insurance. It was the sort of work an aspiring young Catholic lawyer from a Catholic law school could expect to get; there was little point then in anyone but a Protestant applying to the white-shoe Wall Street firms. Still, by the time he went into private practice in 1940 he had begun making important friends.

Shea was neither a litigator nor a legal scholar. Rather, he was the sort of lawyer whom powerful men trusted with their secrets and whom they could rely upon as a go-between. He was adept at putting people at ease, and despite his outgoing nature, never offending. He was the kind of man other people liked; he could not pass a baby carriage without stopping to take a peek at the child and saying something nice. He smiled easily and comported himself without pretense. In a world of after-work cocktails and dinners, he held his liquor well; he made a point of knowing the names of bartenders, so that they would make sure that after his first drink they served him only soda water. He conducted a good deal of business on the phone, scribbling on a paper blotter that his secretary deciphered at the end of each day.

His wife, Nora, provided the connection to the sporting world. Her father, Thomas Shaw, had for decades been one of New York's most prominent "turf men," a polite way of saying bookmaker. Gambling on the horses was then legal, and "Long Tom" Shaw—he was tall and angular, a former bicycle racer—was a presence on the racing circuit in his Rolls-Royce convertible, sporting a diamond stickpin. Among Shaw's friends were Tim Mara and his sons, who owned the New York Football Giants. But aside from a brief flirtation with a semipro football team, the Long Island Indians, Shea's interest in sports remained limited primarily to golf—his handicap was twelve—his children's events, and watching the occasional polo match. Instead, he joined the sorts of boards that brought him into contact with useful people—the Brooklyn Democratic Club, the Brooklyn Public Library, and the Interracial Council—among whom he earned a reputation as a man who could get things done.

Bill Shea set off to bring a new baseball team to New York with what was, by all appearances, an attractive package to sell: the prospect of a new ballpark and a fan base—or, rather, two—that had been abandoned by their teams and were presumably eager to embrace a new club. Granted, Pittsburgh had already said no, and so had Philadelphia. August Busch Jr., the owner of the Cardinals, was not interested in leaving St. Louis, home of his brewery.

But within a week of his appointment, much to everyone's surprise, Shea learned that he had the commissioner on his side. At the owners' winter meeting in Colorado Springs, Frick announced that while the Yankees retained sole American League rights to New York, the National League could return to the city, so long as that club's park was not within five miles of Yankee Stadium. All of New York, and not just Brooklyn, was an "open city." A rare defeat for Topping and Webb.

The timing was propitious. Powel Crosley Jr., the owner of the Cincinnati Reds, had begun talking, loudly, of his dissatisfaction with the meager parking at Crosley Field. His park was a year older and even smaller than Ebbets Field; it sat only twenty-nine thousand. Crosley acknowledged that he had promised to always keep the Reds in Cincinnati, his hometown, but he was not happy about his city's efforts in finding parking spots for his patrons. In fact, he could no longer swear that the Reds would play in Crosley Field in 1958.

"We are under no obligation to stay here," he announced. Besides, he added, the sense among his fellow National League owners "was unanimous that the league should maintain a club in New York."

The story was front-page news in New York. Bill Shea could barely contain his delight. "Maybe," he said, "this is a development that will prove favorable to us."

It did not. Shea had been warned that Powel Crosley was using him to extract more parking in Cincinnati. And no sooner had Crosley issued his threat than the city of Cincinnati offered him 400 additional parking spots. Still, Crosley would not commit to staying. The city then offered to tear down some aging buildings near his park, creating 2,400 more spots. There was talk, too, of building the Reds a new stadium on the Ohio riverfront. In January, Crosley agreed to stay in Cincinnati for five more years.

Undeterred, Shea began 1958 talking like a man who believed that the National League might yet return to Brooklyn in time for Opening Day. "It is quite possible that a club coming here may want to stay in Ebbets Field," he said. "We've presented ideas which make Ebbets Field attractive, even for the future. In coming years, it will be much more accessible than it has been." Robert Moses, meanwhile, was growing impatient with absence of a tenant for his proposed ballpark, and he sent a note to George McLaughlin suggesting that if Shea's committee had indeed come up empty-handed it might be best for all concerned if they simply "fold up."

But Shea was not ready to concede defeat. With Cincinnati out of the picture, he wrote to Warren Giles, asking the league president if he would be willing to invite him and New York mayor Robert F. Wagner to meet with the owners during the July All-Star break in Baltimore to make their case for luring a club to New York. The city now had more to offer than a refurbished Ebbets Field. In late January, the city's Board of Estimate endorsed the idea of building Moses's Flushing Meadows stadium. The members of the board, the mayor explained, had voted their approval in the belief that a new team would indeed come, its identity to be determined when he and Shea met with the owners.

"I am confident," said the mayor, "that the National League will wish to move without delay to safeguard its territorial rights in this great baseball city."

But the league, Shea quickly learned, was in no such rush.

"The invitation wasn't any indication that a franchise was available to New York," Giles told the *Times*. "But there isn't any club in the National League that plans to relocate to New York. I don't see any chance of any of our present clubs moving to New York."

So it was that the trouble that was about to intrude itself on Ford Frick did not come as a surprise. In fact, the heartache about to befall him could have been avoided, and simply. The owners had only to allow New York to replace one of the two teams it had lost to California the year before.

But that they would not do.

And so, on November 12, 1958, at Toots Shor's saloon, the watering hole of New York's sporting elite, Bill Shea rose before a room crowded with newsmen. "Since it has now become apparent that the National League means to do nothing about this," he began, "we have decided to go on a new tack." And with that he announced that a committee he headed was starting a third major league. "In fact," he went on, "it is quite possible we could have a new franchise operating in New York by 1960."

And not just New York. Shea announced that Houston, Dallas, Denver, Toronto, Miami, and Minneapolis–St. Paul might also join his new league. "Prominent citizens in all these cities have assured us they would go all out to gain a major league franchise," said Shea, "and that we could definitely count on the necessary $3 million to $5 million to start a new team." The wording was important: Shea explained that while he hoped the new league would be embraced by the majors, he was prepared, if necessary, to go it alone.

The reaction among the sports chattering class was encouraging, which was no surprise. Whatever good feelings the New York columnists may have once extended toward the owners had evaporated with the departure of the Dodgers and Giants. "The fat cats in the existing loops need to be jarred from their complacency, especially the National League, where smugness has become insufferable," wrote Arthur Daley in the *Times*. Jimmy Cannon pilloried the owners as men who ran the game with "a truculent benevolence as if they were the philanthropic custodians of asylums where mischievous youths were rehabilitated," and then went on to delight in the possibility that the barons of the game could well be undone by the challenge Shea had thrown down.

Ford Frick assumed the injured tone of a man who had never received an invitation to the party. "I still don't get it," he said. "If these so-called responsible parties who are to launch a third major league . . . mean to operate within the scope of organized baseball, or the umbrella as someone called it, why haven't they or the committee come to see me?" They hadn't, Shea responded, because "up to now we have had nothing concrete to offer. If we went to him he would only tell us to do what we are doing now. And what we are doing now is getting the pieces together."

By the time the afternoon papers hit the newsstands, Frick's tone had darkened from aggrieved to incensed. "Baseball," he now declared, "is not going to be sledge-hammered into putting a team in New York because of the threat of a third major league."

The newsmen had many questions, chief among them the source of players and the source of Shea's ideas. They knew that Shea was not a baseball man, yet he spoke like someone who had given the matter a good deal of informed thought. He was vague on both points: The matter of finding players, he explained, would sort itself out. As to the identity of his adviser, Shea was mum, saying only that such a man did indeed exist and that he was a National League club owner. "This man has assured me that a third major league with New York the key city is wholly feasible," he said, "and he also assured me financial backing would not be lacking."

Shea may have been evasive, but he was not dishonest. Branch Rickey still owned a piece of the Pittsburgh Pirates.

DECEMBER: Restoration

He was seventy-six years old and, in his view, insufficiently vigorous and insufficiently employed. He had suffered one heart attack and endured bouts of vertigo caused by Ménière's disease, an inner-ear condition. He walked with a cane but still smoked too many cigars. He now held the lofty-sounding position of senior consultant to the Pittsburgh Pirates, which paid him fifty thousand dollars a year, gave him shares in the team, and came with virtually no responsibilities. The job was a gift from his old friend John Galbreath, the team's owner, who had hired him in 1950 to run the club and who had fired him five years later.

Pittsburgh had been a disaster. Branch Rickey had arrived to great excitement, given what he had accomplished in building championship teams in St. Louis and Brooklyn. He quickly discovered that he did not have the players in Pittsburgh, either in the big club or, more important, on the farm. He had made his reputation by devising a system that would allow him to hoard as many players as he could and then choose the ones who best met his exacting standards. It was not uncommon for a prospect to come to the Dodgers' spring training camp at Vero Beach, Florida, and be assigned a three-digit number; there were so many good players competing for very few positions. It was understood that, despite

Rickey's courtly ways, a bad game meant that someone else would be taking your place the following afternoon. Rickey held opinions on a host of subjects; family dinners were a time for the sort of rhetorical give-and-take with his children and grandchildren in which he would almost always emerge the winner. So it was that he devoted spring training in seemingly equal parts to teaching what he had concluded were the correct ways of doing things ("In a slide to the right, the right foot may erroneously pass the second-base bag two to five feet in advance of the touching foot.") and interminable lectures in the evenings that, at times, veered toward the metaphysical. Not always a big hit with the baseball veterans. Rickey was a man with things to say, some of which he later committed to paper, among them: "Courage is the by-product of form. Form is the horse and courage is the cart." Or, "Generally speaking I don't like the slider. I don't believe in it. The slider devalues more pitchers than it helps." Or, most famously, "Luck is the residue of design."

He looked for young men who displayed what he called "a sense of adventure," a daring on the base paths and at bat. He was not shy about assessing his players' emotional states and was quick to diagnose what he had concluded ailed them: "Without a doubt a confirmed neurotic"; "A blatherhead. Typical low grade Brooklynese. Hedonistic"; or "Obtuse, possibly opaque. I am not sure." His degree was in law, not psychology. No matter. He knew.

Until Pittsburgh. He inherited a team that had last won a pennant in 1927 and that, after finishing second in 1944, typically rose no higher than fourth. The Pirates finished sixth in the year before he arrived. They only got worse under his stewardship; his Pirates finished last four times and seventh once. The nadir came in 1952 when they went 42–112, a winning percentage of .273. Nothing worked. He alienated and then exiled to Chicago the team's one star, Ralph Kiner, because he believed that Kiner, a power hitter, was a one-dimensional player. Perhaps so, but then so crucial was Kiner to the gate that it was customary for Pirates fans to leave Forbes Field after his last at bat, after they'd waited to see if he'd homer again. Rickey signed bonus players who fizzled, veterans past their prime, and young men with great promise—Dick Groat, Roberto Clemente, Bob Friend, Elroy Face, Vernon Law—who would become stars only after he left.

The charitable view about his time in Pittsburgh was that he laid the groundwork for some wonderful Pirates teams. But by then Joe L. Brown had become general manager and made the judicious trades that made Pittsburgh a winner. Brown, a protégé whom Rickey had assigned early on to scour the historically black colleges for talent, departed from Rickey on the question of salary. Rickey, who negotiated hard and well on his own behalf, believed in paying a man as little as was necessary, a good season or no. But Brown thought it prudent to err on the side of an extra thousand dollars in the belief that a grateful man would then feel he had something to prove. "I felt that Mr. Rickey failed to enable those players to appreciate how good they were in contract negotiations," Brown said, carefully, many years later. In June and again in July 1956, Brown's Pirates were in first place. And though they slid to seventh on the final weekend of the season, the team more than doubled its attendance from the paltry 469,000 who came to see Rickey's last Pirates team in 1955.

In the November after his dismissal, Rickey wrote to his children, "I am down but not out—not at all. I think I am on the spring board of happier days." But retirement—he insisted upon calling it "semi-retirement"—brought too many reminders that the game had moved on without him. Old friends from his St. Louis days had died. He now traveled to receive the sorts of lifetime achievement plaques that go to men of whom little more is expected—the Human Relations Award of the National Conference of Christians and Jews, a scroll of appreciation from the NAACP for the work he had done in race relations by signing Jackie Robinson and breaking baseball's color barrier in Brooklyn back in 1947. He advised the founders of the Fellowship of Christian Athletes and joined the president's Committee on Government Employment Policy. Though his name seldom appeared in the papers, he was still invited to appear as an after-dinner speaker. He spoke about "The Perils of Complacency" and "Idleness as the Devil's Workshop" and about the dangers of international communism.

None of it was enough. His connection to the game was now limited to attending Pirates games, serving on the board of the Hollywood Stars of the Pacific Coast League, and observing with growing consternation the changes in the baseball landscape. He had disapproved of the Dodgers' move to Los Angeles—"a crime against a community of three million people," he called it. That the "crime" was perpetrated by Walter O'Malley, who had squeezed him out of his stake in the Dodgers in 1950 and for whom he shared a deep, mutual disdain, did not stop him from attending a luncheon welcoming O'Malley to Los Angeles in October 1957. In truth, it was as close as he now found himself to the center of things.

It is not clear when Branch Rickey first came upon the idea of starting a third league. At the time of Shea's press conference, he had not written about it publicly, and was quoted on the subject only once, briefly, by United Press International, suggesting that if the National League failed to return to New York a third league might be a possibility. The New York papers paid so little attention to his comment that the *Times*, *Post*, *Herald Tribune*, and *Journal-American* did not even bother running the story, brief as it was. One of his biographers, Murray Polner, suggests that he began chatting about the idea in late 1957 with his secretary, Kenneth Blackburn. And yet, in the years to come, Rickey would present his argument for a third league with a clarity and incisiveness that suggested a vision long in the making.

Rickey's opinions generally reflected two imperatives: the legal and the ecclesiastical. He had studied law at Ohio Wesleyan University, but it was the belief in a higher calling that animated his thinking, be it in the inherent value of the stolen base as compared to the home run, the signing of a black man to a major-league contract, or now, in the years of his unhappy exile, the prospect of spreading the game across the land. He approached these pursuits with a fervor that bordered on the evangelical.

All he needed was someone to tell, someone who needed the wisdom and guidance that, it was generally accepted, had abandoned him in Pittsburgh.

CHAPTER TWO

WINTER 1959

JANUARY: Immortality

Bill Shea had been dispatched on his mission with a simple objective: find a new team for New York. Stymied in his quest, Shea had turned to his patron, George V. McLaughlin, who told him to seek out Branch Rickey. Rickey offered hope where Ford Frick, Warren Giles, and the men for whom they spoke had offered none. In the pious Rickey, Shea found a man motivated by a purpose higher than mere expansion: baseball's salvation. Shea and the other big-league supplicants had only to accept his wisdom, and they would be saved, too.

By the early months of 1959, Branch Rickey had so rigorously thought through the nature, structure, and logic behind his new league that he was prepared to commit his plan to paper. His case reflected a mind honed in law school but shaped by a lifetime of Sunday mornings spent first in prayer and then in paying careful attention to his pastors' words. A sermon by way of a legal brief, which is to say that Rickey was as attentive to the fine points as he was to the overarching vision. He began by offering the traditional chastisement—*we are all of us sinners*—an elucidation of shortcomings that men of faith could overcome: "We are rapidly becoming sixteen provincial corporate operations in the entertainment field, with one eye on the cash register and the other on the aroused Congress. Lacking a third eye, we overlook a factor more important than either cash register or Congress, the youth of our nation, to whom baseball owes its very existence."

With that, he began to offer his path to salvation.

Rickey presumed that the men behind the new league would be willing to spend to launch the league; they would need to have pockets deep enough to afford what he estimated would be between three and five million dollars in start-up costs. The more vexing question was the players. Rickey's answer lay in a combination of purchase, draft, and free agency. The purchases would come, as they always had, from existing clubs. Free agency would be limited to any young man not under contract with a major- or minor-league outfit. The draft was trickier. He proposed that, for the first two years, the eight clubs of the new league would be able to draft any player who had made a major-league roster but who had not played in a big-league game. "Thus," he argued, "no present major league club can be deprived under any circumstances of a 'known quantity.'" He also proposed that each of the new teams be able to draft men from the minor leagues, too.

Rickey was quick to acknowledge that his new league would field teams of weaker players—weaker, in the short term, than those in the big leagues. But that, he insisted, did not matter; after all, they would be playing one another. "Competition within the new league will be equal throughout, hence, more often keen than one-sided," he wrote. "This would not be possible to ninth and tenth clubs added to existing leagues." He had seen at the turn of the century how Ban Johnson's upstart American League began surpassing the National League in attendance because it fielded more teams vying for the pennant. "Greatness of any professional team in baseball is a relative thing," Rickey wrote. "It is good if it wins. A tail-end team is always locally bad. The pennant winner is always a 'great' team."

But if every team was to have a fair shot at a pennant, Rickey reasoned, there could be none of the disparity between rich and poor clubs that prevailed in the majors. The remedy he proposed was television. For years there had been talk—and no action—on devising a formula so that visiting teams could share in the local broadcast fees paid to the home clubs. While the major-league owners did share the revenue from national broadcast deals, each owner still kept for himself all the money he made in selling his team's local broadcast rights. But Rickey—who had invented the farm system as a remedy to the advantages enjoyed by the wealthiest clubs—would not tolerate an arrangement that benefited the teams with the largest television audiences. And so he proposed a radical solution: the clubs in the new league would pool 90 percent of *all* their television revenue and divide the money equally.

Rickey conceded that his plan did come with the hint of "socialism"— an anathema to the cold warrior in him. But he insisted it was only fair that a club that provided a share of the entertainment on the field should also share the broadcast receipts, in addition to its customary share of the gate. He believed that after two years of play the newcomers would be ready to play the big fellows in a round-robin World Series, a tournament that would complete their journey to the big leagues.

"The problem is not *can* a third league be formed," he wrote. The emphasis was his. Rather it was which of the wealthy competitors would win the coveted—and in his estimation, essential—New York franchise. In fact, he went on, "the desire for a third league is so strong throughout America, that the great problem of the organizers is not one of inclusion, but *exclusion*. My belief is that the organizers will have sufficient applications to form *two* more major leagues."

But who would lead them to the promised land? Perhaps, he suggested, Ford Frick himself. "He would, given free rein, which he does not have as Commissioner, speak and decide in the best interests of baseball as a national game," Rickey wrote. If not Frick, then perhaps Warren Giles or Will Harridge, who was retiring as the American League president. As for Rickey himself, he begged off. He admitted that he had been offered the post of president of the new league, but had turned it down. "I am 77," he wrote, "and I feel it."

But his protestations—"It is not easy, believe me, to sit on the sidelines by choice"—felt too disingenuous by half. For the moment, he would advise and wait. He could enjoy once again the sensation of being courted, attended, and heard until the time came when he might accomplish what had not been done since 1903, when his hero, Ban Johnson, forced the National League to accept his upstart circuit, the American League, as its equal.

Years later, Rickey, who had long avoided writing about his life and the game—as if committing his thoughts to paper would somehow mark the end of things—at last agreed to write a book. The project, *The American Diamond*, was a pastiche, a rumination on various aspects of the sport and an ode to the men Rickey considered its greatest heroes. He lavished praise on the predictable names—Ty Cobb, Babe Ruth, John McGraw, Connie Mack. But at the top of his pantheon of sixteen "immortals" stood not a player but an executive, Ban Johnson.

"Ban Johnson was the czar of baseball in America," Rickey wrote. "He ruled the game." In 1893, Johnson, a burly and remarkably self-assured Cincinnati sportswriter, was appointed president of the Western League, a minor-league circuit. "Even then, at twenty-nine years of age, Ban Johnson had conceived the idea of a second major league," Rickey wrote. "He became baseball's first successful major-league expansionist." Rickey now hoped to become the second.

He had met Johnson in 1913, early in his career in the front office, and his chief memory of the encounter was of Johnson taking offense at a criticism of one of his managers by another fellow at the table. "No you don't—no you don't," he recalled Johnson bellowing. "He's my boy, he's my boy." Johnson, Rickey concluded, "had no patience with anybody's views contrary to his own."

Yet, Rickey admired him above all baseball men. There is, not surprisingly, a biblical quality—Moses, perhaps—to Johnson's story. A young man of otherwise decent prospects who rejects a career in the press box so that he could save the game from the dark forces then undermining it: drink, gambling, language too coarse for ladies' ears, cheating, umpire baiting, and on occasion, throttling. Only a man with a singleness of purpose and with aspirations transcending his own interests could redeem the sport. "He was a college baseball player, a debater, a law student, a reporter, a ruggedly opinionated advocate of whatever he believed in," Rickey wrote. "Above all, he was a tireless finder and maker of facts to

preface every undertaking. The other fellows' facts were to be questioned
or modified or disregarded. He dreamed baseball almost aloud, but his
dreams did not require psychiatric mastery to find the cause. He was a
supersalesman of ideas—a persuader with economic inducements and a
finished organizer in new fields."

Remove the foray into journalism and what is left is a portrait that
bears a striking resemblance to the author of that tribute.

In fact, Johnson did appear at a time of turmoil in the game. It was
easy to forget that for much of its early history, professional baseball was
a chaotic world, with teams, leagues, and even players' unions coming
and going with staggering frequency. There had been only one constant
since the advent of the professional game in 1869: the National League,
which was born in the winter of 1876 and had managed to fend off every
competitor, and whose monopolistic hold on the sport threatened to
undermine the game's popularity.

By the time of the National League's founding, baseball teams had
become identified not with private clubs but with their home cities—
and so was born the proprietary connection between team and city that
has characterized fandom ever since. Newspapers were hardly neutral in
their loyalties; the *New York Times* referred to the local clubs as "our
teams." One hundred thousand New Yorkers marched in a torchlight
parade to celebrate the American Association championship of the New
York Metropolitans in 1888. The Mets, as they were known, went on to
lose a postseason series to the National League's Providence Grays, in
the precursor of the modern-day World Series.

The American Association had been founded in 1882 as a rival to
the National League. It drew fans by charging twenty-five cents for
admission—half the price of a National League ticket—by playing on
Sundays, and by selling beer at the ballpark; it was nicknamed the "beer
and whiskey league." After two years of hostilities—the first of the nineteenth century's "baseball wars"—the two leagues set aside their differences and agreed not to raid each other's rosters. The National League,
meanwhile, had instituted a practice known as "reserving" contracts for
a set number of players, preventing them from selling their services to
other clubs. "Reserving" kept salaries low and led to the next great baseball war in 1890, when the best players formed their own union—the

Brotherhood—and joined with a group of businessmen to challenge the dominance of the National League. But the resulting Players League lasted only a season. Like the American Association, which also died in 1891, it collapsed when wavering owners abandoned the league for the promise of what so many of them had wanted all along: a place in the National League.

In the fall of 1899, Ban Johnson embarked on a daring plan. He changed the Western League's name to the grander "American League" and began invading city after city that had belonged to the Nationals alone—first Chicago and Cleveland, then Boston, Philadelphia, and Baltimore. The American League played the 1900 season as a minor league, but on January 28, 1901, Johnson declared that it was going major. The Nationals responded by treating him with the same disdain with which they'd regarded the other men they'd co-opted and defeated. First they declared that the upstarts hadn't a chance. Then, seeing that Johnson was not easily bullied, they called upon some of their old foes from the vanquished American Association in the hope of starting a subsidiary league and blocking Johnson from their towns. They also insisted that there weren't enough good players to go around.

None of it worked. The new league charged a quarter for admission, and in 1901 and 1902 attendance was good; of the two leagues, the American offered its fans the better pennant races. More important, the "outlaws," as the papers called the new league, committed themselves to keeping no player under contract for more than five years. Defections were rampant. National League attendance dropped. The Nationals sued, hoping to block its stars from jumping.

"Accepting all this as an open declaration of war, we made up our minds to carry the fight to the enemy instead of waiting for the attack," Johnson recalled in 1930 for an article in the *Saturday Evening Post*. "As a matter of truth, I was without misgivings as to the outcome, for though the National League looked to have every advantage, I knew it was honeycombed with dissension. The American League on the other hand, was so close-knit and harmonious as to have the projectile force of a spear point."

That harmony was Johnson's doing. The men who had joined with Johnson—among them Connie Mack, Clark Griffith, and Charles

Comiskey—had given him leave to rule by fiat. There were none of the defections that had undercut earlier challengers to the National League, none of the weak-kneed owners who wanted nothing more than a place in the senior circuit. Johnson proceeded with the finesse of a jackhammer. He uprooted struggling franchises and relocated them to cities where he believed they might flourish. He hired and fired managers and conducted secret raids on National League rosters, all the while insisting that those who played in his league curb their drinking and their cursing and learn to accept the inevitability of bad calls. Johnson was correct about the divisions among the National League owners, who split between those who wanted to sue for peace and others who refused.

But Johnson was not relenting. Instead, he was plotting his most audacious move: invading the one city deemed essential to success as a major league—New York. He began looking for a place to build a ballpark—imperative, given how insistent fans were that their teams play in new, wooden stadiums. By the time Johnson found his location in northern Manhattan, the National League had surrendered. The two leagues signed an agreement in 1903 that would allow them to exist side by side, in peace, without having their best players stolen, enticed, or induced to jump. The American League franchise in Baltimore relocated to the new Hilltop Park in New York, where in 1907 their second-string catcher was Branch Rickey. They were called the Highlanders until 1913, when they moved to the Polo Grounds and became the Yankees.

The institution that the papers called "organized ball"—two leagues, sixteen teams, ten cities—had meanwhile closed its doors with every reason to believe that they could keep the game for themselves.

FEBRUARY: Allies

Branch Rickey's unhappy exile from the game had come to an end, though not publicly, not yet. But he was back. He was, as he put it, "waist deep in discussions, arguments, possibilities, flying trips, consultations, telephone calls." He was crafting a manifesto, laying out his vision. He wasn't sleeping; he was having a wonderful time. Bill Shea may have been the face of the new league. But it was Rickey who was working the back channels, gauging interest and opposition. He had begun with Ford Frick. The meeting had not gone well.

Frick still believed that the path to expansion lay in adding two teams to each league, and perhaps two more in the years to come, dividing each circuit into two divisions with play-offs preceding the World Series.

Won't work, Rickey told him.

The owners will help the newcomers, Frick insisted.

They may say it, replied Rickey, but they will not do it. The new teams will be left to take on the veterans with the discards and rookies.

"Frick acknowledged the gravity of the situation," Rickey wrote, "but showed that he had not thought through his ideas."

The commissioner pressed on—"a rather one-sided conversation," Rickey noted—even as Rickey began making his case for the need for a radical solution. The number of teams and players, he pointed out, had not changed since 1903.

But where Rickey saw vast possibilities, Frick envisioned nothing but trouble. He wanted to know something of the means and character of the men behind the new league. Where would the players come from? Where would they play? And what sort of pension plan did Rickey and his people have in mind, given that the owners had only in recent years accepted the once heretical proposition that the players have a little something to fall back on in their golden years?

"I tried somewhat desperately to get a word in edgewise," Rickey wrote. "He was voluble beyond understanding. . . . Finally, I said, 'Will you let me say a word?'"

The conversation, however, was just beginning, not only with Frick, but eventually with Warren Giles and Joe Cronin, the new American League president, and with Walter O'Malley, Del Webb, Phil Wrigley, Tom Yawkey, and Calvin Griffith, whose father had managed Rickey when he played for New York. He was back among friends, and if not friends, then certainly men who had known him and perhaps done business with him—always a courtly experience, though seldom easy. These men who had not been happy with his decision to integrate the game (Boston, the last holdout, was about to field its first black player, Pumpsie

Green), but they nonetheless admired him for the clever way he had built his champions. Frick, in his memoir, would write of Rickey's "genius," and that arguably his greatest legacy was producing all the men who learned at his side and who had since risen to positions of prominence in the game, Giles among them. Baseball was so glutted with Rickey protégés that it did not seem unreasonable to assume that the game would be delighted to have him back and would surely welcome his ideas. He was, after all, one of them. Or had been.

Bill Shea, meanwhile, had been on and off the road for months, seeking recruits for the new league. He had stopped in Miami, Atlanta, Dallas, Minneapolis, Toronto, and Denver and was spreading good news: rich and influential people were joining the campaign or suggesting they might. He had met in Toronto with the entrepreneur Jack Kent Cooke, in Atlanta with representatives of the Coca-Cola Company, and in Minneapolis with the Dayton family, the department-store owners. He and Rickey had recruited a powerful friend in Denver, the former governor and United States senator Edwin Johnson, whose son-in-law, Bob Howsam, owned the minor-league Denver Bears. Johnson still had many friends in Washington and was ready to offer his advice and political muscle. Overtures to the majors had also yielded some welcome surprises. Several owners, Shea reported, were ready to help—Tom Yawkey in Boston, Gussie Busch in St. Louis, and Phil Wrigley in Chicago.

Now Shea was heading to Texas, to meet with the members of the Houston Sports Association. Of all the cities that had shown their eagerness to join the campaign, none had been as passionate as Houston, if only because of the man driving their campaign.

The city had first signaled its interest in September 1957, in a letter to George V. McLaughlin that arrived a week before the Giants' final game at the Polo Grounds. It came from a man named George Kirksey, whom McLaughlin would have been forgiven for not knowing. Kirksey identified himself as the representative of a group of prominent businessmen who were interested in bringing a big-league team to Houston and dropped a couple of names that were presumably familiar to McLaughlin. Kirksey wasted little time in getting to his point. "I am writing this letter to inquire whether you think it practical and feasible for you to tie-in with Houston in your efforts to get a major league franchise for New York in the National League." He went on to cite the virtues of Houston, its booming population, its great affection for spectator sports, and its reputation as "the best . . . money town in the south, and in some aspects more attractive than San Francisco and Los Angeles, both of which are race track towns." Better still, he continued, in October the Texas legislature would be voting on a bill to finance a new stadium for Houston. "We would like very much to have your immediate reaction," Kirksey concluded.

He got it within a week. McLaughlin had passed his note along to the mayor. Perhaps there might be something to be gained in throwing in together.

George Kirksey believed that if he stood on a Houston street corner long enough, wealthy men would surely walk by. When they did, Kirksey would stop them. Then he would begin to talk. Kirksey was a man with many ideas, all grand. He was now in his mid-fifties, tall, thin, and with a singleness of purpose that varied with the moment and the company. He had been a sportswriter, and when he tired of that he decided to travel around the world. When he came back, he started writing sports again, until World War II began and he discovered that he could apply his knack for self-promotion to influential people, beginning with the general under whom he served. In his most recent incarnation, he had begun referring to himself as a "public relations engineer." He lived in a two-bedroom apartment that featured the design sensibility of the Collyer brothers: newspapers, books, and magazines stacked so high that they created corridors. Kirksey would spend his evenings racing through whatever he had happened to pick up that day, absorbing the points he needed should the subject of the article or book ever become the subject of debate. His chief rhetorical riposte was to tell people they didn't know what they were talking about. He considered himself something of a dandy. He bought expensive suits that, even in his wife's view, he did not wear well. Nor did he wear socks. He had alienated one wife and was well along in alienating his second.

Kirksey had come to Houston by way of New York, Chicago, Dallas, and Austin, having spent two years at the University of Texas before dropping out. He grew up in a small Texas ranch and farm town, Hillsboro, where his parents ran a boardinghouse that was said to serve the finest food around. Whatever popularity he achieved in high school and college he managed to dissipate by a relentlessness that could drive those around him mad. While capable of generosity, he possessed no apparent sense of humor about himself, nor, it seems, much, if any, awareness. He was easily bored: with ideas, with wives, with jobs. He had a dreadful temper. When he gave offense, it did not trouble him. In every town and place he had ever worked, he left behind bosses who could not stand him.

He arrived in Houston in 1946, a good time for a man who, though no longer young, was still on the make. The city was booming like no other in the country: its population, which had stood at just under three hundred thousand in 1930, was on the verge of doubling, as were the city's dimensions. Houston was not Dallas, a more established city that was, in comparison, East Coast in its sensibility. Houston was a city of oilmen and aspiring oilmen angling for membership in the Petroleum Club. With the oilmen came men in service of their needs, among them George Kirksey, who had concluded that the city needed two things: a publicist to tell the stories of these rich men's companies and a baseball team.

He had covered the game for United Press in Chicago and New York, and he appreciated baseball's pull on a city. Houston was a minor-league town desperate to become major league. It had tried and failed to lure the St. Louis Cardinals in 1952. Legend had it that in 1951 Kirksey was standing on a corner in downtown Houston when R. E. "Bob" Smith happened by. Smith, whose stationery read "Oil Operator," was said to have a daily income of one million dollars and never denied it.

"The Philadelphia Athletics are for sale," Kirksey said. "We can get them for two and a half million."

"Fine," Smith replied. "Put me down for $250,000 and get another nine guys and we're in business."

The Athletics went to Kansas City. But George Kirksey never stopped looking for wealthy men who could help him bring a major-league team to Houston.

And so it was that in January 1957 Kirksey managed to gather thirty-five of Houston's most prominent men in the boardroom of the First National City Bank. By the end of the meeting, he had succeeded in establishing the Houston Sports Association. Its mission was to find a ball club and to build a stadium where the team could play. Kirksey did not wish to be its president. He was, by his nature, a secretive man, happiest arranging clandestine meetings even when secrecy was not required. He understood that he needed a man whom others would follow because they regarded him as one of their own. He found his man in Craig Cullinan Jr.

Cullinan was a Houston aristocrat by way of oil. His grandfather, Joseph Cullinan, had come to Texas in 1897 from Sharon, Pennsylvania, and established the company that would later become known as Texaco. The younger Cullinan had been sent east for school, first to Andover and then to Yale, where he joined the Fence Club and Wolf's Head. He was a naval ensign during the war, and his 1951 engagement was noted in the society pages of the *New York Times*. The family, however, was not without its troubles: Craig Cullinan's father had killed himself after his mother's death, and his estranged younger sister sued him and his brother over the terms of the will. Cullinan was a private man, shy and self-effacing. He had a lot of money, an office and not very much to do. He and Kirksey got along famously.

With the well-born and presentable Cullinan at his side, Kirksey began making important allies, among them the Harris County Board of Park Commissioners. The commissioners were essential in fulfilling a key component of the Sports Association's plan: making it possible for Houston to build a new stadium. The city, like so many other minor-league towns, already had a ballpark. But it was old and small, hardly an inducement for a big-league club. Houston, like New York, would need something new and grand.

The board's report could not have gushed so well about Houston's prospects had Kirksey written it himself. The document was remarkable not so much for what it recommended—yes, a ballpark, and a big one—but for the case it made about all the many good things that came to big-league cities. The report looked at Milwaukee and Kansas City, whose transformations had been staggering. The good news, the board reported, did not stop at the surging attendance. The Milwaukee Association of Commerce claimed that in the five years since the arrival of the Braves their fans had spent $33 million, and not just on tickets: $2 million at restaurants, $900,000 at night clubs, $650,000 at hotels, and—given that the stadium boasted 12,500 parking spots—over a half-million dollars at filling stations. The Braves had transformed Milwaukee into a destination. The Milwaukee Pops were playing to packed houses, as were the productions at the new Fred Miller Theatre. Kansas City, too, was luring visitors; in 1957, despite a seventh-place finish, fully 20 percent of the 900,000 fans who came to see the Athletics play stayed in town overnight.

And those were the happy reports from the merchants, restauranteurs, and innkeepers in cities smaller than Houston. The park commissioners envisioned a sports complex set on five hundred acres, room enough for a stadium and an indoor coliseum. There would be baseball at the stadium, as well as football—college and, perhaps, one day, professional—revival meetings, industrial exhibitions, rodeos, horse shows, and the Fat Stock Show, which was searching for a new home. There would be basketball at the coliseum, along with Ice Capades, boxing, and touring Broadway shows. And there would be no fear of the great complex being a money loser: the teams would pay rent, and the spectators would pay for parking. Houston, the board all but declared, needed this sports complex if it were to reap the great financial benefits that were coming to cities bold enough to build the parks where the big leaguers played.

In early December 1958, Kirksey attended the league meetings in Washington, where he'd pled Houston's case to, by his count, thirteen of the sixteen owners. He'd also spent a good deal of time in the lobbies, chatting up the newspapermen, gleaning what gossip he could. The sentiment, he reported upon his return, was in Houston's favor. Granted, expansion was still a vague and distant dream. But Houston, he declared, was now regarded as the city most likely to land a club looking to relocate; New York had run afoul of a few too many owners, with "its tactics and general attitude." He did not elaborate. Even Del Webb, he reported, was well disposed toward Houston, and had said as much to the other members of his realignment committee, which had jurisdiction over franchise moves. The question, then, was which club, and by what means. A purchase, Kirksey concluded, seemed the best course. He believed the White Sox could be theirs, as could the Cardinals, the Reds, the Athletics, or the Washington Senators. Houston could be a big-league town by 1960. They were that close.

Or maybe not.

Kirksey and Cullinan had been disappointed before, so they knew to hedge their bets. And so after the winter meetings they once again set out on the road, this time to Pittsburgh to see Branch Rickey.

Kirksey returned from two days of meetings with Rickey later that December sounding like a man who had experienced his epiphany. At least, that was the tone he struck in his letters to Rickey. It was fitting that Kirksey worked on a typewriter that lacked a lowercase—all caps, large and small, the better to convey his enthusiasm. If Kirksey was still angling to work a deal to lure an existing franchise, he kept it from Rickey. Instead he wrote to say that he was ready to be of service.

It is difficult to discern what Kirksey loved better: baseball or public relations. He had covered the former but had more recently embraced the latter, and his memos to Rickey reflected less the sensibility of a wire-service reporter than that of an ad man with a product to pitch. In the place of narrative came numbered bullet points, bold and declarative, if rather obvious: *1. Get official recognition by existing leagues; 2. Win early acceptance of public for major-league status; 3. Develop a plan to get players.* But a close reading suggests a more calculating mind at work: the man was not trying to remind Rickey of what he already knew. Rather, his strategy was first to show Rickey how well he had listened and then to lay the groundwork to convince the old fellow that Rickey, and Rickey alone, had to take the lead. Kirksey fairly begged Rickey to complete work on an article—the manifesto—detailing his vision and plan, so that the arrival of new league would be heralded with Rickey's imprimatur in a national magazine. But more than that, he went on, "A Ban Johnson, who'll push the idea with a burning zeal, is necessary for success. You could fill that role if you set your heart to it."

Gauntlet thrown, deftly.

<<<<<

Branch Rickey could spin the tale of baseball with three major leagues. But Bill Shea, attorney that he was, understood that golden words would mean little without the U.S. Supreme Court—and perhaps Congress—on their side. Events of the past two years had given Shea reason for optimism.

The Court had issued no opinions on the constitutionality of a third major league, nor any rulings on baseball since 1953. But in 1957, the justices had been asked to resolve a football dispute and, much to Ford Frick's chagrin, had chosen to append their decision with an admonition about the great game, too. The Court had given Shea a weapon that the owners had been unable to wrest away.

Narrowly read, the matter at hand involved William Radovich, an undersized former offensive lineman for the Detroit Lions, who sued his team for preventing him from playing for a rival league so that he might be able to move closer to his ailing father. The Court sided with Radovich. It held that because the business of professional football constituted interstate commerce, it was subject to federal antitrust laws. The ruling confounded and displeased Bert Bell, the commissioner of the National Football League. "I don't know why baseball is any different from football, hockey, basketball or any other professional team sport that conducts itself properly," he bemoaned. A naive question, given that the Court had just answered it, once again. But this time with a qualifier.

Baseball was different because in 1922 the Court had declared it so. It had ruled unanimously that although professional baseball teams did travel to different states, and although this travel enabled them to make money playing baseball games, the business of baseball did not represent interstate commerce. The ruling came in response to a suit brought against the National League by the organizers of the Federal League, another would-be major league that went into business in 1912 only to expire three years later. The suit charged the owners with having effectively put the fledgling league out of business by so monopolizing the sport that it prevented the formation of competing leagues. The Court, however, was more charitable in its view of organized baseball and effectively granted it leave to operate as a legally sanctioned monopoly.

The author of the Court's opinion, Justice Oliver Wendell Holmes Jr., was a revered figure among legal scholars, which made the ruling all the more baffling. It left generations of otherwise admiring lawyers and judges scratching their heads at its nearly appalling absence of logic. The decision was not challenged until 1953, when a Yankees farmhand, George Toolson, sued to have baseball declared a monopoly after claiming that the team effectively kept him from playing anywhere else after he refused a minor-league assignment. By then a generation had passed since the Federal League decision, but the Court held that, in the absence of legislation changing baseball's rarefied status, the tradition of stare decisis, of bowing to precedent, would have to apply. Four years later, the Radovich case left baseball untouched but not unmentioned.

"If this ruling is unrealistic, inconsistent or illogical," Justice Tom Clark wrote for the majority, "aside from the distinctions between the businesses, that were we considering the question of baseball for the first time upon a clean slate we would have no doubts." His meaning was unmistakable: take away the prevailing 1922 decision and baseball would be subject to the antitrust laws, as football was. Holmes's ruling was left untouched despite the fact that, in Clark's words, it "was at best of dubious validity." But baseball, he wrote, had changed, and Congress had done nothing to address or restrain its growth as a monopoly. The decision, he concluded, "must yield to any Congressional action and continues only at its sufferance." He could not have been clearer had he offered his opinion with a wink and a nod.

It took little time for legislation to be introduced in Congress that would end baseball's antitrust exemption. The sponsor, Republican representative Patrick Hillings of California, declared that his bill would do away, once and for all, with what he called the "horsehide cartel." As it happened, Hillings had hoped to see major-league baseball come to his state and had so far been disappointed. Perhaps, he suggested, his bill would put the West Coast "in a much better position to obtain major league franchises." Hillings had a powerful, if unlikely backer—Emanuel Celler, the Democrat who chaired the House Judiciary Committee and who represented Brooklyn. Celler was not much interested in seeing baseball in California; quite the contrary, he was displeased about reports that his borough's team was considering a move to Los Angeles. Still, the rumors had only confirmed what Celler had long argued: baseball may have been a sport on the field, but it was also a business in need of restraint.

Emanuel Celler, born in the Williamsburg section of Brooklyn, was by birthright and temperament a Dodgers fan. He had watched with growing displeasure their long and maddening dance of departure, and this only heightened his displeasure with the state of the game. He was now seventy-one years old, bald, tall, bespectacled, and a bit stooped. Celler had represented Brooklyn in Congress since 1922 and had been at war with organized baseball on and off for six years. His first public tangle with the game's owners came in 1951 when his committee held hearings on the reserve clause, which bound players irrevocably to their teams and which was protected by the antitrust exemption. "If I thought storms had broken furiously over my head before, I knew better when those hearings started," he wrote in his autobiography, *You Never Leave Brooklyn*. "Never had such controversy raged. Never had so many columns been filled with torrents of words. . . . Here again it was 'Celler is out to destroy baseball,' 'Celler interferes with the national pastime.' If I had the impudence to examine big business, how much greater my impudence to examine organized baseball."

In 1957, buoyed by Justice Clark's admonition and spurred by the looming departure of the Dodgers (a prospect made worse by Dan Topping's insistence in July that no new major-league team could come to New York), Celler set to work writing legislation limiting the antitrust exemption. By early 1958, however, the Dodgers were gone and Celler had been unable to gather enough support for his bill. The only legislation that seemed remotely passable was a diluted version that would grant antitrust exemptions to the owners of teams in major sports, but with a caveat: they would have to prove that any exemptions were "reasonably necessary." Celler believed this condition would protect the players from the owners' arbitrary ways. The burden of proof would be on the owners, who were not pleased.

But the players were happy. In February 1958, J. Norman Lewis, the attorney for their still young and toothless union, wrote Celler that the player representatives were unanimous in backing his bill.

Two weeks later, however, they changed their minds. Several player representatives now suggested that the "reasonably necessary" protection wasn't such a good idea after all. Celler was furious and quick to attach blame. "There is little doubt that the baseball owners read the riot act to the players and forced them to change their position," he said. Celler, it turned out, had been bested by the owners' best friend on Capitol Hill—the ranking Republican on his committee, Kenneth Keating. Keating, who represented upstate New York, was a jovial, silver-haired man who liked to shake hands and give speeches and never veer too far offstage. He was also, from the owners' perspective, reliable and consistent. He insisted time and again that the owners were best left alone, lest congressional interference threaten the very foundations of the game.

The owners were grateful for his loyalty and were happy to prove it. Keating was launching a campaign for the United States Senate in 1958, and among his prominent contributors was Dan Topping.

But even a skillful congressman like Keating could not kill Celler's bill; the chairman still controlled the committee, which voted narrowly to send the proposed legislation to the full House. But the measure had company when it landed: Keating had cosponsored a competing bill granting all the major sports a blanket exemption from antitrust laws. Celler moaned that he would prefer "to see no bill at all" than Keating's blank check. The owners, of course, were delighted—all the more so when the House passed Keating's measure. Now all that stood between them and legal sanction to do as they pleased was the Senate, where forty-five senators had already signed on as cosponsors of Keating's bill.

Still, the chairman of the Senate Antitrust and Monopolies Subcommittee, Estes Kefauver, wanted to give the matter a closer look. "Parts of the bill worry me considerably," he announced. "We must consider what it does to the players, the owners and the public itself." Kefauver had made his reputation as a trustbuster and had taken on the mob in a series of televised hearings on organized crime in 1951. He had twice sought the Democratic nomination for the presidency and was Adlai Stevenson's running mate in 1956. Although he represented the baseball-less state of Tennessee, Kefauver—never shy about the spotlight—was prepared to give the public a show. He invited, among others, Stan Musial, Ted Williams, Mickey Mantle, and Casey Stengel to testify before his committee as it debated the Keating bill.

But it was another, less celebrated, baseball man whose words would resonate during those hearings. Among his fellow owners, Calvin Griffith was not regarded as a clever man. Yet he possessed a power unlike anyone else's. It was not quantifiable in terms the owners understood—dollars—so they did not appreciate it. Griffith owned the Washington Senators, a team he had inherited from his father and that included a small but unique fan base: members of Congress. The owners had only to keep humoring Calvin Griffith—tell him that they took his laments about his meager attendance and tiny park seriously, and allow him to continue performing the annual ritual of personally presenting season passes to the president and First Lady. But instead, all Griffith heard from his peers were complaints about the empty sound of the till when their teams visited his park.

And so it was that on the eve of the owners' midsummer meeting in 1958 Calvin Griffith, weary of the carping, told the *Washington Post* that he was ready to leave town. Minneapolis was promising him a new ballpark and a million patrons a year for the first three years in Minnesota. "I'm really going to ask for advice," he told the paper. "I'm going to ask if it will serve the league if we move, or if it's better to stay."

The American League owners were happy to advise. They shut the door to their meeting room, so no one could hear what they told Griffith. Two hours later, the owners emerged and the sense among reporters was that they'd given the Senators' owner a rough time; one observed that he looked "like a little boy who had been taken to the woodshed for being naughty. He was upset, unnerved and rattled." The owners issued a statement saying that Griffith had, in fact, not asked to move after all. But the damage was done, and the owners knew it.

"This throws us," Del Webb told Shirley Povich of the *Washington Post*. "I am wondering about the reaction in Washington. There are Senators and Congressmen in Washington who may not want to lose their ball club there."

He did not have to wonder for long.

On the Senate floor, one of the Keating bill's sponsors rose to voice his feelings of betrayal over Griffith's words. "It seems to me it comes at an exceedingly poor time when Congress is about to consider legislation on the Senate side, defining baseball as a sport," said Karl Mundt, a

South Dakota Republican. "It seems to me that baseball means to America something more than dollars in the cash registers of those who happen to own the clubs. Perhaps Congress should take another look at the measure now at the desk."

Calvin Griffith, a man born to be underestimated, had succeeded at making members of the United States Senate feel like the fans of the Brooklyn Dodgers. There was, however, one crucial difference: unlike the sorry faithful left behind in Flatbush, Senator Mundt was in a position to announce that he would introduce an amendment to the antitrust bill that would restrict the freedom with which franchises could leave one city for another.

If Emanuel Celler was gloating, he kept it to himself.

Meanwhile, the great and best-paid stars of the game came before the committee to extol the virtues of the existing order, doing so with all the spontaneity of apparatchiks praising the final report of the Fifth Party Conference.

"The men are happy and satisfied with the way baseball is run," insisted Ted Williams.

"If they don't do anything different I don't care what they do," said Mickey Mantle. "I don't think about this stuff very much."

"Do you have any complaints from the players about the reserve clause?" Senator Kefauver asked Philadelphia's Robin Roberts, the National League's player representative.

"No, sir. No, sir," he replied. "When it first came out there were discussions about it not being the thing, and having it thrown out and everything. But after looking at it, and I know a lot of players have, I think players in general agree that baseball must have a reserve clause like it has now."

Kefauver then asked Eddie Yost, Roberts's American League counterpart, why he had told Celler's committee that he favored limiting the clause to ten years.

"I retracted that statement," Yost replied. "Now I am not certain I feel that way."

The star of the hearings, however, was Casey Stengel, who without notes or script kept the gallery laughing and the senators perplexed and the national press corps trying very hard to write down all the many things he said because, really, it was very hard to divine his meaning. He said a good many things that did not remotely pertain to the questions put to him. It was left to Senator Joseph O'Mahoney of Wyoming to concede that Stengel had carried the day: "Mr. Chairman, I think the witness is the best entertainment we've had around here in a long time."

But Stengel and the stars could only buy the owners a brief reprieve. The senators still wanted to hear from Calvin Griffith, who might yet take away their team.

Griffith was not blessed with a gift for obfuscation. He told the committee that yes, he wanted to stay in Washington "as long as humanly possible."

But he could not promise to stay. Then he made matters worse.

"Baseball is a business," he said. "If we don't get enough fans we're going to have to find a way to carry on. We can't leave the franchise to stay here and rot."

He was, of course, not supposed to say that baseball was a business, or if he did, he was supposed to have spoken of its commercial nature as Walter O'Malley had—*a crazy business, but I love it so.* To say that baseball was a business, to say, "We're in baseball to make a profit," was to leave himself and his fellow owners open to questions about money—how they made it and spent it, and whether this was being done fairly. And so the committee began taking Griffith through a review of his accounts, asking how he could plead poverty when, in fact, he was the rare owner who actually paid annual dividends to his stockholders, most of them members of his family. The profits were modest—roughly equivalent to the salary of, say, a general manager, a position Griffith never felt the need to fill because he had assumed it for himself.

Griffith tried hard to make the difficult questions go away. He insisted that, profits aside, he was in no position to compete with the likes of Webb and Topping for the best prospects because he could not afford to pay big bonuses. He was denied the surfeit of cash that came to those few teams that CBS paid for airing their games on the Saturday Game of the Week; unlike the New York Yankees, the Washington Senators did not excite the sponsors.

In the end, he even tried to convince the senators that he knew next to nothing about the legislation that might forever free him and his colleagues from the shackles of legal restraint.

"You don't know why baseball wants this bill?" asked Senator O'Mahoney. "That's what you've just testified, isn't it?"

Ford Frick was handling the matter, Griffith replied.

And what about moving the team to Minneapolis, O'Mahoney asked. Didn't you say you'd never leave?

"I didn't say the Washington team would not be moved in my lifetime," Griffith replied. "I was misquoted."

But wasn't it you, O'Mahoney asked, who wrote an article for the *Post* saying the team "will never be moved from that city and that means forever?"

"If I wrote it, I guess I said it," said Calvin Griffith. "Well, I meant we would be here as long as we can live here."

Two weeks later, the committee voted to table the bill. The full Senate, where forty-five cosponsors presumably still waited, would not vote on the matter before it recessed. The bill, Kefauver announced, was "entirely too broad." Perhaps, he added, something more along the lines proposed by Emanuel Celler might work—granting exemptions where "reasonably necessary."

There matters stood until February 1959, when Senator Kefauver weighed in on the stalled sports bill. The news was all that Bill Shea and Branch Rickey could have hoped for. Kefauver was willing to grant baseball the sorts of exemptions that the Keating bill would have allowed for football, basketball, and hockey. But if Kefauver's bill passed, the days of the blanket exemption were over. Players would not be subject to draft or the reserve clause unless they agreed, in writing. No longer, Kefauver announced, would teams be able to control the contracts of as many as 450 players; each owner would be limited to reserve the services of no more than 80 men. Hundreds of players would then be free to sign with any team they chose—including the teams of a third major league.

Shea would need to decide how to use Congress's muscle, and when.

MARCH: Casey in Clover

Casey Stengel was once again a genius. Not that he had ever doubted it. His Yankees were losing their winter guts in St. Petersburg, Florida, as World Series champions, as they had been for seven of Stengel's ten seasons as manager. The victory against Milwaukee had restored him to the stature he believed was rightfully his: the best manager in the game— now and ever.

The writers treated him accordingly. They followed the team to Florida and arrayed themselves on the steps of the Yankees dugout, notebooks at the ready, prepared for Stengel to speak. He did not disappoint, especially now that the questions no longer focused on what had gone wrong. Instead, the writers wanted to know how Stengel had made things right, a curious and not terribly enlightening line of questioning given that Stengel had explained the nature of his success so many times before. Still, he was happy to oblige.

"Now they say I talk around corners and take you up blind alleys but Ol' Case don't leave anybody there and if we want to talk about my ball team, go ahead and listen," he began. "We got Yogi who you know can catch and maybe play the outfield and maybe he can play first base for us but you never know because he won't be near that bag on account he's afraid of getting his feet stepped on. He's a very delicate fellow even if you can't tell by looking at Yogi. I always did say that Mantle was a sensational ballplayer although sometimes he is not and he has a lot to learn about playing center field. He gets mad when he don't get his hit and he takes it out on the water bucket but he don't harm people. He's just mad at life."

His rumination was, by Stengel's standards, a model of concision. He did not digress or wander off into one of his yarns, like the one about Wilbert Robinson, who managed him in Brooklyn, not putting him in the lineup in the 1916 World Series game against the Red Sox that Babe Ruth started—*even though he was hitting .364 for the series and you could look it up*—because the Babe was a terrific left-handed pitcher before he became a right fielder and Casey never could hit lefties. Still, he rambled as he always did, alighting on this point and that, a player here, a position there, spinning as he always did back to himself. Stengel was not given to speaking in the familiar platitudes of his trade and crediting his players, at least not directly. Rather, he credited them with having performed well *for him* by playing the roles he had chosen in the system he had devised: a man played as long as he performed, and when he stopped performing another man took his place, until the replacement began to fade and someone else took his position. Stengel did things unlike any other manager because he could afford to do so: he could pinch-hit in the third inning, pull a starter in the first, alternate his shortstops, or play his third baseman at first because the Yankees had more good players than any team in the big leagues.

Stengel was sixty-eight years old and looked not a moment younger. Spring was his season, the occasion for his "instructional school," the clinic he had instituted in his second season with the Yankees as a venue for assessing which of the younger men could be of use. He had plucked several fine players from the school, most famously Mantle, whose father taught him to switch-hit and who was that rare Yankee who played the same position every day. He had also discovered Tony Kubek, a young shortstop from Milwaukee whom Stengel also played at third base and in left field. This spring he was trying to choose among his shortstops, a key position in his view—"like you got your quarterback in football. You can surround him with dummies and do all right most of the time. I don't want to insult football, but I said it."

He was trying to teach his young third baseman, Clete Boyer, not to dive for the ball and then throw from a prone position because the ball will sail, and he was trying to decide whether Norm Siebern might fare better wearing glasses and whether the bespectacled Ryne Duren might need bifocals. "We got seven instructors teaching our kids down here and they got lots to learn like how to back up a play or cut off a throw," Stengel said. "Nobody is backing up for the third baseman the other day, and two of our kids are backing up first base and I have to tell them when a triple is hit to right field there is no sense backing up first base at that time and Joe Cronin will bear me out." Kubek might play short or maybe the outfield, and maybe Gil McDougald would play short or third, and maybe Yogi would play left when Elston Howard caught.

Berra was the only other player besides Mantle who could count on always being in the lineup.

Stengel had less faith in his other men. "The rank and file just don't have it to keep going at their best for a full season," he said. "Don't ask me why. Some players blame it on night ball. Some say the caliber of the players has gone back, though why I wouldn't know, because we have better schooling in the minors today than ever before. Maybe the game has speeded up more than we realized. Whatever the reason, there it is."

Injuries, he went on, had been especially useful in helping him see how best to use his men. All the many injuries the team suffered in his first season, he explained, "was one of the luckiest breaks I ever got as a manager. Every time one of my front players got hurt I noticed the feller I stuck in his place would bust out with hits all over the place. Then just about the time he started to peter out he'd obligingly step in a hole or something and another guy, rarin' to go, would take over. From then on I decided I never again would count one player taking care of one position for an entire season."

Unlike the older men Stengel had inherited when he took over the team in 1949—Phil Rizzuto, Tommy Henrich, and Joe DiMaggio, who could not abide him—the new players became *his* players. They came to the Yankees with the understanding that they would play his way and without complaint. And if that young player—or the older ones for that matter—felt bad about it, Stengel did not much care. His Yankees were built around a core of stars—Mantle, Berra, the wonderful left-hander Whitey Ford—and an assortment of other men whom he moved in and out of the lineup depending on his needs and his gut. The only certainty was that a bad game or two would be rewarded with a return to the bench and a nasty aside in the papers. The Yankees had ten farm teams and a ready supply of men that the Kansas City Athletics appeared always prepared to trade away. There was always someone else.

Stengel himself had played such a role late in his playing career when he landed with John McGraw's Giants. McGraw, a harsh and self-important man, played him in center field, or in left or in right and sometimes not at all. "He put me in when and where he thought I could do him the most good," Stengel said years later. No statement better captured Stengel's approach to the game and his sense of himself in it.

McGraw was one of the titans of the game, and people who did not understand Stengel assumed that he had modeled himself after the man known as "Little Napoleon." Stengel was quick to disabuse them. He was, he insisted, his own man, as a manager must be. He had learned from McGraw and he had also learned from the affable Wilbert Robinson, his first big-league manager. But when asked years later to name the smartest manager in the history of the game, he replied, "*I* was."

He had bounced around the small towns of the minor leagues before making his major-league debut in Brooklyn in the final weeks of the 1912 season. He opened the 1913 season in center field in the team's new, modern park, Ebbets Field. He spent six years in Brooklyn and might have stayed longer had he not fought about his wages with the team's owner, Charles Ebbets, who concluded their heated negotiations by trading him to Pittsburgh. He was a decent outfielder and a line-drive hitter who struggled with change-ups and pitches thrown high and inside. Still, he felt himself underpaid, and took his beef to Pirates owner Barney Dreyfuss, who told him to come back when he hit .300. He played thirty-nine games for Pittsburgh in 1918 and then enlisted in the navy.

He had an easy war; he managed the Brooklyn Navy Yard's ball club and made a practice of choosing to play against teams of sailors who had just returned from months at sea and were still likely to be queasy. After the Armistice, Pittsburgh traded him to Philadelphia, but he didn't like the money the Phillies offered, and so he went home, played exhibition games, and gave serious thought to a career in dentistry, which he had studied briefly after high school. Still, he returned to the Phillies and much to his delight was traded midway through the 1921 season to McGraw's Giants, then the wealthiest and most successful team in the game.

He was thirty-one years old and in no position to argue about playing time, let alone money. He did as McGraw told him to do, playing the outfield position with the harshest glare because McGraw had decided that Stengel fielded well in bright sun. Stengel played hard and he played hurt and he played his best in crucial games. He helped the Giants win two World Series in 1921 and 1922 and a pennant in 1923.

And then he was gone, exiled to Boston, being of no further use to McGraw.

He spent the intervening years in baseball limbo. He started managing in the minors in Worcester, Massachusetts, and then Toledo, Ohio, before returning to Brooklyn in 1932, first as a coach and then, in 1934, as manager. His Dodgers finished no higher than fifth in his three seasons, and in 1937 the team, eager to be rid of him, fired him but still paid his salary. Stengel took the $15,000, moved to Texas with his wife, Edna, and began investing in oil wells. He would never again want for money. Boston brought him back in 1938 to manage the Braves; he also owned a piece of the club, having invested $43,000 of the money he had made in oil. He stayed in Boston for six seasons until the team's new owners bought him out and fired him. He spent the early weeks of the 1943 season in a hospital bed after a car hit him during a wartime dimout. A Boston columnist praised the driver who broke Stengel's leg for his service to Braves baseball.

The following spring, Stengel was back in the game, this time in Milwaukee, managing the minor-league Brewers and winning an American Association pennant. He managed next in Kansas City and then Oakland, in the Pacific Coast League, the best circuit in the minors, where in 1948 he won a pennant. He was fifty-eight when the Yankees hired him to be their manager in 1949. He was an odd choice, given the Yankees' lofty history and his own middling past. But the team had finished third in 1948 and had won only one pennant in the preceding five seasons. Webb and Topping made sure that DiMaggio appeared at the new manager's formal introduction, as if his presence might somehow make Stengel look like a Yankee.

DiMaggio thought little of him and made his disdain clear that spring. But if he was under the illusion that Stengel would retreat in his presence, he was wrong. The Yankees were now Stengel's team, and he set about remaking them as he believed necessary. Henrich, a splendid right fielder, had a bad knee; Stengel played him at first. Charlie Keller, a power hitter, had a bad back; Stengel sat him. He would platoon Keller at first and at third and in the outfield. He left shortstop to Rizzuto (who had not forgotten that in 1936 Stengel had dismissed him from a Dodgers tryout as too small; "Go on, get out of here, go get a shoebox"); center field was DiMaggio's, for now. Stengel saw great promise behind the plate in Berra and placed him under the tutelage of Bill Dickey, a coach who had been one of the best catchers in the game. Stengel had never had such a talented team. "But," he later told Harry Paxton of the *Saturday Evening Post*, "I had to find out how to use this talent to win my way." His Yankees edged the Red Sox to win the pennant and then beat Brooklyn to win the first of his World Series.

He won again in 1950, and whatever sense of restraint he might have felt prudent to display was gone. He shifted DiMaggio from his perch in center field to first base, and when he deemed the experiment a failure, shifted him back, succeeding as no one ever had in humiliating "the big fella." He delivered hour-long lectures to his players, baffling the rookies, antagonizing the veterans.

Any lingering doubts about the nexus of the team ended during a game in July 1951 when in the middle of the second inning Stengel sent out a replacement center fielder after DiMaggio had misplayed a ball. He said he only wanted to rest his aging star. But Stengel had already found his own center fielder, Mantle, in whom he saw a challenge worthy of his own bountiful self-regard: to mold the best baseball player who ever lived.

Stengel went through ninety-nine different lineups in 1952, his fourth consecutive championship season. He liked to pinch-hit early; he did not want his big reserve bats waiting for the late innings, as conventional wisdom dictated. And if that meant pulling a man who was pitching well, so be it. "You've got to be an attacker," he said. He won his fifth straight World Series in 1953, a record. His handsome salary represented a fraction of his wealth; there was the oil money, and his brother-in-law had made him a director of his bank, Glendale National. He and Edna had an eleven-room house in Glendale, California, with an enclosed tennis court where their nieces and nephews came to play.

By 1959, Stengel had become the most famous man in the game. He appeared on television and as a banquet speaker. The columnists called his manner of speaking "Stengelese" and took the occasional day off by simply quoting him at length. He posed in a wig, in silly hats, and making foolish faces. Stengel also succeeded in creating a persona—the aging, gravely voiced pixie—that belied two essential truths: Casey Stengel was very bright and had nothing in his life but baseball. His wife said as much. He would spend hours in their rooms at the Essex House, a wealthy man's address, reading everything he could find about every team and player in the game. If he read books or saw movies or shows, he did not talk about them. "All I ever hear around the house is baseball talk," Edna Stengel told the *Los Angeles Times* in an article titled "The Loneliest Man in Baseball." The Stengels had no children. Billy Martin, who acted as if wished he were Casey's son, told Milton Richman of UPI: "I know how much it kills him inside every time we lose a ball game, but he just sits in his office alone, without saying a word." He would stay up until three or four o'clock in the morning, reviewing that day's game. If the Yankees lost, he might not sleep at all.

He would be back at the ballpark in the morning, waiting for the writers; there was nothing he would rather do than talk. He would talk before games in his cubicle of an office at Yankee Stadium—in his underwear; not a lovely sight—and afterward in the clubhouse. When the team was on the road, he held court in the hotel bar, until the writers would fade or retreat to their rooms to file, which was no bother at all; he'd just talk to the bartenders. Not many hours later, the writers would make their way to the hotel coffee shop for breakfast and see him talking with a stranger who might have wandered over to shake his hand and tell him that years ago he had seen him play in Aurora or Shelbyville or Montgomery. Stengel would insist that the stranger join him and would regale him with his stories, pausing only when he spotted a familiar face. "Writer," he'd call out before making the introductions. "This is one of my writers." He hated having breakfast alone.

He was bad with names, or so it seemed. He seldom, if ever, mentioned a player by name. Ford was "the left-hander" and Mantle "the switch-hitter." It was as if the names had escaped him, which seemed odd given that he filled his stories of times long past with the most obscure names, like Kid Elberfeld and Wild Bill Hallahan and even his high school principal, Mr. Cammack. The men who played for him were, collectively, "my players," whose successes he characterized as having played well "for me." He distanced himself when describing their failings and was never crueler than when taking delight in mocking their play for the writers. That spring he had Jerry Lumpe, a second baseman, in camp. He was keen on Lumpe until he decided that his hitting was not up to standard. "He looks like the best hitter in the world until you put him in a game," Stengel told the writers, who dutifully recorded his words.

Lumpe understood the game being played. "You knew why he said it," he said, many years later. "He said it to the writers to say something funny to get in the papers. I knew it wasn't very nice. But that was Stengel."

CHAPTER THREE

SPRING 1959

APRIL: The Crisis of the Old Order

Paul Richards understood why he managed a sixth-place team and why a better day might not soon come. Richards, a wise man with thoughts that extended beyond that day's game, had been managing for eight years, the last four in Baltimore, which in the five years since the franchise's move from St. Louis had seen the novelty of its relocation subside, and with it a decline at the gate commensurate with its ongoing status in the second division. Richards was an innovator—the man credited with having invented the extra-large mitt for catchers of knuckleballs—and a wise tutor of young men, the kindest thing said of managers who have little with which to work. Richards's 1959 Orioles had prospects (the twenty-two-year-old third baseman Brooks Robinson), retreads (a sinecure for the thirty-six-year-old first baseman Walt Dropo), and one player with a reputation beyond the state of Maryland, Hoyt Wilhelm, the knuckleballer. Richards had been around the game long enough to understand that his fellows, stout as he might make them, had little chance for a pennant. Nor did anyone, in his view, but the Yankees. But it is one thing to feel resentful and keep those dark feelings confined, say, to the saloon. It is quite another to go public, in writing, which Paul Richards had felt compelled to do.

"If the American League history for the next decade approximates that of the last, and every sign today indicates that it will, then the league will die," Richards wrote in *Look* magazine, in an article coauthored with *Look*'s sports editor, Tim Cohane. "The cause of the debacle will be strangulation of competition and interest by the overlong dominance of the New York Yankees." Richards proceeded to delineate the ruin the Yankees had caused: all those pennants had meant a drop of interest and with it a decline in attendance across the league, including in jaded New York. In fact, whatever pleasure Del Webb and Dan Topping took in having the nation's largest city to themselves had been tempered by the sight of the stadium on Opening Day 1958, when the Yankees defeated the Orioles before 23,463 paying customers—eight thousand fewer than had attended Opening Day 1957. To make matters worse, in Los Angeles 78,672 people came to watch the Dodgers open their inaugural season in California against the San Francisco Giants.

Richards argued that the Yankees owed their great success, paradoxically, to Branch Rickey, having adopted his ideas about the farm system and plowed their profits back into the organization to pay for scouting and their vast minor-league network. The result was a pool of players so deep that they were never in want of prospects. The rules allowed this, to a point. A big-league roster, Richards explained, was limited to forty men. But by gaming the system only slightly, a team could assemble an entire network of minor-league affiliates whose sole purpose was to be a repository, finishing academy, and, when necessary, holding area for men on the way up or down. The richer a team, the more extensive the network. Rickey had devised his system as a remedy to the wealth of the New York teams, only to see New York turn his innovation to its singular advantage.

But Richards was not merely carping; he was prepared to offer a solution, one sure to please everyone but the fellows in the Bronx: an unrestricted draft. Each big-league team would be compelled to live with no more than its forty men under contract. All the rest would revert to *independent* minor-league teams from which the big leagues would each year draft the best men. The minor leagues, he went on, would be saved. And parity, a quality the game had seldom known, would be achieved. Richards conceded that the Yankees would not welcome his proposal but beseeched them to think broadly, for the sake of the league and the game. "The Yankees themselves must come to realize that, in the long run, the only thing that can be good for them is what is good for baseball," he concluded. "That is why action is needed now. Unless is it taken, the American League, as we know it, won't be around very long."

The Yankees' response came from Del Webb. He did not address Richards's specific points, nor did he offer a rebuttal. Rather, he went after Richards himself for having had the temerity to criticize the way his team went about its business. He did not do Richards the courtesy of even mentioning his name. "This man tried to manage then tried to run the whole thing," he said. "He didn't do either one very well. His team finished fifth last year and now he's trying to tell us how to run the league."

The rest of the league remained dutifully mum. The oddsmakers established the Yankees as 2–1 favorites to repeat as league champions. But in the Bronx, merely winning was not enough. The Yankees were expected to reign with a hauteur that, in a sporting sense, captured the image of class. The man charged with ensuring they continued doing so was the general manager and custodian of their myth, George Weiss.

Weiss was now in his early sixties. He was round, balding, thin-lipped, and perhaps the most disliked man in the game. The players did not like him and the opposing general managers did not like him, but Weiss did not seem to mind. He had been with the team since the days of Babe Ruth and had assumed control of the day-to-day operations of the team when Webb and Topping bought out their original partner, the bibulous and explosive baseball innovator Larry MacPhail, in 1947.

Weiss crafted a team in his own image: smart, remote, and success-ful. The Yankees won a World Series in 1947, before slipping to third in 1948. It was then that Weiss made his most audacious move, hiring Stengel, whom he had known since they were young men running teams in the Eastern League two decades earlier. Weiss had dropped out of Yale when his father died, went into the baseball business, and built prof-itable winners in New Haven, Connecticut, and Newark, New Jersey, before Ed Barrow, who had built the great Yankees dynasties of the 1920s and 1930s, hired him to run the new farm system. Weiss was an exacting boss, calling scouts at odd hours to make sure they were scouring the countryside for prospects and not sequestered in a tavern. If the scouts resented him, the writers found him an easy man to join for a drink and a chat.

What charm he exuded, however, vanished with his promotion to general manager. Weiss retreated ever more to the office and to his box seat behind home plate. He worked long hours, supervising every aspect of the Yankees operation. He moved the team's offices from a small suite overlooking Bryant Park on Forty-second Street to an entire floor on Fifth Avenue that could accommodate all the new people he hired to run his ever-larger enterprise. Weiss understood more than most executives that the game was becoming a bigger business—even if he was not inclined to say as much to the investigators on Capitol Hill. The Yankees were averaging a profit of more than one million dollars a year. Running the team meant making sure the food was good in the exclusive Stadium Club and that operating revenue continued to grow, even with the unwelcome rise in salaries.

Weiss was not alone among general managers in keeping a distance between his players and profits; Rickey, admired as he was, was a notorious cheapskate when negotiating all salaries but his own. But Weiss stood apart in his refusal to pay a man what he appeared to be worth. In 1954, he famously traded away one of his best pitchers, Vic Raschi, after Raschi held out rather than suffer a pay cut. Raschi had won twenty-one games each season from 1949 to 1951 and sixteen in 1952. Then, at age thirty-four in 1953, he went thirteen and six, a fine season that Weiss nonetheless decided demanded a reduction in wages. Raschi refused to report. Weiss traded him to the Cardinals. The message was clear: make a fuss, even if you are an ace, and you are gone, because there are many good men in the minors who will play on the cheap.

From time to time, a reporter would make his way out to Weiss's home in the hope of coming back with a story about the human side of the man who, in more charitable moments, was called "Lonesome George." Weiss and his wife, Hazel, lived in a large white two-hundred-year-old colonial in Greenwich, Connecticut. They had a poodle named

Yankee and no children. Hazel Weiss was something of sculptor, and after an exchange of pleasantries and wifely complaints about her husband's long hours she would retreat to her studio while George led guests to his large second-floor office. The room was filled with memorabilia from a lifetime in the game but of a decidedly arid sort. Weiss saved bats and balls, and he also saved contracts that he liked to show off. "This contract was discussed pro and con," he'd begin, showing off the first $100,000 contract signed by Joe DiMaggio. He also kept the salary roster for the 1932 team: Lou Gehrig made $23,000, and Frank Crosetti, the shortstop who now coached third base for Stengel, made $12,000. "Rookies today," he'd be moved to complain, "are practically getting what the stars got in the early thirties." The stories would inevitably read like earnest attempts at making a beauty queen sound smarter than she appeared, and they could not dispel the sense that George Weiss might as well have been overseeing the production of toaster ovens, such was his regard for his players.

"George is the most impersonal man I have ever known," an admirer of Weiss told *Sports Illustrated* in 1954. "Maybe he doesn't mean to be, maybe he doesn't know how to be any different, but he simply has never realized that ballplayers are also personalities."

This ignorance applied, most shamefully, to black men. Weiss did not sign his first black player, Elston Howard, until 1955—eight years after Jackie Robinson's debut in Brooklyn. Years later he would insist that he was no bigot; he just hadn't found the right man—although, he confessed, Vic Power, a black minor leaguer from Puerto Rico whom he traded to the Athletics, did become an All-Star. Power, he later said, "did not turn out to be the man we wanted."

Of all the men who played for Weiss, it is safe to say that none wanted to be wanted more than Billy Martin. And it was in his treatment of Martin that Weiss revealed a good deal about how he wished his team to be seen. Martin was regarded by the beat writers as a young man adept at managing up. He had first sidled up to Joe DiMaggio, and when DiMaggio retired he turned his affections toward Stengel, who had managed him in Oakland and who liked the fire and consuming need to win that compensated for what Martin lacked in stature and athleticism. Stengel treated Martin as he might a pet, and Martin did not seem to mind. Martin may have been at turns fiery and, when the situation called for it, obsequious, but he was not a Yankee, at least not in the estimation of George Weiss. He was not unrestrained in his habits, dignified in his bearing, and private in his emotions. He liked to have fun, and he liked to have fun with Mickey Mantle, who had never quite shaken the image of a country innocent lost in the big city. Given Mantle's growing fondness for the nightlife and the bottle, Martin was ever more regarded as a bad influence and therefore expendable. It did not help that he was hitting only .241 on the night in 1957 when he, Mantle, Ford, Berra, Kucks, and Hank Bauer went with their wives to see Sammy Davis Jr. at the Copacabana. A fight broke out; Martin stood accused of nothing more than turning twenty-nine; Bauer, the ex-marine, was alleged to have thrown the key punch. But when Martin came to the stadium the following day, Bobby Richardson, a milk drinker, had been penciled in at second base.

His inevitable banishment came several weeks later in Kansas City, in the sixth inning of a game against the Athletics. Martin was told to report to the clubhouse, where Stengel met him. "Well, you're gone," he told Martin. "You were the best little ballplayer I ever had. You did everything I ever asked." Martin's eyes filled with tears, but he said nothing. It would take years before he forgave Stengel, sure that if Stengel had tried, he could have saved him from the wrath of George Weiss.

The irony of Martin's exile was that it suggested that the Yankees were an organization so conscious of its reputation that it would countenance nothing that might sully the brand. But the standard of probity that applied to the players did not apply to the owner.

It was the rare man who could count among his friends both the mobster Bugsy Siegel and FBI director J. Edgar Hoover. But such a man was Delbert E. Webb. In 1959, he was arguably the most powerful, if least understood, figure in the game. Walter O'Malley was still consolidating his influence in the National League, where despite a decade of success on the field and off, the Dodgers did not dominate their circuit as the Yankees had for a generation in the American League. Webb was powerful because the Yankees were powerful; the rest of the league was, for all practical purposes, dependent on the Yankees for a fair share of their revenue.

Of the team's two owners, Dan Topping was the more visible, a familiar face in the cozy world of the New York sporting elite. Topping was a man born into money, a champion amateur golfer who married well and often—among his six wives was the Olympic skating champion and box office sweetheart Sonja Henie. He had had a stake in professional football teams but had otherwise played the role of what the papers called "the wealthy sportsman." Webb, on the other hand, was seldom seen at the stadium, except for his annual World Series sojourn when, after the last out, he would descend to the clubhouse and beam for the cameras as Stengel mugged and preened.

Webb was otherwise on the road, overseeing the many projects being built by the prominent construction firm that bore his name. The Del E. Webb Construction Company had by 1959 achieved the sort of ubiquity associated with the U.S. Postal Service. It had built, variously, high-rise apartment buildings in Phoenix; Veterans Administration hospitals in Denver, Kansas City, and St. Louis; vast aviation plants for Howard Hughes (a friend, though by now seldom seen) in California; factories in Florida, California, and Washington, D.C.; schools in California; air force bases in Texas; entire planned communities in Arizona; and a great many hotels in California, Arizona, and Nevada.

Webb was a man of exacting, if curious, habits. He had divorced his high school sweetheart after a thirty-four-year marriage and now shuttled between his suites at the Beverly Hilton Hotel (which he had built), the Mountain Shadows Resort in Phoenix (which he had also built), and the Waldorf-Astoria. He seldom stayed anywhere for more than a few days and so kept a full wardrobe in each suite. He owned 150 suits, 90 pairs of shoes, 52 pairs of golf shoes, and, as he once put it, "a helluva lot of hats." He was six-foot-four and two hundred pounds and ordered his ties extra long. He took most of his meals in the coffee shops of the hotels he built, and he ate the same dinner every night—steak, a baked potato, a dish of vanilla ice cream. He had stopped drinking years earlier after a doctor advised him to cut back from the twenty bourbons he drank every day. He did not smoke and placed no-smoking signs and ashtrays outside of each of his identical offices. He logged between

50,000 and 125,000 miles a year in the air but had sold his corporate jet and, with no desire to be ostentatious, flew commercial. He had a fleet of black company Fords; an employee who once parked a tan car in the company lot had the vehicle towed and repainted. Webb insisted that all of his employees use the same desk calendars and have the same lettering on their office doors. He also insisted on daily reports from the field.

He enjoyed a wonderful press, which is often the case for men of humble origins who make good. Webb's rise was the stuff of myth: the westerner (he grew up in Fresno) who wanted nothing more than to be a ballplayer but was forced to take up carpentry when his father's sand-and-gravel business failed. The young Webb bounced around the semi-pro company leagues, pitching, catching, refusing to see that he was overstaying his time when he developed a sore arm at twenty-one; he was finally forced to give up the game at twenty-five, when he contracted typhoid. He lost one hundred pounds, spent eleven weeks in the hospital, and, upon his discharge, began repairing doors and houses.

He endured years of struggle that only enhanced his legend—his wife took the orders, he built and never turned down work. He was also lucky; he had based himself in Arizona, which was then beginning to boom. And he was smart, cultivating important friends. By the 1930s, he had expanded his operation to twelve states and opened offices in Los Angeles. He also began spending a good deal of time in Washington, where he befriended, among others, President Franklin D. Roosevelt. He built schools, houses, and hotels, but it was the war that made him rich.

His first major government project was Fort Huachuca, an army post spread over 149 acres in the Arizona desert. He finished the job in ninety days and for his punctuality was rewarded with contracts for ordnance depots, Marine Corps bases, hospitals, radar schools, and, in what would be heralded as a feat of engineering, the Poston Relocation Center near Parker, Arizona. The camp was situated in a stretch of desert so remote that it was described as "a part of Arizona God forgot." Webb took to the task with what had become his customary precision and zeal, and within three weeks, and with crews working double shifts, had built three thousand units that would effectively imprison ten thousand Americans of Japanese ancestry. Washington was so pleased with his work that he was rewarded with a contract to expand the camp to accommodate another twenty-five thousand detainees. If he ever felt bad about his role in what would later be regarded as a singularly shameful moment in American history, he never said so.

At the end of the war, he began turning his attention to Nevada and the rapidly growing city of Las Vegas. In 1946, beset by cost overruns of a purportedly dubious nature, the owner of the Flamingo Hotel, Bugsy Siegel, hired Webb to finish the job. Years later, Webb would joke that he had taken the job having never heard of the man, but Siegel assured Webb that his reputation for violence (he claimed to have killed a dozen men) should not concern him. "We only kill each other," Siegel said. Webb would insist that Siegel was reliable with his payments, which was odd given that shortly before Siegel was shot to death in 1947, he stopped payment on a $100,000 check to Webb.

Webb stayed on in Las Vegas. He built a second hotel, the Sahara, and bought a stake in the Mint. Through it all, there was no suggestion, at least in print, that it might be unseemly for the owner of a major-league baseball club to have ownership stakes in several gambling casinos. Instead, Webb was regarded as the picture of moral rectitude.

The FBI, meanwhile, had opened a file on Webb during the war. There had been allegations that his firm had been defrauding the government through its many contracts with the army and navy, but the bureau found no basis for the charges. Webb's name surfaced again in January 1951, in a memo from J. Edgar Hoover himself. Webb, he wrote to his chief deputies, had called from Phoenix, hoping to see the director on his next visit to Washington. "I told him I was almost certain to be here and that I would make my time available to him whenever it was convenient for him," Hoover wrote. The file also noted that "Mr. Webb is known to the Director on a first-name basis. In January, 1952, he was given a copy of 'Our FBI.'"

The only person apparently troubled by Webb's association with gambling was the baseball commissioner, Albert "Happy" Chandler. So unsettled was Chandler by even the appearance of an association with gambling that in 1947 he suspended Dodgers manager Leo Durocher for a year for merely being seen in the company of reputed gamblers. In

1950, Chandler turned his attention to Webb, as well as to Fred Saigh, the owner of the St. Louis Cardinals. This, from a job-security point of view, was unwise.

Happy Chandler had been Kentucky's governor and later a U.S. senator when in 1945 the owners hired him as commissioner to succeed Judge Kenesaw Mountain Landis, who had died four months earlier. Despite an apparent inability to resist launching into "My Old Kentucky Home" at banquets, Chandler was a man with sharp political elbows. The owners had been compelled to accept Landis's autocratic ways when they hired him in 1921 in the wake of the Black Sox scandal, but if they thought that Chandler's bumpkin affectation suggested pliability, they were wrong. Chandler levied fines and blocked trades and did not allow the owners to do as they pleased. Nor, he believed, did he endear himself to many of them when he sided with Branch Rickey in Jackie Robinson's signing.

In 1950, Chandler began hearing about Webb's stake in the casinos he had built and dispatched his executive secretary, Walter Mulbry, to investigate. But Mulbry was an old friend with ambitions far beyond his station. Hoping to curry favor with Webb, he tipped off the Yankees owner about the commissioner's suspicions.

In December 1950, the owners met in St. Petersburg and voted unanimously not to extend Chandler's contract when it expired in sixteen months. Chandler, an otherwise astute politician, was caught off guard. He had assumed that his friends among the owners would protect him. But he had not counted heads and, more important, had not understood the influence of Del Webb. In truth, Webb's task was a simple one: he needed only five of the sixteen owners to block Chandler's reappointment. He and Saigh, who was having trouble with the Internal Revenue Service, found the allies they needed. Chandler appeared before the owners, pleaded for his job, and lost. He tried again in February 1951, with the same result.

Webb, for his part, made no secret of his role in Chandler's firing. "Perhaps we need a different type of commissioner—a top executive with a big business and preferably a legal background to meet the new problems of our game, which has grown into such a big industry," he said, without an apparent concern for how his words might sound to those on Capitol Hill who would later challenge the antitrust exemption. "I don't think we need a commissioner merely to club us over the head and keep us in line. That is a by-gone stage of the baseball business."

Years later, Webb would take particular satisfaction in his role in ousting Chandler, whom he dismissed as a fool. "If I've never done anything else for baseball I did it when I got rid of Chandler," he told *Sports Illustrated* in 1960. "It took me about 48 hours to get enough votes to throw him out. It was the best thing that ever happened to baseball."

Webb, as it happened, was made chairman of the committee charged with finding a new commissioner. If Walter Mulbry had hoped to ascend to the post—as Chandler suspected he might—he was sorely disappointed. The owners fired him, too. In the end, Webb's committee did not select a commissioner who possessed a background in business or in the law. They chose Ford Frick.

Whatever pleasure Fred Saigh took from Chandler's dismissal was short-lived. In 1952, he was indicted for income tax evasion and later went to prison. But Webb's influence only grew, which, Chandler wrote, would not have happened had his watch been extended.

"If I had remained commissioner," he wrote, "I would have banished both Del Webb and Fred Saigh, owner of the St. Louis Cardinals, from organized baseball."

The accepted and endlessly repeated line on Del Webb was that he was a man of mystery, a remote if successful businessman whose intentions regarding baseball were unclear. In truth, the writers paid him little mind, and as a result allowed his imprint on the game to go unquestioned and seldom challenged. But time and again, in crucial moments, when decisions about the fate of franchises and the future of the game were at stake, Webb appeared from behind closed doors, having made sure things went his way.

By the spring of 1959, it had become clear to those who bothered to look that Del Webb saw baseball not as an enterprise in and of itself, but, like casinos, hotels, and military contracts, a source of revenue for his ever-growing empire. The construction business, he learned early on, is a perilous enterprise, with contractors—even big operators like himself— subject to being underbid, outmaneuvered, and politically outmatched. It was therefore no surprise that Webb had begun buying land in California and Arizona, thereby reducing his dependence on the whims and contracts of others; he could build what he wanted on the land he owned. Baseball was changing and, beginning in 1953, relocating. There was talk of Webb's selling the Yankees so that he might one day purchase a West Coast franchise. He dismissed the rumors, which, in truth, missed the point. The West Coast beckoned, and Webb, who had become a wealthy man by shrewdly positioning himself for the next big contract, saw in all the ferment the chance not to acquire property—he already had the Yankees and the influence they brought—but to build, and without a commissioner meddling in his affairs.

MAY: Fall from Grace

Casey Stengel had not managed a last-place team since August 4, 1940, when his Boston Bees (the once and future Braves) beat the Cincinnati Reds in the first game of a Sunday doubleheader and finally dragged themselves into seventh place, twenty-nine games out of first. He was then fifty years old, in his third year in Boston, and once again managing a loser. It was the same season the Yankees last found themselves in the cellar. New York had finished third that season, after winning the previous four World Series. Yet another troubling omen for the current reigning, stumbling champs.

Stengel's men had started the 1959 season poorly and had risen no higher than fifth since late April, when speculation on their woes began appearing in print. There was talk that their poor play was merely a continuation of the midseason swoon of 1958 that had so vexed and angered Stengel; maybe those final three World Series victories against the Braves had been an aberration. Yet, as much as their rivals delighted in the Yankees' struggles, no one really believed that the team's poor play would continue much longer.

But it did. The Yankees were not pitching well—Ford had a sore arm and had been merely competent; Turley, a star last fall, had thus far been a disappointment. But more striking were the team's pallid turns at bat. None of the regulars was hitting .300, and the team seemed incapable of generating power. Berra was hitting .225. Skowron was hurt again. Mantle, who'd had such a good spring that Stengel himself began talking about his becoming the game's first $150,000 player, had a mere five homers by the second week of May and was once again getting a nasty earful from the fans at the stadium.

The local columnists, who had never experienced so bleak a baseball spring—just one home team and a lousy one at that—took to seeking second opinions on what ailed the Yankees. They asked Phil Rizzuto, who was now a broadcaster and inclined to be a booster, but even he concluded that *these* Yankees, unlike *his* Yankees, seemed unable to take advantage of their opponents' mistakes. His old teammate Tommy Henrich, now a coach for Detroit, claimed that the Tigers were no longer intimidated by the prospect of playing New York. "They'd see us and you could feel them sag," he said of his time in the Bronx. "But now—when the Yankees lose and look bad, and it goes on for a while— now the opposition begins to feel, 'Hey, just a minute. We're as good as they are. Maybe anybody can win all that money.'"

Stengel's pal, the wise and gentle White Sox manager Al Lopez, placed Mantle at the core of the troubles. Lopez was the manager who had broken Stengel's pennant streak with Cleveland in 1954, and his White Sox were now a half game behind the first-place Indians. "Mickey is the most talented, natural ballplayer I've ever seen, but he hasn't capitalized on his gifts," he told Murray Robinson of the *Journal-American*. "I don't like to say this about any ballplayer, especially a great one like Mickey and only 27 years old, but I don't think he'll last very long as a topnotch star." Perhaps, he suggested, Mantle might take a cue from his much older teammate, the forty-three-year-old Enos Slaughter, and take better care of himself.

The Yankees hit bottom on May 20 against the Tigers, who had also started slowly but had been recently rolling and were now eager to cede the cellar. Frank Lary, a pitcher who seldom lost to the Yankees, was scheduled to start, and the prospect moved Stengel to commit the heresy of countering with a pitcher other than his best. He gave Ford and Turley each an extra day of rest and instead dispatched Bobby Shantz to keep the Tigers at bay. And while no one was suggesting that Stengel was conceding the game, his choice seemed the action of a man who thought it wise to wait and fight another day. Shantz, no slouch, had too little that afternoon, and the five relievers who followed him had even less. The Tigers were up 13–2 when the Yankees tacked on four in the bottom of the ninth on a rare but meaningless display of muscle by Mantle and Berra, who homered back-to-back before Norm Siebern brought a merciful end to the afternoon by grounding out to first. The Bombers' sixth loss in seven games. They were now in last place, percentage points behind Detroit.

The writers approached the clubhouse warily, unsure of the state in which they'd find Stengel. He had been grouchy for weeks, grousing about his players even as he tried to affect the behavior of an encouraging leader—*We'll get 'em tomorrow, boys*. But the players had let it be known, anonymously, that the old man had been laying into them when the clubhouse door was shut. "Some of the kids don't know if they're coming or going," confided one veteran. "Casey gets on them for something he doesn't like about their playing and the criticism makes them twice as jittery as they were in the first place."

But now, as the writers squeezed into Stengel's office and arranged themselves around his desk, he tried to keep his darkest thoughts to himself. He offered a barely veiled threat to the pitching staff—"The pitchers will have to do a little better or you won't be watching them around here"—but took pains to praise Shantz. He rambled on for fifteen minutes and then paused for questions that did not come. The writers would later confess that having expected something volcanic, they were not quite sure of what to ask. "You fellers are as quiet as the ball club," Stengel told them. Later, those who thought better of their reticence discovered that the moment was lost. Stengel retreated to the Essex House and informed the desk that he would be accepting no calls.

He was right about the players; they had nothing to say. They dressed quickly, knowing that Stengel would divert the newsmen long enough for them to make their escapes. But a few had spoken as the cellar loomed, among them Gil McDougald, a thoughtful man whom Stengel had brought up from the minors in 1951 and who had known nothing but winning. Milton Gross of the *Post* had reached him earlier that week at home in New Jersey after the Yankees had dropped the second of two against Kansas City, 10–0, yet another dispiriting afternoon. McDougald had come home, fixed himself a drink, grilled a steak, watched Dinah Shore on TV, and begged off baseball pillow talk with his wife. By the following morning he was feeling chattier, though hardly happier. He was seeing new and different things, and they troubled him.

"There's no life in the club," he confessed to Gross. "It's pretty quiet on the bench. There's not much to yell about. When you're winning there's noise. You're riding the other club. This way it's not good for the club. It's got to have life. Now nobody wants to pep it up. They know it would be false." McDougald was beginning to see what happened to losing clubs, how the crystalline delight that came with always winning could so quickly transform into melancholy and self-doubt. Gross had never heard him sound so dispirited. "When you see balls dribbling through the infield the way they've been doing against us you've got to start wondering," he said. "When you can't hit you begin wondering if you ever could hit."

After the loss to Detroit, the Yankees had the following day off, before heading south for a weekend in Baltimore. "It'll be a long year, a long hot summer if we don't get out of this before our next road trip," McDougald had told Milton Gross, when seventh place seemed a comfort. "We could be in real trouble by then."

The Yankees lost the opener against the Orioles and came within an eighth-inning single by Jerry Lumpe of being humiliated on a no-hitter by Hoyt Wilhelm. Stengel locked the clubhouse door and for three minutes lit into his players. When the writers ventured inside to assess the damage, Stengel turned on them, too. Someone asked whether he and Ford had, in fact, rudely brushed their way through the photographers as they boarded their train from Penn Station the day before, a harmless question, really—Ford had already admitted that he had been in no mood to pose; Stengel had retreated to his drawing room, pulled the shades, and locked the door. But the query ignited Stengel.

"What's the matter with you? You're just looking for trouble," he snapped. "Do you have to lose a game to have people following you all over the world? The Phillies lost eight games in a row. Why don't you follow them?" Actually, nine. But hardly a comparison he'd want to make.

Stengel caught his breath and seemed to have regained his equilibrium when someone asked what he had said to his players.

"I said five words to them," he said.

"Would you tell us what words you said?" asked Leonard Shecter, the wiseacre from the *Post*.

"No, I won't tell you. That's why I keep the door closed if I want to." And then he was off again, this time after Shecter, who, in Stengel's view, appeared to have forgotten that he was one of *his* writers and therefore should confine himself to perpetuating the Stengel legend through extensive, verbatim quotation. "You want to find what I said? You want to join the club? I'll give you a uniform."

He stopped and headed to the showers, only to return minutes later, naked and still boiling. He called out to his players: "And I just told Shecter he's been running the club for three years. I asked him if he wanted a uniform." The players asked Shecter where they'd be playing tomorrow.

"I managed an eighth-place ball club before," Stengel said, "but here you lose a few games and they're looking to lynch you."

For ten years he had made himself the story of the Yankees—feeding the writers, keeping his players' names out of the papers—and so now, inevitably, the photo on the back pages of the tabloids was not of Mantle or Ford or Bauer, but of Stengel's forlorn and craggy mug. The slide into last place had also brought out old antagonists whose comments were seldom sought when Stengel was winning and eternally wise. Billy Martin, banished two years earlier to Kansas City and now with the first-place Indians, had been at the stadium two weeks earlier for the start of what would be yet another three-game Yankees losing streak. He had made a point of hurrying past the Yankees' clubhouse door while Stengel could be overhead inside, lashing into his men. Rain had postponed the day's game, and Martin, who had never gotten over his being cast out, asked Pete Sheehy, the clubhouse man, if he knew the real reason why the game had been called.

"Why?" asked Sheehy, who'd always liked Martin.

"We scared the Yankees so much last night they're afraid to show up today."

Martin went on to talk about how good it felt to be wanted and appreciated, and how naive he had been to think that all he had to do in New York was please his manager.

"I loved Casey Stengel like a father," he said, "and the one time I needed him he didn't come through for me."

But if Martin's barb was laced with sadness and regret, there was nothing but contempt from Jackie Robinson. Robinson hated Stengel, whom he believed to be a bigot. He now wrote a column for the *Post*, which he often used as a forum on race relations. But as the Yankees sank, Robinson turned back to baseball, to offer his assessment of the locus of the team's woes. "Any club so demoralized by constant needling and unnecessary harassment by its manager is bound to fall far below its capabilities," he wrote, adding that he had played for Charlie Dressen, who could be a harsh critic but never slammed one of his men in print. Stengel, he went on, "obviously isn't concerned that any player would deeply resent his making public the criticisms that should have remained a family affair." Robinson then offered a vaguely worded but nonetheless damning conclusion: "On a club where the players no longer respect their manager you'll find though they may work for individual achievement they find it difficult to put out for a team effort."

Things were so bad that it fell to the game's most vulgar and caustic voice, Leo Durocher, to offer words of consolation and sympathy.

"You know what gets me most about this whole thing?" he said. "It's hearing the old man booed. They boo him when he was winning, but somehow you don't mind it then. This is a great man—nine of out 10 pennants. Some of it has to be his managing. Damn, how I hate to see him get booed when he's losing."

<<<<<

George Weiss had vanished from view as his team sank, and the writers assumed this meant he was trying to work a trade that might inject life into the club. In Baltimore, just as they began flexing their muscles— winning 13–6 and 9–0 after the loss to Wilhelm—they slid again, dropping the finale, leaving them to trudge back home, still a last-place team. Stengel was shuffling men in and out of the lineup and in various positions around the field, as if he were poring through catalog of fabric swatches. All to no avail. Weiss, meanwhile, was now discovering what it was like to have to deal from a subordinate position. His detractors were having a wonderful time; none took greater pleasure in his discomfort than Frank "Trader" Lane, the Indians' general manager, and the new owner of the White Sox, Bill Veeck. Veeck had Al Lopez, the manager the Yankees coveted. And better still, he was now in first place. But Lane and Veeck had been bruised enough times to appreciate that Weiss would not have to go wanting much longer. They could snub him, but there was one team to whom he could always turn for a sympathetic ear, and deal.

Veeck called Lane. "Get ready," he said, "Arnold Johnson just called me. The Athletics are making a deal with the Yankees."

"Naturally," replied Lane. "Don't they always. Who for? Maris?" Roger Maris, the Kansas City right fielder, was hitting .328 with ten home runs. He had also just had an emergency appendectomy.

"No, not Maris," said Veeck. "Apparently, at this time the Yankees don't want an appendix-less player."

So Weiss settled for Hector Lopez, who could hit for power and play almost anywhere, and Ralph Terry, a pitcher the Yankees had sent to Kansas City in 1957, presumably to get the training he needed before being summoned back to the Bronx. In return, the Yankees delivered Jerry Lumpe, Tom Sturdivant, and Johnny Kucks.

"Congratulate Mr. Weiss for me," Lane said. "I admire him for his astuteness. All it's done is make the Yankees stronger and Kansas City weaker."

Lane confessed that he, too, had designs on both Maris and Lopez but was advised by Kansas City that neither man was available. "I'd just like Johnson to do one thing for me—refund my telephone charges.

They come to $181.32, besides the wear and tear on my nerves. It must be nice to have a friendly club to operate with."

In his excoriation of the dangers of the Yankees' dominance, Paul Richards had neglected to mention an element essential to their success: they were the only big-league club for whom another big-league team operated essentially as a farm team. The deal between New York and Kansas City was the fourteenth between the two clubs since 1955, bringing the number of players that had shuttled between them to fifty-two. No other pair of teams even approached that level of commerce. The traffic had picked up after Del Webb's pal Arnold Johnson bought the Athletics and moved the franchise from Philadelphia.

Under Johnson, Kansas City became the place where the Yankees sent the inexperienced, the untested, and the unwanted, like Billy Martin. Johnson's general manager, Parke Carroll, had worked for the Yankees and once boasted to Bill Veeck, "I don't have to worry. Weiss has promised to take care of me."

The relationship between the Yankees and Athletics was so comically dubious that it had prompted Emanuel Celler to call Johnson to testify before his congressional committee in 1957. "There's been a lot of gossip about our club and another club in the American League," Johnson told the committee. "We aren't anyone's 'farm club' or country cousins."

He had a difficult case to make. Of course, he said, he had made all those trades with the Yankees. "They have the ballplayers," he said. "I'd say the whole second division doesn't have the players the Yankees have in their farm system. We've made as many deals as the rest of the league put together and never made one without trying the other six clubs. So far, I haven't been able to make a single deal with Chicago or Boston."

A pity. But then again, Johnson was not a business partner of Charles Comiskey II or Tom Yawkey, as he been for years with Webb and Topping.

In 1953, Johnson was, among his other titles, vice president of the board of the Automatic Canteen Company of America, the firm that brought the nation the vending machine, and whose officers included Topping and Webb. Johnson was forty-six years old, tall, beefy, and with a reputation in his native Chicago as a wizard at finance. His particular gift was to buy things, real estate mostly, while spending barely any money of his own. Among his holdings were the Warwick hotels in New York and Philadelphia. He also owned Yankee Stadium, the land beneath it, and, in Kansas City, the minor-league park where the Blues, a Yankees farm team, played.

Johnson actually owned Yankee Stadium only briefly. On December 17, 1953, he bought the two ballparks and the land from Topping and Webb for $6.5 million, a bargain, considering that the properties had recently been appraised at $8 million. He then immediately sold his new purchases to the Knights of Columbus, a Catholic fraternal organization that was looking to expand its holdings. The Knights then leased the properties back to Johnson, who, in turn, leased them to Webb and Topping. This all happened in a single day. And when it was done, Johnson had secured for Webb and Topping a lease that, given the write-off against their tax bill, would end up allowing them to stay in the stadium essentially rent-free. The Knights, the *Times* reported, made a profit of $1 million. More details of the deal emerged a year and half later, in the *Saturday Evening Post*, which reported that Johnson had spent only $500,000 of his own money to buy the properties. The balance came in the $2.5 million down payment from the Knights and from a $2.9 million second mortgage on the properties secured by Webb and Topping—who had essentially lent Johnson the money to buy their ballparks and land. The loan, however, was to their advantage: the *Post* went on to report that with the sale and the lease the capital gains advantage to the Yankees owners was $1 million apiece, given that their total capital investment in the Yankees was about $4.25 million.

So it was that in the summer of 1954, Arnold Johnson, whose interest in baseball had to this point been limited to a boyhood rooting for the White Sox, but who was now the Yankees' landlord, announced that he had offered $4 million to buy the Philadelphia Athletics. He planned to move the team to Kansas City, where the Yankees held the territorial rights and where Johnson held the lease on the ballpark.

The Athletics had been part of the American League since 1901, and for almost all that time had been owned and managed by Connie Mack, who had left the dugout only in 1950, when he was eighty-seven years old and still dressed for games in a suit and a high-collared shirt, as if Woodrow Wilson were still president. In fact, the Athletics had last won a pennant in 1931 and in the years since had been hibernating deep in the second division. The team was also bleeding cash. By the time Johnson appeared, seemingly out of nowhere, Mack and his aging sons, Roy and Earle, were looking to sell, though not necessarily to move. The Mack brothers were divided on the question of relocating. Roy, the younger, wanted to stay in Philadelphia, despite the fact that the mayor's "Save the A's" campaign had fizzled, embarrassingly; only 328,000 people came to see the team play in 1954 at, fittingly, Connie Mack Stadium. "Roy talks big, but we don't have a dime," said Earle when he learned that Roy was hoping to put together a group of local buyers to keep the team in Philadelphia. But three days after Johnson made his offer, a consortium of eight Philadelphians who were committed to keeping the Athletics in town matched his bid. Connie Mack, now ninety-one, frail, and sequestered in his apartment, kept his tongue as his sons and the money people battled for the club.

The motivation of the local fellows could be explained by latent civic pride. But left unasked was the question of why an otherwise astute businessman like Arnold Johnson would want to buy such a woeful team. Later, Johnson would insist that he had always wanted to own a ball club—and "pass it on to my son. I bought the A's because I love baseball, not for the purpose of making money." Not in Philadelphia certainly. But perhaps in Kansas City. And if not there, maybe Los Angeles, where in the midst of the haggling, Bill Veeck, the iconoclastic owner who had sold the St. Louis Browns the year before, resurfaced, plotting his return. Veeck had been lining up his own backers—among them the hotelier Conrad Hilton—in the hope of staking a claim to California for the American League. Even so, Veeck understood that his chances of success were remote. "I had little confidence that I was going to get the Yankee vote," he wrote, "especially since Webb and Topping were the men who brought him [Johnson] in to do the bidding."

By October 1954, three months after Johnson had first made his play, the issue had become less a question of Johnson versus the Philadelphians, or Mack v. Mack, and instead whether the Yankees would get what they wanted, which was Johnson in charge, the Athletics in Kansas City, and Veeck out of the picture so that the team—and by extension, the league—could fulfill Del Webb's vision of westward expansion.

Webb had been keen on California for years as potentially fertile baseball ground. But potential, he was quick to say, was all he saw. Los Angeles had thus far disappointed him. It was he who had tried to stall the transfer of the Browns to Baltimore in 1954 in the hope that monied people in Southern California might be able to pull together the ten million dollars he believed it would cost to buy and settle a team into a new ballpark. He did not regard the vast Los Angeles Memorial Coliseum as a suitable venue for baseball; tiny Wrigley Field—home of the Pacific Coast League's Los Angeles Angels—was at best a stopgap that, as he hinted to Veeck, he would be happy to retrofit with additional seating.

After the Browns moved to Baltimore, Webb told the *Los Angeles Times* that he "had the St. Louis franchise available for 48 hours" but that Baltimore "had a park, unlimited money, the mayor." Los Angeles, he carped, "didn't put their money where their mouth was." He advised Angelenos to start showing up en masse at Pacific Coast League games to prove themselves worthy of a big-league team. Yet now, a year later, another medium-sized city was doing what, to Webb's chagrin, Los Angeles could not: showing themselves ready to spend what was necessary to get a club; Kansas City voters, in fact, had just overwhelmingly approved a bond referendum that would pay for converting Blues Stadium into a big-league park.

Webb was not alone among the American League owners in eyeing the West Coast, if only to get there before the National League. But now, his less influential colleagues were feeling emboldened: if they could block Arnold Johnson's plan for relocating the Athletics, they could, at the very least, bloody Webb's nose.

"I'm not for Kansas City," declared Spike Briggs, who owned the Tigers. "Anything the Yankees are for I'm against." He had a vocal ally in Clark Griffith, who at eighty-four still owned the Senators and who had known Mack since Ban Johnson recruited them for his new league in 1901. Only three votes among the eight owners were needed to block the move. Baltimore and Boston, Griffith believed, would join Detroit and Washington in the insurrection.

The owners gathered in Chicago in mid-October. Veeck prudently remained in the shadows, knowing that his mere presence was enough to offend and scuttle the plans of his investors, among them now a Texan named Clint Murchison. Veeck thought he could swing the deal, win the Athletics from Johnson, and lay claim to California. But even he was stunned when the votes were tallied. "I thought it was a mortal cinch for us," he told the *Los Angeles Times*. Clark Griffith, it turned out, elected not to attend the meeting, instead sending his son, Calvin, who, despite orders to the contrary, voted with Webb and Topping. Spike Briggs left before the meeting ended, ostensibly to host a buffet dinner for his new manager. Another vote lost. Johnson would get the Athletics, who would move to Kansas City, which had promised him a million patrons in the first season.

There was, however, one more bump. Roy Mack went back to Philadelphia to break the news to his father but along the way decided that he had never agreed to sell in the first place. Instead, the Macks accepted the local offer. Johnson threatened to sue, but this was not really necessary. Although the league rules did not require approval of a sale—only a move—the Philadelphia buyers wanted the owners' approval. They did not get it. The Yankees, reportedly joined by the Indians and Orioles, blocked the sale to the Philadelphians. They did not explain why. A week later, Johnson appeared at Connie Mack's apartment with a check made out to him for $604,000, a down payment on his club. The Philadelphia buyers were waiting in the lobby to see the heartbroken patriarch—he had been unable to eat for three days—when Johnson emerged, the deal done.

The Yankees, in a seeming act of generosity, decided not to charge Johnson for invading their territory and forcing them to relocate their minor-league team to Denver. Johnson promised the league that he would sever his ties as the Yankees' landlord within ninety days. Kansas City bought Blues Stadium from Johnson. Del Webb's disappointment with Los Angeles's inability to present itself as a viable big-league city—"I can see no prospect of a definite nature of going to California"—was ameliorated by Arnold Johnson, who awarded the Del E. Webb Company the $3.5 million contract to add twenty thousand seats to Blues Stadium.

Three years later, Congressman Celler was still curious about the terms under which Johnson had divested himself of the Yankee Stadium lease. The ninety-day promise he had made had, in fact, not been met, and only when charged with a conflict of interest by Clark Griffith did Johnson at last sell the company that bore his name and held the lease.

"Personally, I never thought it was a conflict of interest," Johnson told the committee. "To me, it was a real estate deal. The Yankees had their lease. I didn't see where it affected anything on the field of play. Frankly, I thought the league would give me some liquidating time."

He went on to complain he was given only forty-five minutes during a league meeting lunch break to sell the company to James Cox, a lawyer who was also his closest friend. The price was $385,000, which in Johnson's view seemed a shame, given that he believed the corporation was worth between $3 and $6 million.

A skeptical Celler wanted to know what proof he had of this sale. Johnson replied that he had only a note, written in pencil by Cox, as evidence.

A "scrap of paper," snapped Celler.

Do you have anything else to support your claim? asked the committee counsel.

"Only my integrity as a businessman for over the last thirty years," he replied. "I'm independently wealthy. I don't have to make deals like that."

JUNE: The Temptation of Charlie Weeghman

The Yankees managed to extricate themselves from the cellar, but only barely. By early June, they hovered at .500 and slid between sixth and seventh place.

The news from New York, however, was not all bad.

As the Yankees sulked their way to Baltimore, Bill Shea emerged with good tidings for the city's beleaguered baseball fans: the new league was coming, and soon. In fact, he went on, there might well be a new club in town as early as 1961. In five weeks, or maybe six, he went on to say, the work of assembling the franchises of the new league would be complete, bringing teams to "every part of the country that does not now have major league baseball." Just which cities he could not yet say. But New York would be among them. It had to be; the men from the other cities had made it clear to Shea that without New York they were out.

It is tempting to fall back on the metaphor of herding cats to capture the work that occupied so much of Bill Shea's time in the spring of 1959. He had made his case for the virtues of the new league and had found audiences in city after city. But the men who now appeared ready to sign on did not necessarily trust one another. Denver's Edwin "Big Ed" Johnson, a political man, was suspicious of Toronto's radio magnate and sports impresario Jack Kent Cooke, who seemed cool to Rickey's plan for sharing television revenue—essential if the league was to succeed as Rickey had envisioned. "Jack Cooke's violent opposition to turning over a large share of TV revenue to the league is disconcerting," Johnson wrote to Rickey. "It leads me to believe that he is more interested in grabbing the Detroit franchise than in Montreal coming into the third Major League." But Johnson was confident of Houston's intentions, as well as those of Minneapolis, though "previously," he noted, "they had mental reservations."

For his part, Cooke was leery of New York's intentions, and so, too, were Houston's Craig Cullinan and Johnson's son-in-law and partner, Bob Howsam. They were so concerned that New York was using them—concocting the league merely as a ploy to extract a National League franchise—that they wrote to Shea to insist on the city's commitment to the third league. His good word, they advised, would not be enough. They wanted to know where the money would come from, and they wanted proof that New York would foreswear all temptations from the majors and vow that the new ballpark in Queens would be the home of the third league's anchor franchise. In fact, without a contract they would not proceed. "It is unthinkable," they wrote, "that the third major league can be organized with any stability, prestige or permanency unless New York is irrevocably committed to becoming a charter member of the new major league." New York, they insisted, would have to go to the owners and to the commissioner and get them to renounce any claim to the city. Only then would the other fellows ante up.

They got an assist three days after drafting their memo from an unexpected source. Ford Frick, sensing that momentum was gathering behind Shea and Rickey, brought the owners together in Columbus, Ohio, to decide how best to address the growing talk of change. They chewed things over for a couple of days and emerged with an artfully crafted statement that appeared to say everything but, in reality, said nothing. "Since there is no existing plan to expand the present major leagues," the statement read, "the two major leagues declare that they will favorably consider an application for major league status within the present baseball structure by an acceptable group of eight clubs which would qualify."

A moment's pause for a closer look. One: *favorably consider an application*. The implication is that they were ready to say yes to an application. Or, perhaps, that they would be happy to consider an application, which they could then reject. Two: an *acceptable group of eight clubs which would qualify*. Acceptable, they went on, would be cities with populations greater than that of Kansas City, the smallest existing big-league town (population 460,000). All the cities talking with Shea qualified on this score; the smallest city in the loop was Denver, with a population of 846,000. Acceptable also meant a city with a ballpark with a minimum seating capacity of 25,000.

In sum, the statement appeared encouraging. The requirements were hardly daunting, so long as the new league could also come up with players and the money to pay them and their pensions. Shea and Rickey were confident they could fill the roster for their league, even though they did not yet have eight clubs signed on. But more than the wording was the tone and what it revealed about the owners' self-regard. They were regal. The third league was a supplicant to whom they might be willing to condescend to assist.

In New York, Shea responded to the owners' declaration by assuming the pose of the office seeker so eager to display his bona fides as a hard charger that he pulls off his suit coat and rolls up his sleeves. "As soon as we have our own house in order then we will be ready to announce some of our plans," he announced.

Not so fast, cautioned Ford Frick.

"I doubt very much whether such a new league could go into effect by, let's say, next year or even the year after that," the commissioner said.

The newsmen hurried back to Shea for comment. Surely, he told them, the commissioner did not intend to slow the march of baseball progress. "I don't think he meant it that way at all," he said. "He couldn't. Who would be interested in working on a thing five years away?" With that he veered toward the existential. "I may not be alive in five years. Maybe nobody else will, either. Anything we're looking to do will get done quick. We're a lot further along than he thinks we are."

The owners' declaration sent the columnists back to the newsroom morgues, where they blew the dust off the files of the stories written long ago about the last attempt to start a third major league: the Federal League.

Suddenly the name was everywhere, back from the grave to serve as a reminder of what had happened the last time a group of wealthy men threatened the existing order. (The Mexican League of the 1940s lured several big leaguers but was never a rival for the affections of America's fans.) The conventional wisdom had it that the Federal League rose up, as if out of nowhere, to take on the majors; it raided the big-league rosters and caused great havoc before it succumbed to financial losses exacerbated by the First World War. The Federal League did, in fact, pirate the rosters, offering big money to the biggest names. But its birth and, more important, its demise, were far muddier than was generally recognized.

For all that baseball delighted in looking to the past, the story of the Federal League remained, for the barons of the sport, one best left buried, lest they be reminded of the awful results that came when other men insisted on sharing their game. The owners' view was shortsighted, which was as unsurprising as it was foolish. Because much of what happened before was about to happen again.

Had the men who founded the Federal League in 1912 contented themselves with fielding teams of mostly unknown men who represented such outposts as Indianapolis, Indiana; Buffalo, New York; and Covington, Kentucky, the major-league owners might have paid them as much attention as they did the Pacific Coast League or the Southern League. The Federal League emerged from the ashes of the defunct United States League with the loftily proclaimed belief that, in the words of its first president, "there can be no such thing as too much good baseball." Surely, he went on, the nation possessed more good ballplayers than the four hundred employed by the major leagues. Still, for its first season in 1913, a life in the baseball shadows seemed its fate; the Federal League felt so overlooked that it complained to the Interstate Commerce Commission that Western Union refused to carry its scores. The league drew fans in modest numbers—two thousand for the opener in Chicago—and fielded the occasional major-league castoff and such out-from-retirement stars as Cy Young, who was now forty-five years old. What little attention the majors paid the new league was limited to sticking up for those minor-league owners who felt threatened by the coming of the new fellows. Indianapolis won the first Federal League championship. The big-city papers paid this little mind and might have gone on remanding news from the new league to small boxes deep in the sports pages had the Federal League owners not decided that a change in tactics was warranted. They did what men in subordinate positions sometimes do when they feel that violence is the only recourse: they declared war.

That November, the Federal League announced that it was open for business: any major leaguer who had not yet signed his contract for the 1914 season was free to sign with them. And better still, their money was good and plentiful. The new league declared that it did not consider the reserve clause binding and would not impose a similar claim on its players. And lest the major-league owners contemplate going to court to block any such signings, the Federals—or "the outlaws," as a generally hostile press dubbed them—were prepared to challenge the legality of the reserve clause. Nor would the rebels content themselves with small markets. As Ban Johnson had done in waging his victorious war against the National League, the Federals set their sights on the biggest stage in the land: New York. Suddenly, it was as if the nation's sportswriters were being fitted with the gear of war correspondents. Reporters descended on Chicago and New York to stake out the hotels where the rival owners and league presidents were said to be holed up, plotting. Almost immediately, there were reports of signings and defections, and not merely of the little-known players. Walter Johnson was being offered $40,000 to defect from Washington. Ty Cobb was being lured with $75,000 for a five-year deal to abandon Detroit. Joe Tinker, the shortstop in the storied

Cubs double-play combination of Tinker-to-Evers-to-Chance, turned his back on Dodgers' owner Charles Ebbets, who had paid $25,000 to bring him to Brooklyn, and signed a three-year, $30,000 deal to manage and play for the Federal League's Chicago franchise. By January 1914, eighty-three big leaguers had signed with the Federals, as had another forty-four men from the minors. So widespread were the defections that in the American League only the White Sox and Athletics were spared. New York was in. Then it was out. Brooklyn was in, and there was money behind the franchise from the owners, the Ward brothers, who named the team after their bakery, the Tip-Tops.

The major-league owners tried ignoring the new league, then disparaged the quality of the men who'd defected, then announced some less-than-stirring signings of their own. They plotted futilely to keep the Federals out of the big cities, even as the outlaws anchored themselves in St. Louis, Pittsburgh, and Chicago. The majors even solicited an opinion from the Pennsylvania attorney general declaring the reserve clause legally defensible. Ban Johnson, who at first suggested that a baseball war might be the tonic needed to cure the owners of their foolish spending, now declared that any player who bolted would not be welcomed back to his American League. The majors went to court, seeking injunctions to block the signings. But even this went badly; on the eve of the season, a federal judge in Michigan ruled that the reserve clause was a wholly one-sided contract and therefore illegal.

On Opening Day 1914, 25,000 people filled the Federal League park in Baltimore to watch the locals take on the men from Buffalo. Meanwhile, across town, the New York Giants were playing their final exhibition game of the spring against the minor-league Orioles and their young pitcher Babe Ruth. The Giants drew a thousand spectators, many of whom were believed to have been turned away from the sold-out Federal League contest. It was much the same story in city after city: 9,000 for the opener in St. Louis, 16,000 in Indianapolis, and 21,000 in Chicago, 3,000 more than the new park's capacity.

The ballpark in Chicago had risen quickly that winter on the corner of Clark and Addison streets, staking a claim to the North Side; the Cubs still played on the West Side and the White Sox on the South Side. The day was brisk and the wind whipped off the lake, yet so many people tried to cram into the stands that the gates were locked a half hour before game time, forcing people to watch from the rooftops of the buildings across the street. After the Ladies of the Grand Army of the Republic marched across the field carrying a great American flag and rockets were launched as the banner was raised, the team's owner, Charles Weeghman, walked to the center of the diamond, where he was presented with a silver loving cup in honor of what he had accomplished in the six months since he had put up $26,000 to buy his way into the new league. A fitting tribute, because it would not be a stretch to say that no man better captured the spirit and meaning of the Federal League.

Charlie Weeghman wanted to be a man of significance. He began his climb in modest circumstances, as the ten-dollar-a-week "coffee boy" in Charlie King's, a lunchroom in the Chicago Loop. King, he would later say, "took a fancy to me" and promoted him rapidly. Weeghman saved his money, and when he and his partners had saved $2,800 he decided to open his own restaurant. On the day he opened, Charlie King died, robbing Weeghman of a patron and a competitor. Weeghman's first restaurant begat a second and a third, and in short order he owned a string of ten establishments serving cut-rate meals, day and night. He was ready for more. He opened a billiard room and a movie house and earned the nickname "Lucky Charlie." By this time he was in his late thirties, a handsome man with dark hair, deep-set eyes, and a great desire to assume the life of a sportsman. His first venture was to establish a three-cushion billiard league, with franchises in, among other cities, New York, Chicago, and Pittsburgh. But baseball was the great team game, and he wanted in. In March 1911, he tried to buy the St. Louis Cardinals. The deal fell through. But Weeghman was not done.

The Federal League's Chicago franchise had managed to finish the 1913 season—no mean feat—despite losing $12,000. The league's new and bold president, a fellow Chicagoan named James Gilmore, prevailed upon Weeghman to buy a stake in the team. Weeghman signed on and was quick to join the baseball war. Or so it appeared.

The first temptation of Charlie Weeghman took place in the fall of 1913 and came in the form he most desired: a big-league club. The St. Louis Browns could be his, if he abandoned the outlaws. The Browns were alluring only in that they played in the American League: they had finished 1913 in the cellar both in the standings and in attendance, and they had gone through three managers that season alone. Weeghman publicly turned on his prospective partners and complained that they were not backing up their talk with money, and if they did not start spending he would quit on them. The owners spent; the deal still fell through. For the moment at least, the Browns remained under the ownership of Robert Hedges, who left the running of his team to his young manager Branch Rickey, whom he had appointed just after Labor Day. Rickey was also the team's second vice president, business manager, and director of player development, a job at which he was devising ways to corral as many unsigned minor leaguers as he could. He was also angling to buy a piece of the club.

Charlie Weeghman decided that if he wasn't going to own a big-league franchise he would make his Federal League club *feel* major league. He spent like mad—he would later estimate that he sunk three million dollars—and built a winner. His team, the Chicago Whales, played well in its new park in 1914, finishing second to Indianapolis for the pennant. The season had been a good one for the entire league; every team had had its run at first place. Half the teams had made money, which kept the league on par with the majors, where it was understood that only first-division teams turned a profit. That fall, rumors flew that Kansas City was out and that New York was in, but in the end the Federals set up shop across the Hudson River, in Newark, for 1915. The new club's owner was the sort of man whose wealth made the new league feel all the more substantial, the oilman Harry Sinclair. But the arrival of Sinclair did not stop Charlie Weeghman from lusting for more. And in the autumn of 1914 he was once again tempted by the major leagues.

This time the lure was the Cubs. In October, newsmen tracked down Weeghman in Cincinnati, where he was meeting with one of the Cubs' owners, and the Reds' president, Garry Herrmann. Weeghman slipped out of town and headed to New York, refusing to say a word. But a deal was in the works, and by the time Weeghman returned to his Chicago office, he found several of his Federal League colleagues waiting for him, demanding an explanation. Weeghman emerged and offered assurances that he would "do nothing that is not satisfactory to the other club owners." But the talks were not limited to Weeghman's desires: he was, in fact, enmeshed in peace negotiations that would spell the end of the Federal League.

The Wards of Brooklyn were said to be negotiating to buy the Dodgers, and failing that, the Phillies. Phil Ball, who owned the St. Louis Federals, wanted into the majors, too. Charlie Weeghman, ever the dreamer, had boasted only weeks earlier that if he could get all the interested parties in a room for fifteen minutes, all of their differences could be resolved. But now, much to his chagrin, he saw that his interests and those of his colleagues were not necessarily the same.

"You know how it is in any business," he lamented to the writers who'd camped outside his office. "One day everything seems going along nicely the next day somebody bobs up with a kick." It was unclear whether the kick came in the refusal of one of the Cubs' owners to sell, or in the Federal League owners reminding him that he had an agreement with them, or in Ban Johnson's refusal to take back the men who had deserted. But the peace talks ended and with them, for the moment, Weeghman's longing for a big-league team to call his own. He tried assuaging his disappointment by sending $6,000 to Walter Johnson, the first installment on a promised $45,000 deal. But Johnson decided to re-sign with the Senators and after selling a herd of steer, sent the money back.

In the winter preceding their third season, the Federals concluded that no amount of raiding, spending, and competitive baseball would bring them what they truly wanted: parity with the majors. The big leagues—or, as they were then called, organized baseball—were still taking them to court to block the signings of the players the Federals coveted. The moment had come to challenge the big leagues' stranglehold on the game and the men who played it. The Federals wanted to invalidate the 1903 pact between the two major leagues—the National Agreement—and to do that, they would need to go to court and make their case that baseball was, in fact, a business run as a monopoly in violation of the Sherman Antitrust Act. To prevail, the Federals would need to make their case to a judge who had shown himself to be a foe of the trusts. They found him in federal court in Chicago, where he had made his name by fining Standard Oil a whopping $29 million. But the judge came with risks: Kenesaw Mountain Landis had a penchant for the theatrical, and he loved the Chicago Cubs.

Landis looked like everything he was not: restrained, prudent, and
wise. He had a great shock of white hair and a well-lined face that
appeared incapable of a smile. The very picture of a judge, biblically
speaking. But Landis was a bigot adept at playing the fool, as he would
famously display several years later when he insisted upon trying Kaiser
Wilhelm in absentia for the sinking of the *Lusitania*. Landis ruled by
whim and with a certainty in his views that gave the illusion of great
intelligence. He would free confessed felons for whom he felt sorry yet
would order federal marshals to hold witnesses in his chambers when
he was displeased with their testimony. He liked to see his name in
the papers and ruled in ways that were sure to bring him attention,
most famously in 1907 with his decision in the Standard Oil antitrust
case, when he levied the biggest fine ever imposed and ordered John D.
Rockefeller to appear in his courtroom to answer his questions. Rockefeller did not come to Chicago, and Landis was left to harangue him
from afar. The United States Supreme Court overturned his ruling—
not the only time it did— and twice resolutions were introduced in Congress calling for his impeachment. Undeterred, Landis fashioned for
himself an outsized persona about whom others could not help but talk
and sometimes cackle. Tucked in the pantheon of Landis stories is the
tale of his admonition of a man who wept at the prison sentence that
Landis had imposed on him.

"Please, judge," the man said. "I can't do it."

"Well, that's all right, sonny," Landis relied. "Just go along with the
man and do the best you can."

The baseball trial was all a showman like Landis could have asked for.
Each morning, the gallery filled to overflowing, with six hundred people
filling a room that normally held only two hundred. The nation's press
squeezed its way into his courtroom, along with the moguls of the game.
The trial went on for four days, during which the two sides took turns
presenting themselves as the saviors of the game: the Federals from the
rapacious ways of the big-league owners; the majors as the guardians of
the order that had delivered the game from the chaos of its early years.

Landis was, relatively speaking, the picture of restraint; there were few interruptions and little mention of his customary rolling of the eyes. But he twice seemed to tip his hand. The first came when an attorney for the Federals referred to the work of ballplayers as "labor."

"As a result of thirty years of observation," Landis snapped, "I am shocked because you call playing baseball 'labor.'"

The second instance also came in questioning an attorney for the outlaws. "Do you realize," Landis asked, "that a decision in this case may tear down the very foundations of this game, so loved by thousands?"

But if the big leaguers walked out of his courtroom believing that his statement foreshadowed a favorable decision, they were to be disappointed. Landis promised a speedy ruling. Days passed, and then weeks. When the wait began being measured in months, it became clear that Landis had no intention of rendering a decision and instead had decided to leave it to the warring leagues to try to settle the matter themselves. It was in this unexpected silence that the third and final temptation of Charlie Weeghman began.

All through the spring and summer of 1915, the talk was of peace just around the corner. It took many forms. There was talk of a deal being worked out between the Federals and Ban Johnson in secret meetings in St. Louis. Then of a deal to be brokered by Landis himself. Then of an arrangement that would allow the Federal League's St. Louis Terriers' owner Phil Ball to buy the Cardinals and, of course, Charlie Weeghman to buy the Cubs. There was talk of a deal between the Federal and American leagues that was reportedly rejected by the Nationals, then of a deal contingent on the Federals being absorbed into organized baseball as a third major league.

Meanwhile, almost everyone was losing money. Things were so dismal in the Federal League that in Newark, which had drawn twenty-five thousand for its opener, the price of bleacher seats was cut to a dime; the rest of the league soon followed suit. Kansas City was on track to lose $35,000, and Baltimore was rumored to be on its way out of the league. But the majors were hardly doing much better. Only on the North Side of Chicago was there reason for celebration. Charlie Weeghman's Whales won the pennant by a percentage point on the last day of the season, and were the only team in the league to make a profit. Weeghman challenged the World Series champion, the Boston Red Sox, to a championship series. He was rebuffed. But he had not stopped trying to broker the deal that would at last bring him to the big leagues. That fall, reporters tracked him to New York, where he holed up in talks for three weeks before returning to Chicago, only to turn back around and head back east, this time stopping in Cincinnati. Now rumor had it that he was poised, again, to buy the Cubs, with Harry Sinclair getting a stake in the Giants as the Nationals and Federals combined owners in Brooklyn, St. Louis, and Pittsburgh. But as with all the other talks of a settlement, the deal fell through and with it came the news that Landis was once again delaying his decision.

The death of the Federal League was foretold the day that it staked its claim to New York. The announcement came in November 1915. No longer content with an outpost in Brooklyn, where the Tip-Tops now found themselves struggling after the death of their co-owner Robert Ward, the Federals announced plans for a fifty-five-thousand-seat stadium that would rise on Lenox Avenue and 145th Street, in a still largely undeveloped patch of Harlem. The park would be the grandest in the game—larger than the Polo Grounds, larger than Comiskey Park, on the South Side of Chicago. Harry Sinclair was rumored to be the money-man behind the franchise.

But the news did not deter Charlie Weeghman from setting out for New York in early December. His trip would coincide with the meeting of the National League owners, and he did not deny that he might see them when he was in town. "I cannot state our present plans," he said. "But look for a hot session in which several important matters will be threshed out."

Indeed, the final weeks in the life of the Federal League were a time of great speculation and a good deal of travel, all of which involved Charlie Weeghman. He was on the train from Chicago to New York— dubbed the *Baseball Peace Special* by the *Chicago Tribune*—with the league presidents and big-league owners; he napped while Ban Johnson played hearts. He was at the Waldorf-Astoria, where the important men of the game gathered to see if they could come up with a deal. "Give us a couple of hours in that assembly room," he said, "and we'll pretty near have the wrinkles ironed out." In truth, he was up to his eyeballs in negotiations and had been for weeks, shuttling between Chicago and Cincinnati, working the long-distance phone lines to see how he might yet squeeze himself into a stake in the Cubs. He had never been so close. Everyone wanted the war to be over, with the exception of James Gilmore, the Federal League president, who had invited Weeghman to join his enterprise and who was not ready to see his circuit vanish. But the sense in the corridors outside the meeting room was that Gilmore's men had abandoned him and were no longer paying him much mind.

The snags, which seemed great and vexing in the heat of negotiations, turned out to be minor in the end. The deal was going to happen and the Federal League was going to die, and all that stood in the way of resolution was determining who owed whom how much. The talk of merger, of consolidation, and of new teams joining the big leagues did not make it out of the Waldorf. The Federal League would go out of business; the players who had jumped to the outlaws would be welcomed back; the Federals would honor the contracts of the men the majors did not want; the suit still pending in Landis's court would be dropped. And the big leagues would emerge from the war looking just as they had before the fighting began, with two exceptions. Phil Ball would become owner of the St. Louis Browns, and Charlie Weeghman would at last have the Cubs. They would play not on the West Side, but would come north, to play in his park.

In the months to come, the players would watch, helplessly, as their salaries were cut now that they had no place else to take their services. The citizens of Baltimore, finding themselves once again out of big-league baseball, filed suit against the majors, claiming that the owners' monopolistic control of their sport had excluded them. The suit would take years to work its way through the federal courts until arriving before the U.S. Supreme Court in 1922. The twin legacies of the Federal League: the Cubs in what would later be renamed Wrigley Field and the lawsuit that unintentionally led to baseball's antitrust exemption.

Perhaps if Charlie Weeghman had remained true to the Federal League, things might have gone differently, because Weeghman had been the most successful of all the Federal League owners; the league could not survive without him. But Weeghman was merely the embodiment of the curse that doomed the league from the moment he signed on. He wanted what Ban Johnson had wanted when he founded the American League and what every man who had ever spent his money on a baseball franchise wanted: to be a member of the club. What made membership in the major leagues so alluring was the promise of exclusivity. It took no time at all for the new members to insist that the doors be locked behind them—witness Johnson himself, who abandoned his rebellious streak the day he signed the National Agreement and who in the subsequent years assumed the role of baseball's high priest, which he played with overbearing zeal. In fairness, Johnson cared deeply for his league—"the great American League," he always called it. But it is hard to detect in Charlie Weeghman a comparable loyalty to the Federals. Weeghman's commitment was deep and single-minded and defined so narrowly that it had room for nothing but his own desires. Welcome to the club.

In addition to the cities that lost their teams in the peace deal—Baltimore, Buffalo, Indianapolis, and Kansas City—there was another loser in 1915. Branch Rickey was out in St. Louis the day Phil Ball walked into the Browns' offices. Ball replaced Rickey with his own man, Fielder Jones, but allowed Rickey to stay on for a year, ignoring his suggestions about how best to develop players. There was talk that Rickey would quit the game to practice law. A year later, Rickey enlisted in the army. He never bought a piece of the Browns.

He returned to St. Louis after the war and went to work for the Cardinals.

CHAPTER FOUR

SUMMER 1959

JULY: Beware the Ides of March

The true voice of the baseball establishment was not that of the commissioner, Ford Frick, but rather was found in the newspaper columns and dispatches of Dan Daniel, who wrote for the *New York World-Telegram* and the *Sporting News*.

Daniel loved baseball dearly and had been covering the game for a living since 1911. He was born Daniel Markowitz, but his editors, uncomfortable with too Jewish-sounding a byline, lopped off the surname. He had started his career at a time when the giants of the press box—Grantland Rice, Ring Lardner—had fashioned a working life built around taking in a game in the afternoon, retiring to the hotel for dinner, repairing to their rooms to write, and then heading back down to the lobby to schmooze with the players and managers. Daniel was the rare scribe who did not drink. Early on, he had seen how liquor had ravaged the careers of too many men—in the Chicago press corps in particular—and vowed that dissipation would not be his fate. He was a husky man with a deep, raspy voice, and the unsmiling photograph that accompanied his prosaically titled "Daniel's Column" made him look like a retired leg breaker. He told a wonderful story and he had a million of them.

He had begun writing in pen and ink and was the first man on the staff of the *New York Press*, his first full-time employer, to use a typewriter. He was a very fast writer, so fast that he believed that if a story did not come to him quickly, it was best to walk away. He style veered toward the rococo; the men he quoted did not speak; they "vehemed" and "exuberated." He wrote every day for the *Press* and later for the *World-Telegram*, and, most important, three times a week for the *Sporting News*. He helped broker the deal that got Babe Ruth his $80,000 salary in 1930 by reminding the Babe that it was unseemly to be holding out for $85,000 when people were lining up at soup kitchens. The Babe, it seemed, was only vaguely aware that the nation was in the throes of a Depression but did not think it untoward to have Daniel serve as the go-between in his negotiations with his boss, Colonel Jacob Ruppert. Such was extent of Daniel's access and influence.

Daniel was the same age as Casey Stengel and, like the Yankees manager, not a happy fellow in the summer of 1959. The world he had known as a young man was long gone. He blamed the game's troubles on the advent of night baseball, when the rhythms of work changed and it became necessary to scurry down to the clubhouse after the game, gather what quotes he could, and then climb back five or six stories to the press box to write because the elevator man would have already gone home. But time, experience, and exposure had boosted Daniel to a rarefied position: the man to whom the secrets were entrusted. Given the feudal nature of the game—fiefdoms, serfs, indentured servitude, a figurehead monarch—Daniel's tenure in the press box and access to the powerful owners (Topping, O'Malley, and especially Del Webb) granted him his lofty post as the purveyor of edicts, the shaper of sentiment, the voice of the unseen hand. If the *Sporting News* was indeed, as it fancied itself, "the Bible of Baseball," then Daniel was its chief and most influential prophet, the voice of the past, and ever more the man who could foretell the future.

Talk of Bill Shea's third major league was growing, and excitement, in some quarters, was building. But Houston's George Kirksey, who had assumed for himself the mantle of chief publicist, was worried that the story was fading and that events were slipping perilously out of their control. Where, he wanted to know and soon, was Rickey's article, the essential document that would lay out before the world the rationale for the new circuit? There was, in Kirksey's always fevered mind, less and less time to get things in order before the moment came to make formal their league's establishment. Kirksey wanted a Manhattan unveiling, perhaps on Monday, July 27—no big games that day. But before then, he cautioned, it would be necessary to tamp down the growing chorus of doubts emanating from one too many out-of-town columnists: "a financial bust," predicted Bill Rives of the *Dallas News;* "It will take these towns about three years before they can get respectable, acceptable baseball," cried Al Abrams of the *Pittsburgh Post-Gazette.*

So Bill Shea, wise to the ways of power, went to the source, such as it existed in baseball, and sat down with aging, beefy, and, as he was about to discover, suspicious Dan Daniel.

For a man who presented himself as the most accessible and transparent of lawyers, Bill Shea was now playing a game whose goals were difficult to discern. He had traveled and worked long and hard to establish his new league and corral the men who would lend their names and those of their cities to his crusade. And then he did a curious thing. In early July, Senator Estes Kefauver offered his help. Specifically, he offered to apply the cudgel of his committee and its very public hearings to the collective heads of the owners, so that they might loosen their grip on the sport and allow the new league to blossom. An appealing offer, given that the threat of the end of the antitrust exemption was the only power that could move the owners. "I don't believe baseball will permit the formation of a third league," Kefauver told Shea and offered to begin hearings immediately.

Shea thanked the senator, and then he turned him down, publicly.

"I asked him to hold the hearings in abeyance because we are in no position to advise on any bill at this time," Shea told the *Times.* "We must get together with the major league owners to reach an understanding."

An understanding?

"I believe that baseball had made an honest statement at Columbus," he said.

Either Shea believed that the owners, facing the mere threat of congressional action, were ready to make a deal to incorporate the third league—and he did not wish to antagonize them—or he had another deal in mind, which is what Dan Daniel was beginning to suspect.

Daniel chose the narrative conceit of a direct examination to air Shea's views and—it now appeared—his own considerable skepticism. For reasons he did not explain but which in the years to come would only burnish his Delphic credentials, he referred to Shea's New York franchise as "the Mets."

DANIEL: Suppose, when your Third League people meet with the club owners of the majors after the Aug. 3 All-Star game you are turned down by them. Do you still have "outlaw" notions?

SHEA: No, we do not plan so-called "outlaw" activity, nor do we believe that, after having invited us in, the major leagues would throw us out.

DANIEL: Well, what if they throw you out, what then?

SHEA: We would go to Washington for legislation which would break the baseball monopoly and for the commissioner to give us official approval. However, I am convinced that Organized Baseball is sincere in extending a helping hand to us and appreciate how much we can do for the good of baseball.

Daniel and Shea's conversation was intended not so much for Daniel's many readers as it was for the men who had arrayed themselves on both sides of the lines of a battle that Shea hoped to avoid. Shea was telling the owners he did not want a fight. Daniel, speaking for the owners, was probing to see how far they could push. Not too far, cautioned Shea. Congress awaits. Be warned.

Daniel had one other piece of business to attend to: the needs of the Yankees. Webb and Topping were not pleased about the prospect of the Flushing stadium and were hinting, none too subtly, that they'd be happy to have the third league's New York entry as a tenant, should they choose not to play in one of the parks that O'Malley and Stoneham had abandoned.

DANIEL: Have you been looking at Ebbets Field?

SHEA: Yes, but only as a temporary location while the Flushing Meadows Stadium is being built.

Not the answer Daniel wanted to hear, but music to the ears of Cooke, Cullinan, and the others.

A week later, Daniel spoke. "New York's chances of again getting a second representation in the majors were revealed to me today as far stronger than is generally suspected. But not through organization of a third league."

This is what he saw: In August, on the nineteenth precisely, and in New York most likely, seven men would meet—Frick, Giles, Cronin, and the owners Lou Perini of Milwaukee, Tom Yawkey of Boston, Bob Carpenter of Philadelphia, and Webb's man, Arnold Johnson of Kansas City. They would sit down with Bill Shea and his people. They would ask two things: could Shea deliver his promised monied people to bankroll a New York club; and would the City of New York promise to build the Flushing stadium? If the men from the majors heard the answers they sought they would grant two wishes: a National League franchise for New York and a second one for Houston, to keep the numbers even. The American League would then extend its reach to California, with a team in Los Angeles and a tenth team, perhaps in Toronto.

Daniel did not wait for the smoke of prophecy to clear before explaining himself. He had spent hours talking with Shea, he wrote, and had come to believe that he was a clever young man—Daniel figured Shea for thirty-eight; he was actually fifty—who could spin a fanciful tale "that could sell you the Brooklyn Bridge. You leave him with the feeling he has that third league all ready to go."

But Daniel did not believe him. He had concluded that Shea hadn't a clue as to the complexities of organizing a baseball league and that he would never find the two hundred players he needed to fill the rosters because—and this was key—the owners were not going to help him. "Are the owners of the NL and AL going to make gifts to Shea and the rest of that talked-of league of their most promising replacements? Not a ghost of a chance, most emphatically."

And he believed that Shea knew this; his replies were too broad, too vague. "I got the impression that Shea wasn't joshing and that expansion was his No. 1 goal," Daniel wrote.

Dan Daniel had seen into the future and into Bill Shea and had concluded that the new league was a ruse, a bluff. And Daniel was calling him on it, just as he was foretelling what he believed would surely come.

"It has to be expansion. New York will give the impetus to that in the NL, and Los Angeles will urge the AL to make its too-long-delayed move into California."

There was one last piece of business. The Flushing stadium. It would not happen, Daniel wrote. The new National Leaguers would rent space at Yankee Stadium from Webb and Topping just as the new American Leaguers would have Walter O'Malley as a landlord at the ballpark he hoped to build in Chavez Ravine.

But the problem with being a soothsayer is that it is one thing to foretell and quite another to be heard. In Shakespeare's *Julius Caesar*, Caesar is warned once, then twice, then a third time to "beware the Ides of March." But Caesar, an arrogant soul, does not listen. "He is a dreamer," Caesar tells Brutus of the prognosticator. "Let us leave him." The game, with an assist by Brutus, does not end well.

The owners had heard Dan Daniel, as had Shea and his followers. But this did not mean they heeded his words.

Daniel, too, had not listened well; he had made a prophecy on incomplete evidence. He had not understood that standing behind Bill Shea, guiding him, filling his head with his own vision of the future, was a friend of many years, Branch Rickey.

The Continental League came to life on July 27, 1959, at the Biltmore Hotel in midtown Manhattan. It was a grand event. Shea and his people sat before the many newsmen who, having heard the outlines of the plan, dutifully returned to their typewriters and pounded out dispatches that by the following morning had given the new league what it sought above all else: legitimacy. Dan Daniel may have offered his dark prophecy—and did so again. But the collective wisdom of the nation's press corps was that Shea and his people were serious and determined; the Continental

League was no sham. George Kirksey, who'd been worrying himself into yet another frenzy, could have been no happier had he written the copy himself.

"What impresses me is the dream of baseball hasn't perished in this country," wrote Jimmy Cannon, who had recently moved his syndicated column from the *Post* to the *Journal-American*. "We are glad people and baseball is part of our national joy. We still want it in our cities and important people are willing to risk fortunes to buy it for their hometowns.

"There will be a third league, all right. The people running it are big league."

And then came the caveat that was on everyone's mind.

"But," he concluded, "how can the players be?"

Many questions were put to Shea and the others that day. There were, after all, only five cities represented—New York, Houston, Minneapolis–St. Paul, Denver, and Toronto. Where were the others?

Fear not, replied Shea, we are deluged with requests. He rattled off the names of interested cities: Buffalo, Montreal, New Orleans, Dallas–Fort Worth, Seattle, Portland, San Diego, Indianapolis, Atlanta, and even San Juan.

And will the majors welcome you?

"I believe in the good faith of the major leagues," he replied, "and that they will not go back on commitments they have already made."

And who will bankroll you?

Mrs. Joan Whitney Payson is the money behind New York, he said, and she was joined by such deep-pocketed fellows as George Herbert Walker Jr., Donald Davis, and Mrs. Payson's banker and omnipresent escort, M. Donald Grant. Craig Cullinan was part of Houston's petroleum elite. Jack Kent Cooke had made millions in all sorts of ventures, and the folks from Minneapolis included the brewers of Hamm's beer.

But where will you play?

There are parks in all these cities that need only to have seats added, Shea replied. And where there are no stadiums, they will be built.

And where will you get your players?

"If the major leagues cooperate with us," said Shea, "we won't have a bit of trouble getting players."

And that, for the moment, is where the matter was left. The mood in the room that carried the newsmen back to their desks was too buoyant to be undermined by doubts about a plan contingent on the word *if*. It is difficult to discern what moved the press corps more—the desire to believe that they were witnessing, as Denver's Edwin Johnson called it, "an historic moment" for the nation's game, or the sight of those men at the dais and the working stiff's belief in the power that came from men with money.

Emanuel Celler was delighted by Shea's announcement—Congress, he said, was "duty bound" to help the newcomers. So was Estes Kefauver, who said, "This is a great forward step and will go a long way toward returning baseball to the American people—where it has always belonged." Better still, the most powerful man in the Senate, Lyndon Johnson of Texas, proclaimed that the "announcement spells the advent of a new day in the historic American pastime." Johnson's state, after all, was in line for one club and possibly two. A new day, indeed.

The owners, meanwhile, kept their thoughts to themselves and left it to their respective league presidents to keep the good feelings tamped down. "Any steps they take should be real slow," said Joe Cronin, while Warren Giles suggested that a mere five teams hardly constituted a league. But the truer sense of the mood among the owners came from a surprising source, in as much as he was an employee—Jimmy Dykes, the manager of the surging Tigers.

"Oh sure, everybody will say they're willing to help the third league to keep Congress off their backs, but you won't find anybody willing to give up anything they could possibly use," he said. "I don't see how the Continental League can make it."

Shea ignored Dykes's comment and instead focused his attention on Giles and Cronin. "I wish that these guys would check with Ford C. Frick, the baseball commissioner, before they go popping off like that," he said. Then, lest anyone think that their words carried weight, he added, "In any event it will be existing major league club owners we do business with and not the league presidents."

Shea was about to set off for Washington for the hearings that he had succeeded in getting Kefauver to delay, and which were now scheduled to begin the following day. There was, however, one more matter left hanging. Who was going to be in charge of the new league? United Press was reporting that Branch Rickey himself was being lured out of retirement to lead the Continental League.

Shea replied cagily. "Rickey," he said, "has always been an exponent of the new major league and he is a very fine man." Better not to mention that the day before, Rickey had finally gotten through to John Galbreath, the Pittsburgh owner—he'd been trying to place a call to him for days—to let him know that he was ready to sell his shares of Pirates stock.

Galbreath asked if it was money he needed, because if so he'd be happy to extend a loan.

No, Rickey said, he did not need the money. He wanted his freedom.

Was he thinking of throwing in with the new league? Galbreath asked.

"I told him very quickly that I had exactly that in mind," Rickey wrote in a memo, recounting the conversation. "But that I could not do it with the ownership of this Pittsburgh stock."

Galbreath, eager to dissuade Rickey, tried to play on his sense of loyalty. "He mentioned that he had always stood by me from the time he first met me," Rickey wrote.

Rickey would not play. "You fired me from my present job and you know it."

Galbreath said nothing. Rickey again asked to be allowed to sell.

"I wished to be free to do work, if I wished, with the Third Major League," he wrote. "He seemed to know something about that in advance."

Bill Shea had learned a good many things during his yearlong education on the nature and workings of the major leagues. He now understood that beyond the talk of players, ballparks, and pensions lay a greater, seldom mentioned impediment in the path of the Continentals. A new league, he had learned, threatened the owners in a way that few could fully appreciate, if only because it reflected not a worry of the moment but of the future. Shea had shared this early on with the men he had recruited.

"Mr. Shea pointed out that one of the most difficult problems connected to the third league movement was the deep interest of the present major leaguers in Pay/TV," Craig Cullinan wrote in his recap of Shea's first meeting with the Houston Sports Association. "He said that the existing 16 clubs would like to divide the country among themselves and reap the golden harvest of this almost certain financial bonanza."

In the summer of 1957, *Television Age* reported that it had surveyed baseball fans among eight hundred New York television-viewing families and discovered that fully 40 percent of them would be willing to pay to watch major-league games. A third said they'd be willing to pay a quarter a game; some said they'd even pay a dollar. The pollsters extrapolated and concluded that based on 346,000 TV sets wired for paid service, and at twenty-five cents a game, the Brooklyn Dodgers alone would make $86,700 a game—or $8,843,400 for an entire season of seventy-seven home games and twenty-five televised road games. The report confirmed what Walter O'Malley had long believed—that, as he told the *Wall Street Journal*, Americans "were ready" to pay for television, and that pay TV represented salvation for men like himself. It was imperative, then, that the Federal Communications Commission stop equivocating and allow paid telecasts to be carried over the nation's airwaves. "Until the government legalizes pay TV," he told *Newsweek*, "the best any baseball man can do is come up with a stopgap." In truth, O'Malley had been a believer for years, having already opened his heart to the pay-TV impresario Matthew J. Fox; he even had Fox as a guest at his private club in room 40 of the Hotel Bossert on Montague Street in downtown Brooklyn.

Matty Fox was a short, pudgy man with colossal dreams. He had married a beauty queen—Miss America 1951—and became a vice president of Universal Pictures at the age of twenty-five. (It didn't hurt that his sister had married the president.) A year later, he somehow managed to convince Indonesia's finance minister to grant him the monopoly rights to all Indonesian imports and exports with the United States. The plan failed to pass muster with the State Department. So Fox, who had made his early money on 3-D movie glasses and the little plastic pipes through which children blow soap bubbles, moved on to television.

No sooner had television begun its remarkable growth across the country—6,400 sets in 1946; 40 million ten years later—than men like Fox began thinking of new ways to make money from the medium. Sports, like old movies, had been an early television staple, given how desperate the stations were for programming. And sports, especially in New York, meant baseball. A combined fifty million people watched the World Series between 1951 and 1956, for which Gillette paid baseball a relatively paltry six million dollars for the broadcast rights. In the meantime, teams negotiated local contracts with their own sponsors, their profits dependent on the deals they cut. But these arrangements were, at best, modest.

But in the spring and summer of 1951, the great possibilities of television were revealed in three hundred Chicago homes, when Zenith unveiled Phonevision, the first pay-per-view network. For three months, viewers who had signed on to be part of Zenith's experiment saw an average of 1.7 movies a week for which they paid a dollar a show—double the average price for a movie ticket. Zenith claimed that the figure represented triple the average family's weekly movie-house attendance. In 1953, a California firm, Skiatron, conducted its own pay-television experiment during off-peak hours on WOR in New York. The following year, the company petitioned the FCC to allow it to deliver its signal on rarely used UHF stations. That same year, Matty Fox, who already owned the rights to RKO's movie library, bought Skiatron. By 1957, Fox had positioned himself so well that the Los Angeles City Council was deliberating whether to grant Skiatron the franchise to install the city's first closed-circuit system.

At congressional hearings in the summer of 1957, Horace Stoneham testified that the soon-to-be-transplanted Giants had already reached an agreement with Skiatron to carry their games exclusively for paying customers. Skiatron, he told the committee, had guaranteed "quite some more" income than the team was now making in its local television deal—somewhere in the neighborhood of $125,000 a game. The next day, Fox testified that he could wire San Francisco for less than $6 million and Los Angeles for about double that amount. He also testified that he had entered into agreements in escrow with the Dodgers and the Giants to carry their games on his pay-per-view network, should they relocate to California. With that, he went on to talk of the good things that would come with pay television—and not merely for men like himself. Television, he told the committee, was "a poor man's medium" and he, for one, had no intention of hurting the common man. Rather, he wanted to give viewers "something extra." No one would have to buy a new television or have their sets converted; Skiatron's signal would come through a decoder box attached to existing sets. A computer punch card would unscramble the signal—all for three dollars a month. "We trust the American public," Fox said. "Our customers won't have to pay in advance."

Still, some members of the committee were skeptical. New Jersey representative Peter Rodino told Fox that he'd been getting letters from unhappy people who had assumed that the only price they would have to pay to watch television was the cost of their sets.

"Who had the right to make that guarantee, the set makers?" countered Fox. "In Milwaukee there is no baseball on TV. If I bought my set in New York, then moved to Milwaukee, could I claim I was being deprived of free TV? After all, any club owner today can stop televising his games. Then the fans have nothing."

With that, Fox returned to what he did best: selling. Pay television, he advised the committee, was the coming thing, and despite the disappointment registered in Peter Rodino's mail, America would be willing to pay.

"We estimate," he said, "that 85 to 90 percent of TV homes would be willing to buy our service."

The pitch had impact. On the day of Fox's appearance, Skiatron was among the five most active stocks traded on the American Stock Exchange, with 30,100 shares traded and the price per share up a dollar on a day of otherwise sluggish trading. The following day, the Los Angeles City Council approved Skiatron's contract to wire the city for pay television.

Asked if he owned stock in Skiatron, Walter O'Malley said that he did not. But, he was quick to add, "If it ever develops to its potential, I very sincerely intend to."

AUGUST: Big Ed's Dilemma

The best thing that ever happened to Bob Howsam was Janet Johnson's agreeing to step out with him for a Coca-Cola at the Sink, the malt shop at the University of Colorado. He liked her and she liked him, and from that first soft drink sprang a courtship that would lead to the very long marriage that drew Howsam into the orbit of Janet's father, Edwin Johnson. Howsam was the son of a farmer and assumed that he would one day become a beekeeper. His father-in-law had other ideas.

Big Ed Johnson was six foot four and carried himself with a commanding beefiness that befit his position as perhaps the most powerful politician in Colorado. He had come to the state from Nebraska in 1909 to convalesce from the bout with tuberculosis that had ended his dream of being a railroad man; he had made the climb from track worker to telegrapher and dispatcher when his doctors advised him that mountain air might restore his fragile health. He and his wife moved to rural Colorado, where they lived in a cave, presumably against doctors' orders, while he and his Swedish immigrant father built their home in the middle of nowhere. Johnson found work teaching school, ran for school superintendent, and lost by five votes. He never lost another election. He was elected to the state legislature in 1922, then as governor in 1932, and United States Senator in 1936. He served for three terms before returning to Colorado, where he was again elected governor in 1954.

His politics reflected the sensibilities of a man who appreciated the wisdom of being a friend to industry—highway construction was a Johnson passion—and was against anything that so much as hinted at foreign entanglements; he twice called out the National Guard to keep Mexican immigrants from entering the state. He was a Democrat who opposed the New Deal as well as America's involvement in World War II. Johnson possessed a sanctimonious streak: he introduced legislation to license movie actors, the better to impose standards on their dubious sense of morality; he had been particularly appalled by Ingrid Bergman's affair with Roberto Rossellini—"an apostle of degradation," he called the

Swedish actress, adding, for good measure, "vile and unspeakable." But he did like baseball. And that is where he saw his son-in-law.

In 1947, he had brought the husky, round-faced Howsam with him to Washington to serve as his administrative assistant. Six months later, the sports editor of the *Denver Post* called to say he needed help in reorganizing the Western League, a Single-A minor-league circuit. It was not uncommon for sports editors and columnists to perform double duty as sports promoters and boosters. Nor was it regarded as unseemly for Johnson to serve as the league's unpaid president, a position that allowed him to choose a new administrator. Howsam had played baseball in high school and might have played college football had he not contracted pneumonia. That was good enough for Johnson, who ordered him back to Colorado to take charge of his league. "That was my father-in-law," Howsam later wrote. "You didn't refuse a request from him."

Over the next twelve years, Howsam absorbed many lessons about the baseball business. He soon became the owner of the league's Denver franchise, and learned, at turns, how to fire a manager, identify talent, peddle concessions, and curry the favor of the politicians he needed to finance a new ballpark. His father-in-law was helpful with that one, while his mother, father, wife, and brothers helped sell the tickets. In time, Howsam's Denver Bears were playing in a new ballpark—it would one day, in an expanded form, be renamed Mile High Stadium—and doing so well that in one season they outdrew the St. Louis Browns and Philadelphia Phillies. He was keen on promotions and stunts, once inviting the citizens of Yuma, Colorado, to bring jackrabbits to the ballpark so that his players could chase them around the outfield. In 1951 the *Sporting News* named him minor-league executive of the year. He won the award again in 1956, this time with a Triple-A team; when Arnold Johnson moved the Philadelphia Athletics to Kansas City, Howsam bought the minor-league Kansas City Blues for $90,000 and brought them to Denver, where they won the 1957 Junior World Series. Howsam and Big Ed Johnson were pleased but also restless. One night after a Bears game, the two men sat in a car outside of Johnson's Denver apartment, talking of the future. Howsam would later recall that he was sure he had heard Branch Rickey say something about the wisdom of starting a third major league. That was all that Johnson, a man of great and sudden enthusiasms, had to hear. He advised Howsam to call Rickey in the morning. And when the sun rose he telephoned to make sure that his son-in-law had placed the call. Howsam met Rickey in Columbus; Rickey spun Howsam's head with visions of a new league and advised him to get in touch with Bill Shea.

Rickey succeeded in making a convert not only of Howsam but also of Johnson, who by the summer of 1959 had at long last retired from political life. Big Ed was seventy-five and still liked to feel that he could flex his muscles, especially on Capitol Hill, where Estes Kefauver's committee was about to convene.

On the morning of July 31, just four days after Shea's press conference at the Biltmore Hotel, Big Ed Johnson took his place at the witness table before Kefauver's committee. He had returned to Washington to speak of the evils of organized baseball and had torn into the owners with the sort of zeal he had displayed toward Ingrid Bergman and her love child. Baseball, he told the committee, was a rotten business that espoused high ideals it had no intention of fulfilling, among them the routinely and grossly violated forty-man player limit written into the leagues' charters. "There are good rules, logical and reasonable, and absolutely sound but no club in either league makes any pretension of living up to them," he testified in his opening statement. "The Commissioner of Baseball, the honorable Ford Frick, and everybody else is familiar with these Major League illegal operations and yet no one does anything about it. I cannot understand such flagrant dishonesty."

Johnson had come not merely to excoriate, but to plead for help for the Continental League; it was Johnson himself who had given the new league its name. The committee, he warned, would be well advised to heed the warning that Tigers manager Jimmy Dykes had offered about the owners' empty promise of cooperation. "I hope this committee misses not one iota of this red hot tip-off," he said. "It is exactly what will happen if Congress does not get on the backs of the National and American leagues well equipped with lash and spurs. Thank God for Jimmy Dykes—he knows our big brothers!"

Then he gave way to Branch Rickey, who contradicted everything he said.

The old man ambled into the hearing room wearing a bow tie and a well-beaten Panama hat, and carrying a cane that he used. He took a seat behind Johnson, perched the cane around his neck, and stared at the back of Big Ed's neck. He took notes on a big pad and chewed on an unlit cigar.

When his turn came, he tore off the wet end of his cigar, put it in his coat pocket, and lit the remains of his stogie. He placed the cane on the witness table and began to speak without notes: "Senator Kefauver, and members of the committee, I have no prepared statement. I didn't know how to do it."

Like fun, he didn't.

He rambled on for a while longer, telling a story designed to ingratiate himself with the committee, all the while affecting the humbleness of "a country boy without any high school education" (his law degree went unmentioned) before arriving, at long last, at his true purpose. "I wish I were worthy of the time of this committee to answer every single question that I have heard in the last several minutes directed to Senator Johnson. Some of my answers would be at variance with his."

Such as regarding the owners' duplicity and venality: Rickey did not want a war. He still hoped to sway the owners, so that they would embrace the new league.

"You can be a fish in a puddle and think the world is made out of water," Rickey went on, "but you don't take the Western League and think all baseball should be castigated as phony." (Read: Big Ed doesn't know what he's talking about.)

He continued, "This is a basically honest game, supported and owned by honest men. Gentlemen, there has been maligning of some of the very great sportsmen in this country that is unfair and leads the general public to believe amiss about them. Do you think Gus Busch, Powel Crosley, John Galbreath, my good friend Wrigley or Mr. Yawkey, or Del Webb—oh, it is unkind not to include them all—that they are the definition of sportsmen who would for forty years make phony deals?"

Let it be noted that none of the senators thought to raise a hand and ask, say, about the many sweetheart trades between the Kansas City Athletics and the New York Yankees. Perhaps they were too stunned by Rickey adding an exclamation mark to his point by slapping his cane on the table.

"Mr. Griffith and Mr. Connie Mack, my great good friend Mr. Griffith, my second manager as a player of the Yankees"—this would have been Clark Griffith, not his son Calvin, the present owner of the Washington Senators—"I knew them well." Paraphrasing Hamlet while playing Polonius, the windbag.

He was speaking less to the senators than to the owners themselves. He was reminding them that he was one of them and had been so since they were boys going to the ballpark with their fathers, his contemporaries. He was vouching for their integrity, such as it was, and telling the members of the committee, and by extension both houses of Congress, that as much as he appreciated the attention they were paying to his game, their services would not be needed. "I would like to discuss with you the feature confronting us that it seems to me we can solve our problems, leaving me without the apprehension some of you have that baseball itself cannot put its house in order," he said. "It can. It should. In my judgment it will. It is not sufficient to say it will not do it because it has not done it."

There was supposed to be time for questions. Curiously, the time had vanished. "Oh dear, I haven't touched on these other things," Rickey said, "and you have not honored me with questions, and I haven't given you the chance I get."

And with that his work was done.

Ed Johnson held his tongue and most certainly his pen. Johnson did not hesitate to commend his thoughts to paper; he had terrific penmanship and wrote in green ink. But no letters of complaint or befuddlement followed, at least none kept by Rickey, who saved every letter from every Kiwanis Club and plumbers local that invited him to speak. But then again, Johnson was a political man and appreciated that while Rickey (and by extension, Shea) was playing a game with which he disagreed, he and the other "founders" needed the old man, and badly. More than George Kirksey's urgently requested "article," they needed *him*—to be their face and, more important, their voice—because without him they were merely five prosperous men left to bang on the clubhouse door, begging to be let in. So whatever thoughts Ed Johnson had of taking Rickey by the arm and bellowing, *"What are you playing at?"* he apparently kept to himself. This was made clear in the days and weeks that followed, as the men of the Continental League pleaded with Rickey to lead them.

Rickey remained flattered and a little coquettish. "These people are definitely unanimous from one end of them to the other, with almost tears in their eyes,—I have to say it that way, to have me become President of the new league," he wrote. "I don't want to be president. My age is against it, my inclination is against it, and the fact that I own approximately 1,000 shares of the Pittsburgh club is against it."

They told him to make whatever demands he wanted, and they would meet them. He told them he would need an assistant who would require a $40,000 salary and a generous expense account, and that he would need to be free to locate the league headquarters wherever he chose. Yes, they told him, whatever you want. And still he demurred: "I do not want the job of President. I do not intend to take it if it can be possibly avoided." Still, he wanted to be a part of things, but in a way that, it now became clearer, would allow him to retain his shares of Pirates stock. He could be an adviser; his contract with John Galbreath, he believed, would allow this and keep him free of accusations of a conflict of interest. And he wouldn't lose any money.

The founders of the Continental League were surely men of significance, but they were prepared to subordinate their considerable egos and allow themselves to be led by Branch Rickey. The danger in this strategy—one that was made clear the moment Rickey settled into his seat at the witness table and began his deep and interminable rumble—was that his would be the dominating voice. He would speak for them to the owners, to the press, to the public. That was all well and good, so long as his interests and those of the men he led remained as one.

Ed Johnson's problems, meanwhile, were not limited to Branch Rickey. His son-in-law Bob Howsam had fallen under the spell of another man: Lamar Hunt.

The two had met in 1958 when Hunt came to Denver to talk about baseball. Hunt hoped to bring a team to Dallas. Howsam told him he hadn't a chance. But Hunt was a persistent young man. He returned a year later with a different proposition and sport in mind: would Howsam be interested in joining in his new venture, a rival to the National Football League?

Lamar Hunt was twenty-six years old, and his father, H. L. Hunt, was one of the world's wealthiest men. Though a slender, bespectacled man, he had played football at the Hill School in Lawrenceville, New Jersey, and at Southern Methodist University. Hunt had been the sort of child who liked to read the attendance figures in the daily box scores. His first sporting venture was a batting cage replete with a watermelon stand. He later opened a driving range that failed. Having been advised to forsake baseball, he turned to football and approached Bert Bell, the commissioner of the National Football League, about bringing a team to Dallas. Bell turned him down. He then tried to buy a franchise so he could move it to Texas. He had heard the Chicago Cardinals might be for sale, and that the league was eager to see the team move. But the Cardinals' owners rejected his offer, just as they had rejected those of several other suitors. On his plane ride home—Hunt, a frugal man, flew commercial—he decided, as perhaps only the very young and fabulously wealthy can, that he would start a league of his own. Soon after he landed, he called a friend, the Houston oilman Bud Adams, and asked if he wanted in. Adams agreed, and soon Hunt was off to find others who might join in, among them Bob Howsam.

The timing, from Howsam's perspective, could not have been better. He owned a stadium that, much to his chagrin, remained idle for too many months. He needed another sport, and football would do nicely. Hunt's band quickly expanded to include Minneapolis–St. Paul, Los Angeles, and New York, and Hunt was so pleased that he thought Bert Bell might be, too. He went to the commissioner, told him what he had been up to, and asked if he might be willing to be commissioner of his league as well. Bell declined. But Hunt and his group, Bell quickly saw, might be of use, especially on Capitol Hill.

Professional football had also fallen under congressional scrutiny and was in a position far weaker than baseball's. The Supreme Court, after all, had ruled against the NFL in 1957, declaring it a monopoly and subject to antitrust laws for its unfair treatment of William Radovich, the lineman whom the Detroit Lions had kept from playing in a rival league so that he might be closer to his ailing father. The league was eager to retain the protections the law had allowed, in particular its own version of the reserve clause and the draft of college players that it insisted maintained the competitive balance that baseball so sorely lacked. Bell, who held more sway among his owners than Ford Frick did with his, was eager to show what an enlightened operation he ran. His game was on the upswing and had been since 1950, when the NFL merged with its postwar rival, the All-America Football Conference, a short-lived circuit whose owners had included Dan Topping and Branch Rickey. Attendance had risen 40 percent from 1950 to 1957, and television helped, too. The wider the broadcasts the higher the attendance, even as the league banned coverage of home games. Bell wanted the draft, no part of pay television, and the freedom to be left alone.

But now new people wanted in, and their appearance suited Bert Bell's needs nicely—so nicely, in fact, that he used the occasion of his testimony before Kefauver's committee to announce that a new football league was about to be born and that the NFL would be delighted to serve as its midwife. He was vague on the particulars. Lamar Hunt, meanwhile, sat in the gallery, letting Bell do the talking. He remained silent for two more weeks before surfacing in Chicago—a fitting choice, given that it was his failure with that city's Cardinals that led to his plan—to announce that he was forming the American Football League. Play would begin in 1960 in six cities, among them Denver, where Bob Howsam was identified as the owner.

Bill Shea was furious. He called Ed Johnson and harangued him about his son-in-law's foolishness in dividing his loyalties. But Bill Shea was no longer the man in charge. So Big Ed took his troubles to the new boss, Branch Rickey.

Rickey had hemmed and hawed and dithered about the sale of his Pirates stock. And finally, in mid-August, John Galbreath agreed to buy back Rickey's shares for $200,000, the same price that Rickey had paid for them in 1951. He was free. Two days after Lamar Hunt's announcement of his new football league, the Continental League's founders gathered in Bill Shea's Manhattan office and unanimously elected Rickey their president. With that crucial piece of business finally done, the founders rose and followed their president uptown to the Warwick Hotel, where Frick, Giles, Cronin, and the selected group of owners awaited them. The augury of Dan Daniel had come to pass.

"Baseball history shouts for expansion," Dan Daniel cried out once more. "But our magnates too often have had deaf ears."

The two sides gathered in the Walnut Room, on the mezzanine. Frick and Rickey faced each other from the far ends of the conference table, and in a gesture of good intentions, several of the opposing camps' representatives sat side by side. No one wanted to appear in the mood for a fight. The Continentals had come with a limited agenda: they wanted only recognition and help.

"We want your cooperation," Rickey told the major leaguers. "We need your cooperation. We demand your cooperation."

Two hours later, the doors opened and Frick's assistant, Charley Segar, emerged to advise the waiting reporters that the conferees were breaking for lunch. The talk, he added, had yet to move from the general to the specific.

And who, the reporters wanted to know, had been talking other than Rickey?

"I'd say he's been doing most of it," Segar said. "And I don't say that laughingly."

The afternoon session began after an hour's break and once again took place behind closed doors. Finally, shortly after four-thirty, Segar emerged to announce that the big-league owners favored expansion through the new league.

As vague as the communiqué sounded, it was just what Rickey and his people had hoped to achieve—a statement that reinforced the owners' support of their intentions. Now all they needed were three more cities. And assistance in getting players. And stadiums large enough to meet the owners' demands. And all in time for a projected Opening Day in April 1961.

Almost four years had passed since Branch Rickey's words had been deemed quote-worthy. But his election as president of the Continental

League was front-page news, and his appearance across the bargaining table from the commissioner had immediately restored the position he shared with Casey Stengel as the bottomless repository of good copy. Suddenly, he was being quoted everywhere. The *Times* dubbed him a "Man in the News"—"Still Pioneering at 77," read the headline—and dispatched a reporter to his suite, where a crowd of newsmen had gathered to watch him eat lunch and listen to him spin a fanciful and, as always, eminently reprintable vision of the future.

"It's October 1963," Rickey began. "The Yankees, let us assume, win the American League pennant, the Chicago Cubs prevail in the National and the Houston Continentals win in our league. The series opens at Yankee Stadium with New York playing the Cubs."

He poured himself more coffee, relit his cigar, and described what would happen in Game Four when Houston would play Chicago at Wrigley Field. A round-robin tournament. Three teams. No fewer than eight games. Maybe as many as eleven.

"Judas Priest," he said, "I'd like to see that."

But wouldn't the public be bored by so many games?

"Bored? Why, the fans will devour it. Baseball fever runs from one end of this great land to the other."

But where will you get your players?

"The same place the Yankees get them," he replied. "Good Lord, the world is full of baseball players. We'll draft them, we'll secure waiver rights to them. We'll purchase them. And we'll get them from the free agency field the way the Yankees got Mantle."

But will the majors demand a high price for players?

He picked up a teaspoon. "If you ask me $10 for this spoon I'll tell you to keep it and start for the door. Darned if you won't say, 'Wait a minute.' Then we'll bargain a little. We'll be generous in purchasing players, but not spendthrifts. There are almost as many surplus players as there are teaspoons."

He allowed that it would take several years before the new league's prospects developed into worthy players. But that did not concern him. He was ready to offer steady work to those men whose services the majors no longer required, players like Enos Slaughter, who was forty-three and still hanging on with the Yankees. "We'll pick up all the Slaughters in the country. We'll take the Darks, the Musials, the Williams, the Dicksons, the Wertzes."

He folded his arms across his chest and lit a new cigar. "You know, the major league owners may think they own baseball, but they're wrong."

It was not only the writers who were now seeking an audience. His league was now fielding requests from cities all over the country—among them, the city that his old nemesis, Walter O'Malley, had claimed as his own, Los Angeles. The application came from an advertising man, who was writing on behalf of a small group of well-placed suitors: the actors Jack Webb and Chuck Connors. Better still, the men marked down as the group's president and first vice president were, respectively, Dean Martin and Frank Sinatra.

The Continental League was so cool that even the Rat Pack wanted in. *Ring-a-ding-ding*.

SEPTEMBER: O'Malley in Bloom

There was a new team in Brooklyn, and it played at Ebbets Field. The team was called the Stars, and its connection to the Dodgers pulled at the heartstrings. Its sponsor was Roy Campanella, who was then thirty-seven and since the winter of 1958 had been confined to a wheelchair, paralyzed from the neck down.

His Stars were a rescue mission, a wincingly late-in-the-day attempt to see if there might still be life in an institution whose days were numbered the moment Branch Rickey signed Jackie Robinson: the Negro Leagues. Only one was left, the Negro American League—and its mere existence was remarkable, given that even the Boston Red Sox, who'd held out longer than everyone else, now had a black player, Pumpsie Green. The league fielded six teams filled with men who, despite the encomiums about the potential that appeared in the black press, were not destined for the majors. The Negro American League had been dying for years, and now its longtime president, Dr. J. B. Martin, was conceding that he did not see how the circuit could last another season. Five clubs were losing money and attendance was dropping so precipitously that the league's historic signature event—the East-West All-Star game—drew only seven thousand patrons to its traditional home, Comiskey Park. Martin had hoped that the game might draw twenty thousand. "I've been doing everything I can to keep them playing," he told Lee Jenkins of the *Chicago Defender*, "but it looks hopeless."

Campy returned to Ebbets Field on a rainy Sunday in July. Perhaps it was the weather that limited the crowd to three thousand. But even a visit by the Kansas City Monarchs, once the premier team in the circuit, drew only seven thousand to Yankee Stadium on a weekend when the Yankees were out of town. The Stars played a doubleheader against the Memphis Red Sox, and though they were drubbed in both games, Campanella, ever ebullient, tried to see the good that might come from his team. "The youngsters have shown a lot of ability," he said, the drizzle dampening his face. "It is our hope, in a humble way, to keep baseball alive in Brooklyn." Yet even a late-August appearance by Satchel Paige drew only four thousand spectators, and by then the players themselves were getting restive. After losing to Paige and the once-vaunted Monarchs, the Stars filed into their clubhouse and stripped off their uniforms, a protest, presumably over money. Meanwhile, Paige, who was now well into his fifties, struck out three in three innings of work and announced that he was available should a big-league team want him. "Anyone will do," he said. "Even the Yankees."

But Paige was not the answer, not for all the problems that still plagued Casey Stengel's men. The trade that brought Hector Lopez and Ralph Terry from Kansas City had yielded little. Terry lost far more often than he won, and Lopez, though a fine hitter, was a sieve at third base. Bill Skowron was hurt, Whitey Ford's arm ached, and Bob Turley was no better in September than he had been in May, when he was dreadful. The team had escaped the cellar only to join the pack of middling squads. They had spent most of the summer slipping between third and fourth place and by Labor Day were fifteen games behind the first-place White Sox, barely at sea level, a .500 club.

Stengel, who had spent a miserable sixty-ninth birthday at Comiskey Park watching Early Wynn hold his team to a single run, had foresworn any further attempts at encouragement. Everyone disappointed him, even Tony Kubek, whom he had once adored, and Bobby Richardson, who seldom offended. "Those two think they can hit the ball out of the park every time they come to bat and they swing for the fences," he carped. "I tell 'em to push the ball. Hit to the opposite field. They better do what I say or they won't be around." He spared no one, not even old friends. He ripped his pitching coach, Jim Turner, for his staff's collective failure to pitch inside. The harshest criticism, inevitably, was directed at Mickey Mantle—"I don't want him to look at recent pictures of himself because he'll see how lousy he is. But he ought to take a lot of batting practice." He went on and on about how he tried to teach Mantle, and how Mantle would not listen because all he wanted to do was hit the ball as far as he could. "Now why wouldn't he learn to drop a bunt towards third the way the third basemen play him? Maybe the tough time he's having this year will convince him to try some things," Stengel moaned. "And why wouldn't it help it if he could add a thing or two to his attack and hit a home run too." For the record, Mantle would finish the season batting .285, with thirty-one home runs, twenty-one stolen bases, and seventy-five runs batted in. Not good enough.

The digs were relentless and came even at unexpected times and places. When the team honored Yogi Berra with a gift-filled "night," Stengel used the celebration to further distance himself from Mantle, the player who was to have been the monument to his wise tutelage. "Outside of DiMaggio," he told the crowd, "the man behind the plate, Berra, is the greatest player I ever managed." The players said nothing, at least those who were still on the team. But Enos Slaughter, whom the Yankees had shipped to the Braves in early September, surfaced in Milwaukee to tell a pregame national television audience that as much as he believed Stengel's players were well advised to heed his advice, they had stopped listening. The Yankees, he said, "think Casey Stengel is in his second childhood."

But Stengel and the Yankees were ever less the baseball story, even in New York. By September, the columnists had repaired to the West Coast, where they could observe close up the race for the National League pennant and allow themselves to recapture the past.

<<<<<

All that Walter O'Malley had dreamed of was coming to pass. The legal roadblocks standing in the way of his new ballpark at Chavez Ravine had been cleared—the voter referendum had been won and the lawsuits resolved in his favor. In May, the last residents of Chavez Ravine were forcibly removed and their tents torn down, a nasty piece of television drama that would leave the city's Mexican population seething for years to come. Finally, on September 17, O'Malley and three thousand spectators made their way out to the empty, hilly tract in downtown Los Angeles and watched as bulldozers began leveling the land where his ballpark would rise. The $600,000 earth-moving contract had gone not to the Del E. Webb Construction Company, but a rival firm, Villard Construction, which now stood to win the deal to build the stadium, a disappointment for Webb, who had flown his club out from Kansas City so that they could play an exhibition game at the Coliseum on the night O'Malley chose to honor Roy Campanella. Even Buzzie Bavasi, O'Malley's longtime general manager, had no idea why O'Malley had presumably done Webb dirty on the stadium deal. O'Malley maintained strict lines of responsibility and made it clear to Bavasi that his job was to handle the players, and O'Malley would not seek his advice about how to make and spend his money.

The players' work on the field, which had so disappointed him during the team's maiden season in California, now pleased him immensely. On the night after the groundbreaking at Chavez Ravine, the Dodgers not only moved back into second place with a 4–3 win against the Braves, but also surpassed two million in attendance, the best in the big leagues. All the while, O'Malley held firm in his refusal to televise all but a handful of Dodgers games. He was not about to let people see his games on television for free—not when there existed the possibility of one day charging them to watch.

The Dodgers had drawn 1.8 million fans in 1958, second to Milwaukee's 2.1 million, and the team had started slowly in 1959. But by early summer, they were in a pennant race, and a dandy one at that. They slipped in and out of first through June and July, and even when they fell back to third they were never more than five games out. Their opponents were the defending National League champions, the Milwaukee Braves, and, better still, their old, transplanted antagonists, the San Francisco Giants. It was as if the crosstown rivalry that for decades had filled Ebbets Field and the Polo Grounds had been re-created on the far reaches of the California coast. As August gave way to September, the three teams remained joined at the hip and the crowds at the Coliseum swelled, never so much as when the Giants came to town.

The Dodgers headed north to San Francisco, where they swept a weekend series at tiny, sold-out Seals Stadium, knocking the Giants out of first and putting themselves in a position to clinch the pennant on the final weekend of the season in Chicago. So grateful was O'Malley to his 2,071,045 paying customers that, as a gesture of goodwill, he rewarded his newly loyal patrons the gift of free telecasts of the last two games from Wrigley Field.

They lost on Saturday but won on Sunday, finishing in a tie with the Braves, forcing a best-of-three play-off for the pennant. The Dodgers took the opener in Milwaukee and then headed back to California, hoping that with a win they could take the title.

This was no longer the Brooklyn team that O'Malley had insisted upon moving intact to California, because, he reasoned, Los Angeles had wanted the Brooklyn Dodgers, and that is what they would get. Pee Wee Reese had retired (he now coached), Carl Erskine started only three games all season, and Carl Furillo had been replaced in right field. Yet, as much as Los Angeles had taken to its own star, Wally Moon, the old faces had not vanished entirely. Duke Snider, who was thirty-two, still played center field, and thirty-five-year-old Gil Hodges was at first. Johnny Podres, Don Drysdale, Roger Craig, and the woefully inconsistent Sandy Koufax started, and Clem Labine still appeared fifty-six times in relief.

The Dodgers were trailing 5–2 going into the bottom of the ninth of the second game when they scored two runs on four singles, one of them by Hodges, who was standing at third with nobody out when manager Walter Alston looked to his bench and turned to what had worked so well for so long. He sent thirty-seven-year-old Carl Furillo in to pinch-hit. His fly ball scored Hodges with the tying run.

The two came to bat again in the twelfth. With two out, Hodges walked, then advanced to second on a single. Once again Furillo, who'd stayed in to play right, stepped up. He sent a ground ball skipping up the middle that should have ended the inning. But Milwaukee shortstop Felix Mantilla's poor throw bounced in the dirt. Furillo was safe. Hodges scored. A pennant for Los Angeles, a gift from Gil and Skoonj.

CHAPTER FIVE

FALL 1959

OCTOBER: Days of Reckoning

Casey Stengel was back at the World Series, this time with a pen and a notepad. *Life* magazine had asked him to cover the series, and Stengel, not quite ready to retreat to his desk at the Glendale National Bank, agreed, if only to avoid the ignominy of having to buy a ticket. "I paid my way into other World Series," he said, "and I'll pay my way into this one which I don't like if you was to ask me."

His season had crawled to an inglorious conclusion; the Yankees were eliminated from contention on September 8, and by the final weekend Stengel's banter was reduced to reminding one and all that he would be coming back in 1960—"This is a good place to work," he said— and trying to make sense of his team's collapse. The Yankees finished in third place and won only seventy-nine games, their fewest since 1925. Bobby Richardson was the only Yankee to hit .300, and even he had barely made it. "Only one man in our organization had a really good season," Stengel declared. "He was the bat boy. He had a tree-mendous season and never made a mistake." He blamed Turley and Ford, and Skowron's bad back, and, of course, Mantle. He even took some of the burden upon himself. "The players didn't cross the plate and I didn't manage as well as I should."

The White Sox had won the American League pennant and would host the Dodgers in the series opener. Stengel arrived at Comiskey Park and immediately lost his pencil. Then his pen broke. "I'm gonna have to keep it all in my head," he announced to the writers who had gathered to watch him try his hand at their craft. Note taking, however, proved not so great a hurdle; Stengel posed many questions but provided the answers, too. Still, he did try to talk with everyone, and not just White Sox manager Al Lopez, an old friend, who was all set to answer Stengel's queries with "No comment" and "This is off the record." Stengel, never content with conversational dead space, did not give him the chance. The writers took in his performance a little while longer before turning their attention to the real story of the day, which, as Stengel might have put it, wasn't himself.

This was Bill Veeck's moment, and the White Sox' owner was celebrating it with roses—his ushers had distributed twenty thousand to the women in the crowd—and by tweaking old antagonists like Lou Perini, who quickly discovered that he would need a Sherpa to help him find his seat. "Nobody gave me anything when I was out of baseball," Veeck said. "Particularly Perini." It seemed that the Braves' owner had promised Veeck twelve seats to the 1958 World Series, only to renege. "Not two, not one, but none. Mr. Perini needed my twelve for himself. Okay, now this is the day of reckoning. I'm doing what Mr. Perini wishes he could do. I'm taking care of my fans first."

The beef was not limited to free passes. Veeck had a history with Perini. It dated back to 1953, the year Perini moved the Braves to Milwaukee, a step he might never have taken had Veeck not tried first.

Bill Veeck was the game's great impresario. He did not wear ties, and this was only the beginning of his problems with his fellow owners. He was a man who liked to have fun and who believed, heretically at the time, that people should have fun at the ballpark, too. Veeck had lost a leg in the war and then had an ashtray carved into his wooden prosthesis. He did loud and sometimes foolish things at the ballpark, like sending the three-foot-seven Eddie Gaedel in to pinch-hit for the St. Louis

Browns. He had told Gaedel that if he dared to swing the bat rather than taking four balls (inevitable given his tiny strike zone), he would shoot him.

The other owners regarded Veeck's ideas as akin to promoting Bingo Night at the Vatican. Veeck, a clever man—O'Malley's equal in intelligence, if not in the pocketbook—was quick to lash back but did so with a sharp wit that only further alienated him from the men who had the power to decide his fate. In the winter of 1953, Veeck owned the woebegone St. Louis Browns and wanted to move them to Milwaukee. St. Louis, he had concluded, could no longer support two baseball teams, not with the advent of television and not with the purchase of the rival Cardinals by the beer magnate August Busch. Veeck was a baseball lifer whose father had run the Chicago Cubs. He came of age trimming the ivy at Wrigley Field and won a World Series in 1948 when he owned the Cleveland Indians. He had also come upon the clever strategy of amortizing the value of his players to cut down on his tax bill. If this placed the other owners in his debt, however, they did not show it. And the first to stand in his path in escaping St. Louis was none other than Lou Perini, the owner of the Boston Braves.

Perini held the territorial rights to Milwaukee, where the minor-league Brewers played. Milwaukee had spent five million dollars on a 38,000-seat stadium that could be expanded to seat 80,000. All it needed was a team to come play, and the city was sure it had found one in Veeck's hapless Browns. Perini was not happy about the blossoming affections between Veeck and Milwaukee and decided to put an end to it. He called upon his fellow owners to pass a measure prohibiting the movement of any team into a minor-league city until the end of the regular season, October 1. Milwaukee's city fathers and the Wisconsin state legislature were aghast and issued a proclamation denouncing Perini's attempt to block the fulfillment of their big-league dream. Stalled in Milwaukee, Veeck then turned his attention to Baltimore, which like Milwaukee had briefly been a major-league town but had not had a team since 1902—except for its brief flirtation with the Federal League.

It was now mid-March 1953. Opening Day was mere weeks away when Perini made his intentions clear to the city that only days earlier had lambasted him. The league owners gathered for their respective meetings. Veeck walked into the American League meeting smiling, only to emerge crushed. Two days later, Lou Perini became the owner of the Milwaukee Braves. Baltimore did get the Browns the following year, but not before Veeck was compelled to sell the team to men more to the liking of Del Webb, who like most everyone else did not care for Bill Veeck and was singularly well positioned to do something about it.

In fairness, Webb would not always be hostile to Veeck. Some years later, he learned that Veeck was talking with Phil Wrigley about acquiring his territorial rights to Los Angeles—where Wrigley owned a minor-league team. Webb made it known, Veeck wrote in his memoir, that if the contract for rebuilding Wrigley's twenty-thousand-seat stadium in south-central L.A. went to Webb "I would be getting his vote in any American League meeting." Veeck did not secure those rights. They went instead to Walter O'Malley, whose team now stood in the way of Veeck's achieving a measure of revenge far sweeter than parking Lou Perini in the outer reaches of Comiskey Park.

Stengel liked the White Sox. They pitched well and ran well and fielded well, and the fact that they hit very few home runs did not trouble him. They played the game as it was played when he was young and Babe Ruth was still a pitcher. Stengel loved to talk about the past, especially when there was little joy to be derived in the present, and so it was not surprising that his distillation of the series began with a look back. His theme was heroes, the unexpected ones.

"Now I'm an expert on heroes," he wrote. "I've managed a considerable number of them in World Series competition and once, back in 1923, I was a hero myself. That was the year I hit two deciding home runs against the Yankees for the Giants. And what did everybody say? They said, 'My goodness, did he hit the home runs?'" People, he continued, thought the big fellows like Irish Meusel and Highpockets Kelly would be the heroes, not Casey Stengel, a thirty-three-year-old understudy who'd homered only five times all year. But then, he wrote, "I became the star." His home runs won the first and third games, and then his moment was over. "I'll have to say that before the series ended that

year, Babe Ruth came to bat and got three home runs and wiped away
my two."

The Yankees took the 1923 series in six games, which was just what
the Dodgers would do to the White Sox in 1959. Stengel attributed Los
Angeles's victory to the heroic play of two little-known men—the
catcher, John Roseboro, and Larry Sherry, a relief pitcher. Roseboro
barely hit, but his throwing scuttled the running game of the "Go-Go
Sox." Sherry appeared in all four of the Dodgers' victories, winning two,
saving two, and allowing only one earned run. Together, Stengel concluded, Roseboro and Sherry broke the White Sox's spirit and heart, as
can only be accomplished by men of whom little is expected. "It's a great
thing for the fans in Los Angeles, having a world championship flag in
their park, as I realize everyone is interested in baseball to a great
extent," he wrote. "Being a world champion is a great thing to become
and a sad thing to lose, as I know."

The Dodgers celebrated their championship in Chicago with champagne and a steak-and-caviar dinner that ran so late that at the stroke of
midnight the hundreds of people in the banquet room paused and raised
their glasses to toast Walter O'Malley on his fifty-sixth birthday. He
brought his team back to Los Angeles the following afternoon, and
when their plane touched ground five thousand people were waiting for
them, along with a crew from KTTV television, which was broadcasting
their arrival. Free of charge. A happy week passed, and then O'Malley's
mood took a dark turn with the arrival at his offices of the emissaries of
the Los Angeles Stars, who had come to seek his blessings before proceeding with their formal application to join the Continental League.

Frank Sinatra had withdrawn from the Stars' management team, but
Dean Martin was still on board, as was Jack Webb, television's own
Sergeant Joe Friday, and Chuck Connors, once a Brooklyn Dodger and
now the star of *The Rifleman*. Their emissaries were led by Mark Scott,
a television man, the voice of the minor-league Hollywood Stars. Scott
had first floated his plan to invade O'Malley's turf—the euphemistic
term of the moment was providing "continuous baseball," scheduling
their home games to coincide with the Dodgers' road trips—by such
Angelenos of consequence as Norman Chandler, who owned the *Los*

Angeles Times, and his sports editor, Paul Zimmerman. Both advised Scott to seek out O'Malley to advise him that men of means were lined up behind the Stars.

O'Malley, however, was not pleased to see him, as Scott made plain to Rickey when he called to tell him how things had gone. The Dodgers' owner was, Scott reported, "terribly shocked."

He was "shocked" to learn that anyone would have conceived of such a plan. Who were these people?

Scott declined to name them.

What, precisely, was this Continental League—a question that suggested that either O'Malley had been living in Tibet or that he was being characteristically coy. Who was behind the new league, was New York a part of it, and if so was the city really going to build the club a new ballpark?

Scott demurred.

"Where are you going to play?" O'Malley demanded.

Perhaps, Scott replied, the Stars might be his tenant at Chavez Ravine.

"What next?" asked O'Malley.

Then maybe tiny Wrigley Field. But failing all that, Scott told him, we do know a man who might be willing to part with a hundred acres he owns in the San Fernando Valley. We might build our own park there, much as we'd prefer to bunk with you.

But Walter O'Malley did not want a roommate—even one willing to pay his way in. So he tried to convince Scott of the foolishness of his venture. He went on for half an hour, by Scott's calculation, about the financial perils that awaited anyone unwise enough to get into the baseball business. Why, he alone had just lost forty thousand dollars on the championship game in Chicago. How this happened he did not say, or if he did Scott did not feel it worth repeating.

Have you any idea how much it will cost to establish a ball club in Los Angeles? O'Malley asked.

"We have in mind that it will cost us $5 million," Scott replied.

That would be right, said a surprised O'Malley who, in Scott's view, could not quite believe that the money was available.

But if Mark Scott thought his recounting of his meeting with O'Malley would please Branch Rickey, he was sorely mistaken. Rickey was not happy at all and made it clear to Scott that the last thing he wanted to do was to invade another team's turf—with the exception, of course, of New York—especially the turf of a canny operator like O'Malley. He advised Scott not to count on his help. "I stated to Mr. Scott that I was not going to give out any information of any sort that could be interpreted as remotely indicating an offer on the part of the Continental League on going to Los Angeles," he said, as he dictated the conversation to his secretary, "that we did not have it in mind, and didn't intend to put it in our minds, but we would treat courteously inquiry from responsible persons provided it had Mr. O'Malley's approval in advance."

Scott and Rickey chatted awhile longer about this and that, and then Rickey hung up, having made it as clear as possible, given his ornate language, that Mark Scott and his famous and monied friends were making his already complicated life harder still.

Six weeks had passed since Branch Rickey's coronation as president of the Continental League and the ceremonial gathering with the baseball establishment. But he was still three teams short of a full roster of eight teams, even as Mark Scott was lobbying for Los Angeles to make the cut. Montreal also seemed a possibility, and even distant Honolulu wanted in. Rickey had traveled to Buffalo, which seemed promising, but the prospective owners there had asked what he regarded as far too many questions about the source of players. He had also visited Atlanta, a city that boasted its own "Branch Rickey League." Atlanta's minor-league operator, Earl Mann, had earned Rickey's admiration for his baseball acumen and for having integrated the Southern League in 1954.

Rickey saw great possibilities in Mann and the city of Atlanta; there was, he believed, no more promising baseball town in the country. Atlanta was eager for a team, having already been rebuffed by the Reds, the Athletics, and the Senators. It took Rickey little time to sway the local doubters. As for Mann, Rickey wanted him as general manager of the Continentals' New York franchise, but that would complicate Rickey's dealings with Ed Johnson. Johnson had already gotten a lecture from Bill Shea on "the evils of Bob Howsam's interests in pro football" and had written to Rickey to say that he would get his son-in-law to give up his involvement in Lamar Hunt's American Football League if Rickey would make Howsam the general manager in New York. But what neither Rickey nor Johnson knew was that Howsam was not about to make himself a slave to his father-in-law's wishes. He had seen great promise in Lamar Hunt's scheme and in the future he envisioned for football.

Such were the developments that allowed Rickey whatever sleep he was getting. Because things were otherwise so unsettled, it was a wonder his memos did not include mention of appointments with a gastroen-terologist. New York had still not voted to continue funding work on the Flushing Meadows stadium; the Brooklyn romantics on the city's board of estimate were still hoping the city might instead spend its money on expanding Ebbets Field. The voices and dreams of the Continental League "founders" could hardly compete with the desires and plans of Robert Moses, and the delay in the vote left Bill Shea having to convince the others to keep their faith in New York and its stadium, the linchpin of the whole endeavor. The founders, meanwhile, were growing restless and taking their troubles to Rickey.

Houston was now sensing weak knees among its moneymen, and the hyperbolic George Kirksey was all but begging Rickey at last to sit down and write the article, with Kirksey's help if necessary, that would give the league's boosters a published document that they could use to refute the growing chorus of skeptics. Local sports columnists, he warned, were voicing doubts about the league and, worse still, so was Dan Daniel in the *Sporting News*. Shea, meanwhile, had concluded that the warm feel-ings expressed by the owners in August had turned decidedly chilly; Frick was beginning to question whether the Continental League could be ready to begin play in 1961. Then the minor leagues, which owed their existence to remaining in the good graces of the majors, reported what Shea believed were bloated estimates of their clubs' values, and, by extension, the price the new franchises would be compelled to pay in indemnification fees for invading the minor leagues' turf. "You see cer-tain things under the table," Shea said on a radio talk show. "There are things happening that I don't think are exactly happenstance."

And then, to complicate things further, the American League announced that the time had come to consider expanding.

The rumors had begun during the 1959 World Series, and they swirled around the doughy mug of Calvin Griffith. He wanted out of Washington, again, and this time he was saying that Minneapolis wanted him and had the money to lure him there. The nation's representatives were once again in a tizzy, and none was more exercised than Emanuel Celler, who saw in Griffith's plans to abandon the capital the chance to finally end baseball's antitrust exemption. Celler trotted out the barbs he had been directing for years at the owners—*interested in money rather than sport*. But now he was in a lather, warning that Griffith's flirtation with the Twin Cities "will give me more ammunition and impetus" to get a bill passed in the next congressional session. He also managed to work in a plug for the Continental League, reminding everyone that the owners "say they want to help but they don't. Their protestations are just a lot of malarkey."

At this point it would not have been surprising if the owners had thrown Griffith into the trunk of a car and driven him to an undisclosed location, where he would remain until they had finally gotten Celler and Kefauver out of their hair. Short of that, they made clear to Griffith that the votes to allow a move to Minneapolis would not be there. The Senators' owner retreated, having once again left behind a mess. But this time the people of Minneapolis, who for two years had hoped to lure the Senators to their state and in frustration had thrown in with the Continental League, were not prepared to walk away. Instead, they turned their backs on Rickey, Shea, and their fellow founders, went to the American League, and asked to be granted a franchise.

Shea was furious. "There was never any chance of Washington moving to Minneapolis, and there's no chance of Minneapolis going to the American League," he said. "If the people from Minneapolis continue acting as dupes and be suckered into these things, they could wind up without a team in any league."

Shea also recognized that Minneapolis's gambit could cause the Continental League to fall apart—not because of losing the Twin Cities but because the move might compel the owners to expand. The owners now recognized the risk to their antitrust immunity if they abandoned the nation's capital. If the Senators relocated to Minnesota the American League would be compelled to add a replacement franchise in Washington, along with a second new team to keep the schedule balanced. Expansion, in turn, would deny the Continental League a reason to exist—that is, if the league's founders were not committed to Rickey's vision of a competitively balanced, revenue-sharing, eight-team league.

For their part, the American League owners were delighted with the gift that Calvin Griffith had, inadvertently as always, provided them: the day after Minneapolis made its application, the league president, Joe Cronin, formed a committee to study the possibility of adding teams, a process that could drag on for years. The announcement came the day before New York's board of estimate was to vote on continuing funding for the Flushing Meadows stadium, and Shea saw a dark hand in all of it. "The American League set up this committee only for propaganda purposes," he said, "and to hurt the Continental League."

But the mere talk of expansion was enough to send Houston into an even deeper panic that it had taken the wrong path in its efforts to get a major-league club. Kirksey wrote to Rickey and Shea, begging them to write to his city's deep-pocketed backer, Bob Smith, and assure him that all would be good. "We cannot continue to hold our present position," he wrote, "if the expansion talk is allowed to hang over our head like the sword of Damocles."

There was, however, an even more troubling threat, one that so concerned Rickey that he felt he had no choice but to confront Shea. The other founders did not trust New York. They believed that the city was ready to abandon them once it got the big-league team that Mayor Wagner had originally dispatched Shea to find. In fact, Rickey had it on good authority that the man behind Minneapolis's American League application, Gerry Moore, had told Cronin's people that he was simply trying to get in ahead of the bid that would surely come from New York. No matter that the board of eestimate had approved an additional $170,000 for the Flushing Meadows ballpark; there was a growing fear among the founders that it would be the National League and not the Continental League that would make its home in the new stadium. Even

if the National League didn't expand—adding a tenth club in either
Houston or Toronto in addition to New York—Rickey had heard that
the league would persuade one of its clubs to move to Queens. There
was simply too much "glamour" attached to a New York franchise.

Speculation about New York's true intentions, he continued, had
bred suspicion within the new league: Jack Kent Cooke was stalling on
building a new park in Toronto, and Craig Cullinan's growing doubts
were, in turn, giving the moneyman in Dallas, J. W. Bateson, second
thoughts about signing on. And now Bob Howsam, Rickey had learned,
was trying to lure the American League to Denver because he "doubted
that New York would ever become a member of the Continental
League." Rickey had challenged Howsam, who told him it was not Shea
he mistrusted but the men to whom Shea reported.

"I have often said that if New York is in the pocket the Continental
League can be successfully organized regardless of the defection of any
one or more cities," Rickey wrote in a memo to Shea. The memo was
Rickey at his most lawyerly—three and a half single-spaced typewritten
pages that took the form of a legal brief, each paragraph beginning with
Whereas. The progression of Rickey's argument led, painstakingly, to
this: he needed a commitment from New York—and this time, not just
from Shea, but from the mayor—that the new park would be built for
the Continental League and no one else. Rickey wanted this in writing
or in a public statement. He was in no mood to be played.

"I have given fifty-six years of my life to professional baseball," he
concluded. "Under no circumstances can I permit, if avoidable, my
identification with a needless administrative failure to organize this
league."

A week after Joe Cronin impaneled his expansion committee, he
announced that the league would not be adding teams in 1960. It might
in 1961. Or maybe later. He couldn't say. But the Associated Press was
now reporting that the league was actually planning a radical realignment: a new team in New York, a move by the Senators to Minneapolis,
and a new club for the nation's capital. The league would then swap

franchises with the National League, giving it New York while it took either Philadelphia or Pittsburgh.

"This American League filibuster which I choose to call it, against baseball expansion must collapse from the weight of its own self-interest," Rickey wrote in a statement of denunciation. "I am sure it will fail." He even invoked the ghost of Ban Johnson to show that history was on the Continentals' side: "The National League failed in a similar role as obstructionist 58 years ago when the forward-seeing Ban Johnson organized and launched this same American League. At that time every argument now used against the Continental League was used by the National League against expansion of that period."

But privately, Rickey was not nearly so confident. He was unsure of New York's intentions—no public statement from Mayor Wagner followed his memo to Shea, nor do his copious archives contain the written assurance he sought. And there was something more: Rickey had gone to Congress and vouched for the integrity of the owners, undercutting his ally Ed Johnson to say what he had hoped would so please the owners that they might look favorably on his plan. But then came the talk of expansion and with it the growing sense that the owners did not wish to see the Continental League come to life.

Once again he wrote to Shea. Only this time, it was not to plead for help but to suggest that the future of their new league might well rest on taking a step he had spent all his life avoiding for the chaos it might rain down upon his game.

"In great confidence I say to you that it occurs to me as a possibility that we will never be able to organize on any economic basis with acceptable player adjustments unless we go completely independent of the present major leagues. I regret the thought of such a thing, but evidence multiply and conspire against us so continuously as to leave us only with the alternative of independent action.

"If the boys would approve of such a course then we could indeed become major league overnight."

Branch Rickey, an architect of the establishment, was suggesting life as an outlaw.

NOVEMBER: Calling the Bluff

Walter O'Malley had a recommendation for the men who wanted to bring the Continental League to Los Angeles: get stuffed. They had been hounding him for weeks, spoiling the pleasure he might have otherwise taken in owning the world champions and perhaps in taking a spin out to Chavez Ravine to watch the ground being leveled. But Mark Scott and his people would not go away and would not take the hint when O'Malley stopped returning their phone calls. He made appointments, then broke them; surely, these people could see he was in no mood to share his new town. Weeks went by. Finally Scott got through one afternoon and requested a meeting.

"Don't get tough with me," bellowed an agitated Walter O'Malley. "I've read a lot of stuff you've been putting out."

Scott insisted that his people had been putting out no "stuff" at all, that they had been forthcoming in answering all of his questions, and truth be told, he hadn't been all that pleasant in return.

"If you don't like it," snapped O'Malley, "you can do whatever you like about it."

If O'Malley had elaborated, Scott chose to spare the puritanical ears of Branch Rickey, to whom he recounted this conversation. Despite discouraging Scott's move on Los Angeles, Rickey had taken a liking to Scott and his people, and Scott did not wish to give offense.

In fairness, O'Malley did not wish to sound like a man consumed with greed. He may not have been willing to allow more than token broadcasts of Dodgers games, but he was willing to allow the citizens of Los Angeles the chance to satisfy their desire for "continuous baseball." Just not with Rickey's league. Perhaps, he told Scott, the American League might want to bring a team to town.

Scott listened and went to see Del Webb, hoping that the Yankees' owner might be willing to give his blessing for an expansion club in Los Angeles. It was no secret that Webb was eager to see his league move west, if only to give him the chance to build a new ballpark or two, given that O'Malley had denied him the Chavez Ravine contract. But Webb made quick work of O'Malley's suggestion. The American League, he told Scott, had no plans to move a club to Southern California, not now and not "in the foreseeable future." Nor did Webb wish to see the league expand to nine or ten teams, because that would only increase the number of second-division clubs.

It was an odd thing to say, given that his general manager, George Weiss, was serving on Joe Cronin's expansion committee, weighing the very possibilities that Webb insisted would not happen. Unless, of course, the committee was a ruse, a stall, baseball's Potemkin village of progress. Rickey, who had assumed just that all along, now dictated a telegram to Cronin with a proposal designed to call his hand.

"One or more of these cities in question has been encouraged by certain members of the American League to believe that it could become a member of their League through the granting of a ninth franchise," he wrote in a telegram to Cronin on November 9. "Whether intentional or not, these representations as to being major league in 1960 were misleading and untrue."

Rickey then proposed that Cronin, his committee, and representatives of the Continental League visit Minneapolis, Dallas, Atlanta, Buffalo, and Montreal to see if they might resolve "this confusion." The Continental League owners would be happy to pick up the tab. Rickey's secretary sent the message and then walked a copy over to Ford Frick's office.

The commissioner called, by Rickey's watch, three minutes later.

"You think one way and I think another," Frick told Rickey. He was not happy. "I think we should sit down and talk this thing through. I know damn well the point you have in mind."

Rickey, whether or not he was being disingenuous, noted in his recounting of the conversation that he did not know what point the commissioner meant. The commissioner checked his date book. He couldn't meet with Rickey the following day—he had an appointment for his annual checkup, new doctor, X-rays, the works. The day after wouldn't work, either—it was Veterans Day and people would surely come to call. This surprised Rickey, who had no idea that the commissioner, whom he had known for decades, had served. What about the day after that, suggested Rickey. Breakfast?

"I won't come in for breakfast," said Frick.

How about today? asked Rickey. "Can't you clear today? Why not today?"

"Impossible," said Frick. "I have an engagement this afternoon with George Weiss and Del Webb." Besides, Frick added, "Cronin will call me about this thing."

"Yes," said Rickey. "I suppose he will."

"You know God damn well he will," snapped the commissioner—rough language to direct at a man for whom the profanity continuum stopped at "Judas Priest." But the telegram had nettled Frick, and his anger was racing ahead of his customary sense of caution. "I don't want this thing to go haywire and you know what I mean by haywire."

"I don't want it to go haywire either," replied Rickey.

"I know you don't. Neither of us wants this thing to go haywire. You know what I mean by that."

"I think I do," said Rickey.

Perhaps. But if Rickey was reading Frick correctly, *haywire* meant not a single moment but rather a cascading series of events that might well lead to a baseball war—the first since the Federal League disbanded in 1915. It would happen like this: the Continental League, stymied by the big leagues, would declare its independence and go into business as an outlaw circuit. To extract the players whom the majors held in perpetuity, the Continentals would go to court to challenge the legality of the reserve clause. Both sides knew that the clause endured on the shakiest of legal grounds. A ruling against the big leagues would liberate hundreds of ballplayers, making them free agents who could sign with any team, including the well-heeled owners of the Continental League. Haywire indeed.

It is important to remember, however, that Branch Rickey believed in the reserve clause with a fervor equal to his faith in the Almighty. He had defended it before Congress, and nowhere in his memos or letters to the new league's founders did he so much as hint at challenging the provision that he had used to such great advantage in building his own career and reputation. Nor was he suggesting that the new league organize without it. He had embarked on this venture with the hope of being included under what he called "the umbrella" of organized baseball, a beneficiary, like everyone else, of the right to keep players bound by contract. He wasn't asking the big leagues for Mickey Mantle, Willie Mays, Ted Williams, or Henry Aaron. He just wanted the young ones and maybe a few of the older fellows until the new stars were ready.

But the commissioner, the league presidents, and, more important, their bosses, would not relinquish any players. "I am perplexed somewhat because of the apparent urgency to call me the very minute he read the Cronin letter and then wanted three days time before he met me," Rickey wrote, summing up his talk with Frick. "Can one suppose that the Commissioner needs counsel?" He was, after all, off to meet with Weiss and Webb. "One thing I am very sure about: The Commissioner is now ready to take a position on internal expansion. The whole idea is to defeat the Continental League."

Rickey had called. And in his rashness Frick had shown his hand: he was worried.

But Rickey, too, had ample reason for concern. He now saw how badly he had misread the men whom he had thought of as friends. He had gone to Washington to stall Congress, believing that the owners would appreciate the wisdom of his plan and allow his new league to come to life; like Dan Daniel, he did not believe that the men who ran the game needed Congress to tell them how to conduct their business wisely. But he was wrong and now he knew it. Frick had merely confirmed what Rickey had begun to suspect after consulting with a higher authority: Del Webb.

Webb had advised Rickey that it might be best to hold off for a year before launching the Continental League—all the confirmation Rickey needed that the American League was indeed playing for time, having calculated that delay was a strategy that would doom the new league. Until the Continental League could fill out its roster of eight teams, the big leagues were under no obligation to embrace it or help it; the newcomers were, after all, still in the formative stage. The bills pending in the House and Senate both ratified the reserve clause. If the final measure passed before the league was organized and recognized, the Continental League would be rendered helpless in challenging the big leagues' legal claim on virtually all the nation's ballplayers. The league would die and with it Rickey's dream for the future of the game.

So the American League owners trotted out their president, Joe Cronin, first to empanel his expansion study group, and then to make himself and his people inaccessible. Cronin, once a terrific shortstop, was an affable fellow who took to his assignment by undermining Rickey with kindness. He called the following morning and did his best to barrage Rickey with good tidings. "I have never in my life heard so much solicitude expressed in one telephone conversation in my entire life about my knee, my heart, my wife, my children, my present, my past, and my future," Rickey observed.

Rickey had done enough of this sort of work to know when the moment had come to shut off the platitude valve.

Had Cronin received his telegram? he asked.

Indeed he had, said the league president, and he had sent copies to the members of his expansion committee. He was expecting to hear back from them that very day.

"Well," said Rickey, "I can then expect to hear from you today in answer to my wire."

Sadly, the timing was not good, Cronin replied, hoping for a sympathetic ear. Meetings. Trades coming up. And just so that Rickey didn't get the wrong idea, Cronin made sure to commend to paper his assurance that his league had not been soliciting new members. Minneapolis had come to him. In the days that followed, Cronin would continue to lead Rickey on a merry dance, with Rickey trying as best he could to squeeze from the league president a commitment to expansion or an end to the charade.

Stymied by Cronin, Rickey then took a great risk: he offered to surrender any claim to any Continental League city the American League wanted, and if the American League wanted one of the cities that had applied to the Continental League, he would be happy to stand aside.

If Rickey was bluffing, he was playing a bold, if perilous, hand—risking desertions from those Continental League founders who would leap at the prospect of a spot in the American League. All Cronin had to do was call and commit to expansion, and the Continental League could well collapse.

But he wouldn't—or couldn't; Cronin, after all, was not the one making decisions for the American League. He would not even agree to a meeting; he was "knee deep" in work. The best he would do was agree to make a decision on expansion at the league meetings in early December. Really, he couldn't ask his "boys" to weigh in any sooner on so important a matter.

But Rickey no longer had the luxury of waiting until December or allowing Joe Cronin to play him for a fool. The founders were due in New York later that week, and by the time of their arrival Rickey had devised a counterattack. But first he felt compelled to prepare his people for what could well lay ahead by detailing, exhaustively, the campaign being waged against them.

"I am thoroughly convinced that the American League is completely committed to opposition to the Continental League," Rickey declared in his report. "There can be no doubt about it." The National League was also opposed but thus far without the American Leaguers' ferocity. Unlike Webb, Walter O'Malley was not facing imminent invasion—just a persistent threat of one. Little wonder, then, that it was the American League that had trooped out the ruse of expansion: it was the Yankees, everyone's meal ticket, who were guarding their turf against the twin threats of a new club and a new stadium in their city. "Most of the organized opposition," he wrote, "stems from the New York Yankees."

And why? Because the Continentals had the major-league owners frightened. One National Leaguer had confided to Rickey that the owners now saw that once the Continental League was fully organized and in a position to draft young players it would be at a great competitive advantage: in five years' time, these young men would be ready to supplant the aging, if familiar, stars of the game. "He stated that this point had been discussed and that, of course, meant all major league clubs would quite naturally oppose the Continental League for this reason," Rickey explained. Worse still, from the owners' perspective, all these fine young players might well be playing against one another in the Continental League's new and modern stadiums, like the one in Flushing Meadows, whose progress toward ground breaking only added to the growing displeasure of Webb and Topping.

But Rickey also wanted the founders to know that his own judgment had not always been wise. He confessed that he had been slow in recognizing what a clever strategy the mere hint of expansion could be.

"Your president," he reported, "has been completely in error about the effects of the propaganda dealing with internal expansion. He has always believed that the expansion would be offered but believed that it would be easy to meet and defeat. In spite of the absurdity of it and the complete improbability of it, it has taken hold in the public mind and in the press even among our own people most surprisingly"—he did not mention Minneapolis by name—"and it has upset all my calculations having to do with the completion of our league."

But there was an answer, one that he had already floated by Bill Shea, a strategy so daring that Rickey had heard that the Yankees did not believe that he and his people had the "guts to go 'haywire.'"

"It is becoming ever more evident to me day by day that we may not be able to organize until after October 15, 1960," he concluded, "except on one basis, namely independent organization."

If the founders were excited about Rickey's call to arms, they kept their enthusiasm to themselves. The only hint of dissent came from Big Ed Johnson. He was not necessarily opposed to a fight but wondered whether Rickey's plan wasn't "an emotional approach to a difficult situation." Johnson believed that there was a step short of going outlaw—one that, if Rickey would listen, might make life easier for all of them: the founders needed only to agree on an amendment to the bill now sitting in the Senate, a legislative tweak that would ratify the reserve clause but at the same time limit the number of players under contract. The operative word was *agree*.

Big Ed was not happy with Rickey. Not that he could say so directly; the founders trod around their president with great care. Johnson was displeased that Rickey did not seem to appreciate the urgency in drafting such an amendment and getting it onto the docket on Capitol Hill. Bob Howsam had reported back to his father-in-law that Rickey was under the impression that while the owners were pressing for speedy passage of the antitrust bill, Congress was in no such hurry. Johnson had sent Rickey a proposed amendment in late October, and Rickey had

The crowd outside Yankee Stadium before Game Three of the 1958 World Series between the New York Yankees and the Milwaukee Braves. This game was sold out, but there were empty seats by Game Five. (Corbis)

A forlorn Casey Stengel in the summer of 1959 as his Yankees headed to a rare third-place finish. (Corbis)

Friends no more: Branch Rickey, at left, with George Weiss, the general manager of the New York Yankees. (Corbis)

Ban Johnson, the founder of the American League in 1901, baseball's czar in the early years of the twentieth century, and Branch Rickey's hero. (Corbis)

Charlie Weeghman, the owner of the Chicago Whales, who helped found the Federal League in 1913, and then abandoned it. (National Baseball Hall of Fame Library, Cooperstown, N.Y.)

Justice Oliver Wendell Holmes of the United States Supreme Court, the author of baseball's exemption from federal antitrust laws. (Library of Congress)

Milwaukee's County Stadium, the ballpark that in 1953 became the new—and very profitable—home of the former Boston Braves, and set in motion the departure of the Brooklyn Dodgers and New York Giants for California four and a half years later. (National Baseball Hall of Fame Library, Cooperstown, N.Y.)

Walter O'Malley, the owner of the Dodgers and the wiliest businessman in the game. (National Baseball Hall of Fame Library, Cooperstown, N.Y.)

Casey Stengel and his role players, from left, infielder Gil McDougald, pitcher Jim Coates, infielder Clete Boyer, and catcher Johnny Blanchard. (National Baseball Hall of Fame Library, Cooperstown, N.Y.)

William A. Shea, standing, announces the establishment of the Continental League in New York City on July 27, 1959. Seated from the left are Craig Cullinan of Houston and Jack Kent Cooke of Toronto; in the background is Houston's George Kirksey. (AP IMAGES)

Senator Estes Kefauver, the Tennessee Democrat who presided over the U.S. Senate's hearings on baseball's antitrust exemption in the late 1950s. (Library of Congress)

Representative (and later Senator) Kenneth Keating of New York, the owners' best friend on Capitol Hill. (Library of Congress)

Baseball's Barnum and its power broker: The iconoclastic owner of the Chicago White Sox, Bill Veeck, seated, speaks to Del Webb, the imperious co-owner of the New York Yankees. (Corbis)

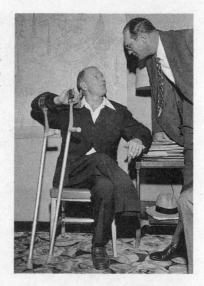

Webb's co-owner, Dan Topping, left, speaks with Arnold Johnson, the owner of the Kansas City Athletics, who kept the Yankees well stocked by trading the most promising players on his second-division team to New York. (Corbis)

The biggest crowds in the history of the game came to the Los Angeles Memorial Coliseum to see the Los Angeles Dodgers play the Chicago White Sox in the 1959 World Series. (National Baseball Hall of Fame Library, Cooperstown, N.Y)

The Yankees' All-Star center fielder, Mickey Mantle, nursing a wound in May 1960, after a fan punched him in the face at Yankee Stadium. (Corbis)

The stadium at the center of the drama: From left, Stuart Constable of the New York City Department of Parks, Branch Rickey, Mayor Robert Wagner, and Bill Shea examine a model of the planned ballpark to be built for New York's Continental League franchise in Flushing Meadows, Queens. (*The New York Times*)

The founding owners of the American Football League strike a pose. Lamar Hunt, the league's founder and the owner of the Dallas Texans, is in the front row, third from the left. Bob Howsam, the owner of the Denver Broncos and the owner of the Denver franchise in the Continental League, is at the far left of the front row. (AP IMAGES)

Casey Stengel and Branch Rickey at a dinner with Commissioner Ford C. Frick in the fall of 1960. (Corbis)

The scoreboard tells it all: The New York Yankees led the Pittsburgh Pirates in Game Seven of the 1960 World Series in the bottom of the eighth inning, when a bad-hop bouncer caught Yankees shortstop Tony Kubek in the throat, forcing him out of the game and setting in motion a chain of improbable events that would cost the Yankees the championship. (AP IMAGES)

The unlikeliest hero: Bill Mazeroski in the Pittsburgh Pirates' clubhouse after his dramatic home run in the bottom of the ninth of Game Seven won the 1960 World Series—the first time a World Series had ended with one swing of the bat. (Corbis)

"Write anything you want. Quit, fired, whatever you please. I don't care." Casey Stengel speaks to reporters on October 18, 1960, after the New York Yankees announced that he was not returning as the team's manager. (Neal Boenzi/ *The New York Times*)

In 1962, the National League returned to New York, and two years later the New York Mets moved into Shea Stadium, their new state-of-the-art ballpark in Flushing Meadows, named in honor of Bill Shea. The stadium was a big hit with the fans and would serve as the Mets' home for the next forty-five seasons. (*The New York Times*)

replied that Big Ed's suggested forty-man limit "did not go far enough"; he wanted to cap the number at thirty. That was fine with Johnson—"I want to go all the way," he wrote—but he needed the league to settle on a number and finalize the amendment so that he would have something to take to his friends on Capitol Hill. But more than a number, or the wording of an amendment, Johnson needed to know that Rickey, Shea, and the founders were prepared to act together. Because if they could not, Big Ed was prepared to walk away.

Johnson wrote to Shea to say that while Rickey had done a fine job "soft-soaping and buttering up the American League" and that while Johnson appreciated his work, the performance nonetheless left Kefauver and his committee "bewildered."

"They were convinced that the monopolistic practices of the major leagues had to be curbed," Johnson wrote, "and I did what I could to encourage that thought." Still, he added, "the committee was dismayed by our lack of unity." Lyndon Johnson himself had written to say that Kefauver was ready to deliver the bill to the full Judiciary Committee, and from there to a vote by the full Senate, where its prospects were bright. "I am alarmed over your thinking that Congress will not enact S-2545 in early 1960," wrote Big Ed, calling the bill by its senatorial name. "That is living in a 'fools' paradise.'"

He was also feeling aggrieved, in the way that self-important men do when they feel their efforts have not been sufficiently appreciated. "I, and I alone, was able to keep the bill bottled up in the Judiciary Committee last summer," he wrote. He had made promises, to Lyndon Johnson and to others, that in return for their agreeing to this bit of obstruction, the Continental League would settle on the terms of an amendment. "I made this pledge," he wrote, "and it will be kept." If the league could not agree on the terms it wanted, "it can anticipate no further interest by me."

Word of Johnson's displeasure, of course, reached Rickey, who felt the need to defend himself. Yes, he wrote to Big Ed, he had resisted his requests to provide the language necessary for the amendment: in truth, he had not wanted to see this bill, or any other antitrust measure, pass. Rather, he had hoped that his testimony might stall the measure so "that baseball would be permitted to clean its own house." But as if he needed further confirmation, he had gone to see Ford Frick, and over the course of a ninety-minute meeting had confronted the commissioner, by his count, three times about his opposition to the new league. "I said to him, pecking away with my forefinger over my heart, 'in here you are positively against a third league and you know it.'"

Rickey now appreciated that an amended bill might be of use but not necessarily for the same purposes envisioned by Johnson and the other founders. He admitted no anger nor any pain of betrayal. Yet it was if the owners' treachery—even as he was vowing for their decency and rectitude—had been an illumination, harsh and inescapable. He no longer wrote of trying to win the owners' blessings or acceptance into their exclusive domain. He wanted only their players. And if that meant the end, for all practical purposes, of the best of the minor leagues, it seemed to him a price worth paying if it allowed the best of those Double-A and Triple-A players to find better-paying work in the Continental League. Going outlaw, he wrote to Johnson, "seems to me, should now be our objective."

The wonderful thing about visionaries is the clarity with which the future appears to them. They imagine it and pursue it and all the rest is in service of realizing the dream. The windiness of Rickey's prose—both spoken and written—cluttered the vision he presented to those whose minds he sought to change. But that did not alter the fact that from the day Bill Shea came to call, Rickey knew exactly what he wanted to happen. The refusal of the owners to see things his way was now reduced to a nuisance—a considerable one, but not enough to dissuade him from believing that his vision for a third major league was wise and correct. To realize his plan he needed players. He had hoped the owners might share some of theirs and that he could convince them that this was in their best interest, too. But, by his own admission, he had waited too long and had delayed unwisely. Now he was prepared to reverse his views about seeking congressional help and insist that the owners hold no more than thirty reserved contacts. He needed a lot of players, because that is how he had always built his winning clubs; he had seen what a weak farm system had done to his plans in Pittsburgh. The means may have mattered to Ed Johnson—a man of process, not a man of vision—but Rickey thought about the end, the league. His league. And if the owners were going to fight him, he would simply go his own way—taking the best of their youth with him.

"I cannot tell you how reassured I am that you have no faith in the American League and the Commissioner," wrote Johnson, relieved that Rickey had seen the wisdom of his plan and the necessity of standing together. As it happened, he had just had breakfast with Senator Estes Kefauver and told him that Rickey was hoping to testify at the next round of hearings in February. He wanted two hours.

"Will the Continental League reach an agreement and present a united front?" Kefauver asked.

Johnson assured him it would.

"You can have two days if you want it," replied Kefauver.

Johnson closed his letter without addressing the question of an outlaw league, as if the matter had never been raised.

The next day, Dan Daniel offered another prophecy: "Brooklyn's return to the major leagues as a member of an expanded American League which would admit Minneapolis–St. Paul as well, will be considered by the organization in its annual meeting in Miami Beach, Dec. 17."

The new stadium would rise in Flushing Meadows. A new team would come to New York, because the Yankees would surrender their exclusive American League rights to the town. In return they would have a rival, which would enrich them just as all the games between the Brooklyn Dodgers and the New York Giants had once enriched those two teams. Daniel estimated that a new rivalry could boost Yankee attendance by a half million paid customers. Del Webb, Dan Topping, and George Weiss knew of this plan and had so far voiced no opposition. Daniel did not explain how the team would be considered a Brooklyn team if it played in Queens; perhaps it was enough that the two boroughs shared a border.

Meanwhile, Lamar Hunt was being tempted with the very thing he had set out from Dallas hoping to find: a team in the NFL. It was not the first time this had happened. He had been offered a team in September, three weeks after announcing the formation of his new league. He would not say who had made the offer but insisted it had not come from George Halas, who owned the Chicago Bears and headed the league's expansion committee. Hunt declined the invitation. Bert Bell, the NFL commissioner, dismissed the story, insisting that no owner was in a position to make such an offer.

But now, suddenly, Bell was dead. He had suffered a fatal heart attack in October during the closing minutes of a game between the Pittsburgh Steelers and the Philadelphia Eagles. The league was searching for a new commissioner, and in the meantime, power resided with the senior-most owners, Halas chief among them. He had still not given up on trying to lure Lamar Hunt into the NFL and eliminate the growing headache of his rival league.

This time he invited Hunt to Chicago. Hunt, however, did not come alone. He brought Bud Adams and Bob Howsam, who despite his father-in-law's assurances, had not given up on the American Football League. Years later, Howsam would recall how Halas sweetened his offer: franchises for Hunt in Dallas and for Adams in Houston.

But what of Denver? asked Hunt.

Not Denver, Halas replied. He did not think Denver was much of a football town. Nor did he offer to help Howsam buy into another team.

Lamar Hunt thanked George Halas for his time and declined his offer. The NFL could have all his teams or none of them. No one was being left behind.

Two weeks later, Halas announced that the NFL would expand to Minneapolis and Dallas. There would be pro football in Lamar Hunt's hometown, but it appeared he wouldn't be part of it. If Hunt wanted a battle, Halas was happy to oblige.

DECEMBER: Three's a Crowd

The baseball owners, league presidents, and commissioner descended on Miami Beach and decamped at the Fontainebleau. It was not quite beach weather, but at seventy degrees with clear skies, it was balmy enough for summer-weight suits and perhaps breaking out a straw hat.

Branch Rickey had also come to town to spoil everyone's fun. Bad enough that he had arrived prepared to confront Cronin about his assurance that the American League would decide, one way or the other, on expansion. But of all the hotels along Collins Avenue, Rickey and his retinue had also chosen to stay at the Fontainebleau. A man couldn't even risk taking a dip for fear of running into one of Rickey's people.

"Providing the rival factions don't get lost in this fourteen-acre playground," wrote John Drebinger of the *Times*, "something lively might develop if they meet head-on."

Cronin took the American League owners to one room and Warren Giles took the National Leaguers to another, where they would also take up the question of expansion. Rickey summoned the Continental League founders to a meeting room to await word of the big leaguers' respective decisions and consider how best to respond. But Bob Howsam had news to share. He had met twice with Frick and had found the commissioner to be nothing like the misanthrope Rickey and Shea had encountered. In fact, said Howsam, he might well be an ally. Truly. They'd talked for two and a half hours, and Howsam had walked away convinced that the commissioner wished to be cooperative and thought that, in Howsam's view, working together was "desirable." The Continentals, Frick had said, would do well to resolve their territorial disputes with the minor leaguers whose turf they planned to invade. And while Howsam's father-in-law was readying the legislative club, Howsam found the commissioner to be anything but frightened. Hurt, yes. Scared, no.

Frick, he went on, was feeling bruised by all the harsh things he'd been reading about himself in the papers.

Too bad, said Jack Kent Cooke. Frick might be hurt but the Continental League men were "mortally wounded."

Dinnertime was nearing when word came that the American Leaguers had reached a decision. Sort of. Nothing definite about the long term, but no new teams were to be added for 1960; they just couldn't agree about 1961. News from the National Leaguers soon followed, and it was more of the same: no plans to expand "at this time."

Rickey and his people were furious to find themselves still in limbo.

The big leaguers had cleverly left themselves room to change their minds; there was no assurance that they would not once again hint at taking in a city or two, a prospect that could split the Continental League before it ever fielded a team or played a game. The Continentals broke for dinner, and when they returned they talked and plotted until midnight before deciding to hold off on a statement until the morning, when they would have the press corps to themselves.

There was another matter left unresolved. Rickey had raised it late in the evening: he wanted their permission to take the owners to court. The suit would be in the name of a single club, but all the Continental League franchises would join as plaintiffs.

The founders decided to postpone a decision. Maybe they were tired. And maybe their president was leading them to a place they did not wish to be.

Ford Frick wanted to be their friend. That's what Bob Howsam had said. Everyone could walk away happy.

The next morning, Bill Shea warmed up the crowd of reporters, photographers, and television people. He took them through the history of the fledgling league and its struggles to endure. As an opening act, Shea played the tough guy and did it well. "I have my own ideas of what we should do in the face of this apparent opposition, as contrasted with their bald promises of cooperation in the United States Senate," he said, "and I feel certain that if we are forced to take these steps, the Continental League will become a reality in spite of the attitude of organized baseball."

Then, with the threat of congressional action and maybe worse hanging heavily, Rickey took the microphone.

"So long as the Major Leagues are able to maintain their absolute monopoly on players and territories," he began, "and further continue their tactics patently employed for the purpose of defeating any organization of a third major league, we will alone find ourselves unable to complete the formation of the Continental League. The answer to our future is presently in the hands of the American League."

No immediate plans for the majors to expand was a sham, he said, a diversion, a bluff. Except this time Rickey wasn't calling the bluff, not yet. First he was raising.

"I've got a little news for you," he told the assembled reporters. "Atlanta is our sixth club." The Continental League was now two cities short of a full roster.

Rickey would spend the weeks after Miami Beach courting Buffalo, trying to revive things in Dallas, and luring Montreal, should its application become necessary if someplace else dropped out. He had fulfilled his promise to Ed Johnson and crafted the wording for the amendment— a forty-man limit, just as Big Ed had originally wanted. Rickey turned seventy-eight years old on December 20, but much to his delight, he barely had time to pause to celebrate. He was planning a January trip to Minneapolis and then on to Houston. No matter that the *Saturday Evening Post* had declined to publish his article about the rationale behind the Continental League, he still had a lovely note from Craig Cullinan, praising his "magnificent" performance in Miami Beach and assuring him that though he may have been critical about "procedure," he still considered himself "one of Mr. Rickey's boys."

Four years had passed since the humiliation of his dismissal in Pittsburgh, four years since the letter to his children vowing that he was "not down and not out" and that he was "on the spring board of happier times."

And perhaps happier times, too, for Casey Stengel. George Weiss had given him all he could have asked for for Christmas. Weiss had scoured both leagues for trading partners and, having come up empty-handed, turned as always to Kansas City. Gone from the Yankees were Norm Siebern, Marv Throneberry, and Don Larsen, who was now even further removed from his one transcendent World Series moment. Banished, too, was Hank Bauer, who had outlived his usefulness. In return came two reserves and Kansas City's right fielder, Roger Maris.

"I know we'll take a lot of ribbing," said Weiss, "but it simply came down to where we couldn't close a deal with any other club."

The old order was not dead. Not yet.

CHAPTER SIX

WINTER 1960

JANUARY: Members Only

Of all the good things that had happened to Branch Rickey since the first of the year, perhaps the sweetest came the night he was mocked. This happened on the night of January 31, when the New York chapter of the Baseball Writers' Association of America gathered for its annual dinner.

Rickey started the day in his room at the Hotel Astor receiving visitors, then reporters, one after the next. The telephone did not stop ringing; he took the calls, or left it to his wife, in case one of the children was trying to get through. He dressed for dinner at five, and then went downstairs and did not have a moment to himself until he finally made it back to his room at midnight. Fourteen hundred guests descended upon the hotel's ballroom and everyone, it seemed, wanted to talk to him—minor-league executives, the major leagues' lawyer, old friends and old players, even the son of George Sisler, Rickey's first star player back with the St. Louis Browns, who had been recommended as having the makings of a fine general manager. George Weiss stopped by to say hello and was pleasant about it, unlike Ford Frick, who was not.

It was, as always, a grand affair—Mayor Wagner spoke, as did Governor Nelson Rockefeller, who hammed it up for the cameras with Ty

Cobb, playing at picking sides with a bat; the governor was lucky that Cobb was now seventy-three and frail and no longer likely to try to win by taking a bite out of Rockefeller's arm. Rockefeller, who late in the game had tried to keep the Dodgers in Brooklyn, now dedicated a portion of his remarks to kind words about Rickey and the Continental League: "His organizational genius in forming the new major league is but another landmark in his most distinguished career."

But this was not an evening for platitudes, and in keeping with the spirit of an event at which the great men of the game became the object of ridicule, Rockefeller allowed himself to have some fun at Casey Stengel's expense. He suggested that the Yankees' manager might make a fine secretary of state—"Ol' Case would get those Russians so confused they'd send Khrushchev to the moon on the next rocket—by mistake." The mayor then took his turn by joking about Walter O'Malley ("He could have at least sent us a post card for Christmas") and about the Yankees' disappointing 1959 finish: "Now we're down to just the Yankees in New York—at the present time that's pretty low."

With the audience warmed up, the politicians yielded the stage to Sal Terini's orchestra and to the writers themselves, for whom the moment had come to perform. There was a send-up of Stengel as a World Series reporter. There was a jingle about the Yankees' poor pitching, set to the tune of an Alka-Seltzer commercial. And then Roscoe McGowan rose to sing. McGowan was blessed with a lovely basso profundo that he now broke out at the expense of Branch Rickey.

There had been a time when Rickey was a fixture of derision at these shows, especially for his legendary unwillingness to part with a dime in salary talks: "You can't take it with you, Mr. Rickey," pleads an underpaid player; "Well, then," replies the wag playing the mahatma, "I won't go."

But for the past several years, Rickey had been a forgotten man. Until now. Once again he had been deemed a worthy object of ridicule. And who better to deliver the blow than McGowan, who came out of retirement to do the show.

"*Ol' Man Rickey,*" he sang, channeling Paul Robeson, "*he just keeps rolling along.*"

With that bit of mockery, the Continental League, on this night at least, had become a part of the club.

<<<<<

Things, in fact, did appear to be falling neatly into place. Dallas, which had spurned the Continentals in November, had returned to the fold. The founders then gathered in Minneapolis, which had seen the error of its short-lived betrayal. "The Twin Cities," wrote Charles Johnson, the sports editor of the *Minneapolis Tribune*, "must go with the new Continental League if they are ever to get major league baseball." Johnson, not alone among sports editors with big-league aspirations, had immersed himself in trying to lure a major-league team to his town. But now, in light of the American League's delaying tactics, he conceded that the prospects had all but vanished of ever welcoming the Senators.

Rickey, eager to soften the disappointment, took the occasion of the meeting to assure his hosts that their Continental League franchise would not be a loser, unlike the American League team they had wanted so badly. In fact, there would be no losers in the Continental League— last-place finishers, of course, but not the perennial fifty-games-out-of-first-by-August laggards that were as much a part of the game as the infield fly rule. Rickey had devised a remedy that, in effect, reversed the very approach he had invented forty years earlier: in the Continental League there would be no individual team farm systems, no harvesting of talent at the expense of everyone else. The new league, he announced, would pool its prospects. It would maintain a central registry and would hold "thrice-yearly drafts by all teams on the basis of a draw."

Everyone would have the chance to win because everyone would have a shot at the best players. And to ensure that the less populous cities in the new circuit would be able to compete with, say, wealthy New York, Rickey was pushing an even more radical plan for revenue sharing, insisting that the founders sign no television deals on their own; rather, he wanted one deal for the entire league with the proceeds divided equally among the teams. A contender in every town. If not one year, then maybe the next.

Still, the Continentals left the Minneapolis meeting a franchise short of a full deck, and so without the recognition of their legitimacy. With antitrust legislation proceeding rapidly toward a vote in Congress, Shea and Rickey headed to Washington, hoping to stall until they could secure an eighth club. Having exhausted the patience of their allies—Kefauver himself announced that he was disappointed with the league's slow progress—they turned to a foe for help: Kenneth Keating of New York. Keating was now a United States senator, and with his ascent had assumed a statesmanlike mien. "I'm dedicated to seeing this Continental League become a reality," he said—this from a man who counted Dan Topping among his campaign contributors. In fact, he went on, he was so eager to help that he offered his services as an "informal mediator" between the major-league owners and the Continentals "night or day." Rickey was so pleased that when a reporter caught up with him at National Airport, he predicted that America would soon see not only a third major league, but a fourth one, too.

But Ford Frick was not happy at all. Keating was an ally—perhaps the owners' most important ally on the Hill. It was all well and good for Frick to offer the Continentals his support because, as Rickey had learned, he did not mean it. But Keating was not supposed to help the Continentals, and certainly not to serve as a go-between. So Frick hurried to Washington to impress upon Keating that his services would not be needed. "Mediator of what?" the commissioner whined to Dan Daniel, who went along for the ride. "Is there any dispute that requires mediation? Have Rickey and Shea abolished my job as commissioner?"

Once again, Frick was the aggrieved party; *he* was prepared to help the new league. After all, was it not he who had declared New York an "open city," blocking the Yankees from laying exclusive claim to the town? "My office in New York is in Rockefeller Center," he told Daniel. "Rickey's headquarters are only a couple of blocks away. Shea is on East 42nd Street. But I have waited in vain for either or both to come up and discuss their problems and clarify their intentions."

He would not have long to wait. Rickey had told Keating that he needed only two or three weeks to complete the league's roster. The eighth team might be Montreal or Buffalo; for the time being, Mark Scott would have to hold off on his assault on Los Angeles. And therein lay a new conundrum for the junior senator from New York: Keating no longer represented a safe Republican district in Rochester, but a state that, like Texas, now stood to gain Continental League franchises in its two biggest cities. Keating may have been happy to oblige the owners, so long as he did not risk alienating his many new constituents.

Rickey was a man of his word. Two weeks after his meeting with Keating, the Continental League invited the press corps to the Hotel Delmonico, where Shea, taking the place of a weary Branch Rickey—one too many late-night meetings—announced that the founders had chosen Buffalo as the league's eighth city. The news came on a propitious day—January 29, precisely fifty-nine years and a day after Ban Johnson decreed that the American League had become a major league. Shea took the moment to remind everyone what Frick had told the Continentals: "Come to me when you have all your clubs and I'll be your commissioner, too."

Branch Rickey, Shea assured the newsmen, would be getting in touch, and soon.

FEBRUARY: Three Perils

Rickey was up early the morning after the sportswriters' banquet. He was at his breakfast table by nine o'clock, once again attracting a crowd. Another long and splendid day filled with people wanting something from him. A man from city hall called his room about a contribution to a charity favored by the Democrats. A limousine arrived to ferry him to Connecticut, where six hundred people were waiting to hear him speak. He was weary when he got to bed at one in the morning. "I was thoroughly disgusted with myself because I was so tired," he wrote to Shea, who was out of town. Rickey sent him two memos that day and four the next; there was so much he needed to tell: "The Baseball Writers' Dinner was 'Continentalized,'" he wrote. "It was almost the red thread running through the entire program." And no need for Shea to ask his office to send the New York papers; Rickey had already called to alert them.

One by one, the job seekers made their way to his room. Some were men who, in a baseball context, were down on their luck and out of the game, but who had known and perhaps worked for him when he was last a man of consequence. One was Billy Southworth, who had managed Rickey's last world champions in St. Louis in 1942. Southworth, who'd also won the 1944 World Series with the Cardinals and a pennant with the Boston Braves in 1948, had been fired by Boston midway through the 1951 season. He'd been having a hard time of it in recent years, especially since the death of his son, a decorated bomber pilot killed on a training mission after making it home from the war. "He will be a manager in the Continental League," Rickey advised Shea. A good feeling to once again be in a position to dispense favors.

Southworth departed and soon it was noon, time to head to Rockefeller Center, and call, as promised, on the commissioner.

"Well, sir, you've got a tough job—tougher than you think," Frick said in greeting. ˙

"Very tough, Mr. Commissioner," replied Rickey. "No doubt about it. It has been tough."

"Not like it's going to be," said Frick.

"If it gets worse, and more serious, the Continental League will need a better man than me."

"You may be able to do it. It could be done, I know that. But it's a tough job."

"What strikes Mr. Commissioner as the immediately tough job you have in mind?" asked Rickey.

"Well everything, but particularly two or three things," replied Frick. "Now, let's get into it."

First came what the commissioner called "the money problem," which is generally the easiest sort of problem to resolve. It came in two parts: pensions for the players, a relatively manageable fix, and the thornier matter of restitution to the minor leagues for invading their territories. This, Frick explained, also involved bruised feelings, not only among the minor-league operators but also among the major-league owners who controlled these affiliates—particularly in Minneapolis, a Red Sox outpost, and Atlanta, which belonged to the Dodgers.

Why, Frick wanted to know, hadn't the Continentals gone immediately to Boston's Tom Yawkey and asked him how much he wanted for the rights to the Twin Cities? Rickey, in his recounting of the conversation, kept his tongue and allowed the commissioner to offer a remedy: cash. Presumably, a good deal of it; the San Francisco Giants, he reminded him, had indemnified the Pacific Coast League to the tune of $450,000. The sense was that this could be done, and the Dodgers, too, could be appeased. Houston, however, was another matter.

Cullinan and Kirksey had, early in their campaign to lure a club, been offered the local minor-league team, the Buffs. They'd turned the deal down, calculating that the price, both in money and time, would be a distraction from their bolder goal. The team, a St. Louis affiliate, went instead to a partnership that included Marty Marion, the onetime Cardinals shortstop and manager. Marion was happy to off-load the Buffs—for $492,000, a price so high that even Frick had to admit it was woefully out of bounds. Frick had heard that Marion might drop the price by half. Rickey assured him that that report was overly optimistic. Frick, in turn, promised to offer what help he could and told Rickey that his door was always open. Rickey understood that to mean that if he wanted Houston in the league, he would have to deal with Marty Marion himself.

They closed by agreeing to keep the substance of their meetings from the press. But Frick did not seem inclined to end the meeting on an encouraging note. Rickey had put on his hat and was headed to the door when the commissioner offered a final, closing dig.

"You've got a tough job," he said. "I don't know whether you can do it or not."

Rickey did not turn to face him. "Don't try to scare me," he said.

Frick never did get around to raising the second of Rickey's problems. Or perhaps he was not inclined to alert him of Webb and Topping's plans to scuttle his league.

Across the river in Queens, the planned new stadium in Flushing Meadows would be all that Yankee Stadium was not: It would be modern. No pillars. No posts. No long shadows. No monuments in the outfield that generations of children on their first visit to the park thought were tombstones. Worse still, from the Yankees' perspective, it would sit not in the middle of a neighborhood of apartment buildings, but alongside a highway that extended to the single-family homes on Long Island.

And those new patrons would be able to park. Not like those foolish enough to drive to Yankee Stadium, with its measly three thousand places and where custom had it that a parking spot on the street appeared only after forking over a few bills to the fellow who promised to "watch" the car during the game and who was prepared to knock out a window or flatten a tire if his price wasn't met. In Los Angeles, Walter O'Malley was building a ballpark surrounded by parking lots. And now New York's master builder, Robert Moses, was pushing the construction of just such a stadium for a franchise in a league that existed only in organizational charts, a growing bank account, and the fanciful imagination of Branch Rickey.

In fact, the idea of such an arena had become so much the rage that even Frick claimed that what he called "the all-purpose, all-weather, all-year-round sports palace" would be the savior of the game. Never again, he told the *Los Angeles Times*, would teams like the Dodgers or Giants want to abandon their cities, not when they played in such a park. The *Times* offered an artist's rendering of how such a complex might look. Indeed, plans for just such a ballpark were already circulating, the most audacious of which had been developed by a rancher turned civil engineer turned newspaperman named Henry Ladd.

Ladd, a Texan who boasted degrees from two colleges, believed he had devised the answer to every city that wanted a team or feared losing one; he called it "the Stadiseum." Ladd gave his park a subtitle at once worthy of Abraham Lincoln and Earl Scheib, the cut-rate car painter: *For All the People All of the Time at One-Third the Usual Cost.* The Stadiseum would house an arena for basketball, boxing, hockey, wrestling, and tennis; a pool for swim meets and water polo; a convention center with a capacity of 54,000; exhibition halls for auto, garden, and trade shows; a museum called "Our America"; a 21,000-seat theater, a hall of fame; shopping at "the Bazaar of Nations" and "the Nation's Mart"— the nation's "largest merchandise mart"; a hotel with 2,800 guest rooms; 22,000 parking spaces; and a helipad.

At the center of it all would stand a stadium with a seating capacity of a quarter million. And this would be no ordinary stadium. Never again would a spectator in a faraway seat be relegated to an afternoon of bad sight lines. At the Stadiseum, the stands would rotate, making a full revolution of the playing field every twenty-two minutes. There would be football at the Stadiseum, as well as auto racing, soccer, track meets, and, of course, baseball. And with so many spectators, the ticket prices would stay low. The Stadiseum, outsized as it was, had nonetheless drawn attention, even in New York, where in 1957 Deputy Mayor John Theobald wrote to Ladd to solicit details. As it happened, the city had been toying with an aluminum-sided arena spread over fifteen blocks. It was to have been called "Olympic City." But in the end, inevitably, it was Robert Moses's vision that prevailed, and he wanted nothing more than a 55,000-seat stadium whose most attractive qualities were its 10,700 parking spots and the fact that it was new.

Del Webb and Dan Topping were not willing to stand idly by as Moses built a stadium that offered all that they could not. And so they concocted a plan of their own and dispatched their lawyer to float it by the mayor, with a copy to Moses. They proposed that the city take over the Yankees' lease. And once Yankee Stadium became municipal property, the new club could share it with the Bombers. There would be no need for the Flushing Meadows stadium—a relief, presumably, to the taxpayers, or more precisely to the purchasers of the municipal bonds that would fund the project. With its newly acquired stadium, the city could invest in such improvements as additional seating—doubling the bleachers could expand seating to an even 100,000, making it the colossus of ballparks—escalators, and more parking. The city needed only to take the adjoining Macombs Dam park, pave it over, and wait for the cars to fill it up.

The Continentals, of course, did not want to play in Yankee Stadium; Shea had already made it clear that without the Flushing Meadows ballpark there would be no New York franchise and, by extension, no new league. Flushing, like the Continental League itself, represented a future in which ballparks like Yankee Stadium had no place. It fell to Rickey to dismiss any thought of sharing the great cathedral in the Bronx.

"I don't want Yankee Stadium on a permanent basis—it's an antiquated park—and what have they to sell?" he said. "It's an international attraction I'm looking for, something that New York and the nation will be proud of—with ample parking space for the fans. This is progress, and the only way to make progress is to make more progress."

Moses offered the city's response to Webb and Topping in a way that was sure to offend. Neither he nor the mayor replied directly to the offer, although Moses had already written privately to Wagner to dismiss the proposal and identify the scheme behind the plan: "to attack and to bedevil the building of the Flushing Meadows stadium." He then issued a public reply, via the antiseptic instrument of a press release. Moses was not afflicted with Rickey's penchant for circumlocution. For a generation he had done as he liked when it came to demolishing and rebuilding the city, and what he wanted now was a stadium in the geographic center of the city, in Queens, alongside the World's Fair he was planning for 1964. So it was that the operative word in his statement was *will*. As in, the new Flushing Meadows stadium "will accommodate 55,000" and "will be U or horseshoe shaped" and "will require a reliable sponsor." And lest the Yankees have any illusions about undermining Moses, he went on, "We hope Mr. Shea and his group will establish the new baseball league for this most important single usage, that is baseball." There was, however, a caveat: Unlike O'Malley's baseball-only stadium in Chavez Ravine, Moses's park would be built for many games—"football, soccer, cricket, track, bicycle races." Once the mayor and city council voted to extend funding, work could proceed so that the new park could be ready in time for Opening Day 1962. And a 1961 opening was also a possibility, if everyone hurried.

This was not what Webb and Topping wanted to hear. Unable to gain any traction by working the back channels, and having failed to budge Moses when they sent George Weiss to meet quietly with him and the mayor, the Yankees' owners decided that the time had come to take their grievances public. They also assigned this task to Weiss, an odd choice given that Weiss seldom, if ever, had anything to say. The press corps trooped over to the Yankees' Fifth Avenue offices, where Weiss surprised everyone by filling their notebooks with terrific copy.

He first went after Rickey, who had provided the ammunition for an opening salvo. Rickey's use of the word *antiquated* had apparently wounded Weiss, deeply. "It seems out of order for the president of a league without a park, a franchise or a ballplayer to speak about Yankee Stadium," he said. He was just warming up. "Of course anyone who has been to the Stadium pays no attention to what Rickey says. If he does get started he won't even have a good AAA class team." The Continental squad in New York would surely be a team so inferior to his that Weiss, for one, did not think it worthy of sharing the game's most hallowed ground "because the difference would be so marked it would be ridiculous. Do we fear the Continental League? Figure it out for yourself."

But if Weiss and his employers were not fearful, if they were not feeling threatened by the prospect of such a woeful franchise setting up shop in Queens, why did he then feel compelled to lay into the commissioner and the city fathers, too?

How, he wanted to know, could the city treat the Yankees so shabbily, an enterprise that was good for $200,000 each year in taxes? "We should have the right as taxpayers to ask how Flushing Meadows park is going to be paid for. They talk about $15 million. Land improvement and the stadium and highways are going to cost a lot more than that."

And, for that matter, how could the commissioner take sides against the Yankees? "We are the only major league club directly affected by the Continental League," he said. "They come to New York without paying a quarter for territorial rights. Frick declared New York is open territory and he is the only one to declare it. How could he do this?"

Lest there be any mistake about his meaning, Weiss then threw a marker, on behalf of Topping, Webb, and the rest of the American League:

"They say this is open territory. This is our territory."

Frick had warned Rickey that two or three perils awaited him. One was money. One was the Yankees. Now, in Houston, came a third—a dire peril that Frick himself may not have foreseen.

The Continental League owners had come to Texas to lend their presence and support to Houston's flagging prospects. Marty Marion had reportedly offered to drop his price for the minor-league Houston Buffs by half—just as Frick had suggested to Rickey. But even that seemed too costly to Craig Cullinan and George Kirksey, and the two sides remained tens of thousands of dollars apart. No deal meant no club, which meant no new stadium for baseball, football, and the Fat Stock Show. It was a particularly galling predicament for Kirksey, who had been campaigning relentlessly since he first wrote to George V. McLaughlin in 1957, asking if New York wanted to throw in with Houston. The Houston franchise was now in such peril that Mark Scott wrote to Rickey, letting him know that if a vacancy happened to open up, he had a man in Anaheim ready to build a thirty-five-thousand-seat stadium that he'd be happy to rent on reasonable terms.

The Continentals toured the city, met with the potential investors, and concluded that one issue that needed resolution, soon and publicly, was the vexing problem of players. Rickey had made his views clear, or as clear as could be expected from a man who could not resist larding his plan with grandiose talk of how things would one day be. He had wanted to build the league, as he had built his first champions in St. Louis, with little-known men who had proved themselves the worthiest prospects. But not everyone agreed. And as the league meeting began to unfold, Rickey was confronted with the most treacherous peril of all: an insurrection.

In truth, he had come to Houston already knowing that his hold on the league was not nearly as powerful as the one that Ban Johnson had exerted over the fledgling American League. The day after the writers' dinner in New York he had felt compelled to write yet again to Bill Shea, not to boast of his success, but to plead for his help. A crisis loomed and he needed an ally, badly.

People wanted him out. Or, short of that, a role of diminishing influence. He had learned that Cullinan, Jack Kent Cooke, and one of the New York investors, Dwight Davis, had proposed that the league appoint a second in command, an "executive vice president." They even had a man in mind: Trader Lane, Cleveland's chatty general manager and an odd choice, given that he had said many disparaging things about the new league. "This was originally Jack's idea," Rickey wrote. "I was quite surprised to say the least. I asked him directly if he had in mind Frank Lane becoming President of the League. He did."

Never mind that Rickey regarded Lane a poor choice as deputy or successor—he would not, as he put it, "wear well," but might be a suitable general manager for one of the Continental League clubs. Far more troubling was the knowledge that three franchise leaders were conspiring to dilute his power or even to throw him over. "I am extremely discouraged, of course, that a committee composed of the three gentlemen . . . should find it necessary to take over the functions naturally devolving upon the President of the League," Rickey wrote to Shea. Where, for instance, did these three get off making proposals about the number of veteran players on a team? He himself had been giving the matter a lot of thought—"I have a full program to offer on that very point"—and if they were so interested perhaps they'd also like to take up, as he had, such nettlesome points as waivers, salary limits, option agreements, and other details.

Rickey also wanted Shea to know that he had considered walking away. "If it were not for the paramount objective, namely the successful operation of a third major league, and, if further, if it were not for the breach of observance of my continuous identification with the effort to organize the Continental League, and finally, if it is true that this committee represents fully the views of the League as a whole—I would write out my resignation as President of the League and submit it to you for instant and irrevocable action," he wrote. "For the reasons, just stated, I leave no such thing in mind."

No, he couldn't quit, not yet. Just as New York was the essential franchise, he and Shea were the indispensable men, without whom the Continental League could not go on. Rickey had heard enough flattery in his time to be fluent in the language, tone, and pitch. "Without yourself this league could not be born," he wrote to Shea, "and without your continuous nursing it could not survive."

Rickey did not think that Cooke bore him ill will—"Jack had in mind only the kindliest attitude toward me personally"—or that Davis had been more than a follower. Instead, he turned on Cullinan. "Craig," he concluded, "was the insistent one—without doubt."

Rickey had come to Houston to try to save the franchise of a man who liked to be thought of as "one of Mr. Rickey's boys," only to discover that Cullinan was not the only one turning against him.

Rickey was right about Jack Kent Cooke; the Toronto owner bore him no apparent ill will, certainly not regarding Rickey's plan for acquiring players. Cooke, who had learned something of the game as a minor-league operator, was especially keen on the idea of looking south for talent and signing the best players from Cuba, Puerto Rico, and Venezuela. They were plentiful, they were not bound to the majors, and they would come cheap. The Continentals, he now suggested to his colleagues, would do well to establish its own minor leagues. There was talk of taking over the Class-D Western Carolina League, a first step toward harvesting players without commitments to the majors. This was just what Rickey wanted to hear.

But not Bob Howsam. Big Ed's son-in-law also owned a team and, unlike Cooke, he had concluded that homegrown talent and imported Spanish-speaking free agents would not sell. He had broken out his adding machine and concluded that he, for one, stood to lose a half million dollars a year if he fielded a team filled with unknowns whom few would pay to see. The league, he insisted, would collapse if it could not wrest from the big leagues some of the also-rans and minor leaguers whose contracts they held. Like his father-in-law, Howsam believed that the only path to success lay in extracting a player limit from the big-league owners in exchange for federal antitrust protection.

Rickey agreed, presumably. He had acknowledged his failure in reading the owners and in resisting limits on their antitrust exemption. Yet Howsam and Johnson sounded as if they still doubted his faith in their plan. It was a logical and troubling conclusion given how tenaciously Rickey clung to his vision of a league "dominated," as he put it, "by the free agents, the unknowns, the great stars of the future." Granted, an amended antitrust bill might free, by his calculation, 2,200 of the 4,200 players under contract. But these men, it was becoming ever more apparent, did not interest Rickey; they would not be *his* people.

They would not be like all the young men who had passed through his baseball academies, learning and perfecting what he had concluded were the best ways to slide, bunt, and hit to the opposite field with two strikes. The current minor leagues were filled with too many players who possessed none of the "sense of adventure" he wanted to see on the base paths and whose character he had had no hand in honing. Rickey sought to position himself to command not merely a team's farmhands, but the youth of an entire league. They would gather each spring to train together—he already had Daytona Beach in mind as a training facility. And because he would have a say in choosing the managers and general managers, he would be able to impose his view of the game as he believed it was meant to be played. Rickey spoke of the future, endlessly. But it was the past he was trying to re-create, bolder than it ever was. His league would be filled with a new generation of scrappers like Pepper Martin, Leo Durocher, Rip Collins, and Frankie Frisch. It would be a great and enduring gift, to stand with his emancipation of the game: eight cities with Gas House Gangs to call their own.

Howsam wasn't buying a bit of it.

"If you can't get a way to get the minor league players you fail," he told Rickey.

This was insubordination, and Rickey would not stand it.

"You ought not to be in the league," he told Howsam. And with that the old man rose and walked out of the room.

But Howsam would not let it go.

Cooke did his best to defend Rickey's approach. Howsam dismissed his talk of experimentation, and others, who knew less about the game, were beginning to consider what might happen if they fielded teams with men who could not play like the big leaguers.

"Five errors will empty the ballpark," said Dallas's J. W. Bateson.

Which was why, Howsam pressed on, it was imperative that the league demand that Congress force the owners to surrender some of their players. A poor start would ruin them all.

But what of the future, asked Cooke, and all those free agents from the Caribbean?

Won't work, replied Howsam. And neither would going independent, because the press, he believed, would never get behind an outlaw league. One by one, Howsam parried the arguments Cooke was making in

Rickey's absence, all the while building his own case upon a simple proposition: television had changed everything. It had given players faces, and those faces first seen on barroom televisions were now appearing in millions of living rooms across the country. Rickey was talking about all the fine players to be found in South and Central America, but these were not the faces people wanted to see, Howsam argued. Nor would they be drawn to following the rookies from the Western Carolina League, which had, in his view, "too many colored players."

The conversation ended without resolution and without Branch Rickey, who never did return. The leaders were left to consider their next step in his absence. Tabled, for the moment, was the question of players. Instead, the men turned to their own future and how best to conduct their business. Cooke mentioned the vice-presidency plan, but the proposal gained little traction. Howsam suggested that the group appoint an executive committee to run the league's affairs and avoid any potential vacuum in power.

"Mr. Rickey," he suggested, "might not be with us."

Bill Shea, who'd largely been silent, now weighed in. The committee was acceptable, he said, but only to advise the president.

Craig Cullinan suggested delaying a decision until another day.

Bob Howsam was left to return to Denver dreaming not of a league filled as Rickey might have wanted but of a circuit of television stars, of men like Ted Williams, Willie Mays, and the biggest of them all, Mickey Mantle.

MARCH: The Pitchman

The moment had come for George Weiss to exact punishment for the Yankees' failed 1959 season, and he did not shrink from the task. In mailboxes across the country, envelopes arrived bearing contracts that were sure to disappoint; underachievement was a crime whose penalty was a cut in pay. The rules limited teams to reducing a man's pay by no more than 25 percent, and Weiss was not averse to offering as little as the law allowed. But of all the envelopes opened that winter, none was greeted with more chagrin than the one that arrived at the Dallas home of Mickey Mantle.

Haggling had by now become an annual rite with Mantle and Weiss, who had gone at it since the winter of 1958 when Mantle, who had hit .365 in 1957—finishing second for the batting title to the ageless Ted Williams's .388—demanded a $10,000 raise. The team balked; in Weiss's eyes, Mantle had failed to repeat his Triple Crown performance of 1956. Mantle held out again in 1959 until the team granted him the same modest raise it had ponied up the year before. But now Weiss was in no mood to spread cheer. He offered Mantle, who had earned $75,000 in 1959, a contract for $62,000—a 17 percent cut for his role in the team's slide.

One by one, the Yankees took their licks, signed their 1960 contracts and began packing for spring training in St. Petersburg. All save one. "I think I can safely say that, with a single exception, all the players still unsigned will be in uniform," Weiss announced. "I don't think I need to name the one exception."

He and Mantle had talked, and it had not gone well. Weiss suggested that Mantle come to Florida so that they could discuss their differences face-to-face, but Mantle declined, preferring for the time being to remain at home and negotiate by phone. Weiss handed the case to his assistant, Roy Hamey, who had nothing to offer Mantle that might change his mind.

So Mantle stayed in Dallas, and when the mood hit him, stopped in at his new bowling alley, Mickey Mantle Lanes. Bowling, his manager insisted, was the coming thing, and people were so taken by the game that they stopped by to bowl during lunch. And what could be more contemporary than a bowling alley in the basement of a shopping center? People came by hoping to catch a glimpse of Mantle, who might bowl a game himself—he was a 160 bowler—but whose comings and goings could not be predicted. He might be attending to his other business interests, such as the Mickey Mantle motel he owned in Joplin, Missouri.

He could afford to hold out. It was one thing for an ordinary player to be compelled to take the reduced wages Weiss offered. But Mantle was alone among his teammates in having sources of revenue outside the game; there was no need to work at the hardware store, as midlevel players traditionally did in the off-season. Mantle could make money simply by showing up. Television had made him the most popular player in the game.

He was now twenty-eight and as broad as a heavyweight across the chest, back, and shoulders. He was blond, crew cut, and had the sort of boyishly handsome face and grin that could have made him a star in Depression-era second features about the big man on campus.

The Yankees may have slid to third place, but they remained the greatest road show in the game; fans across the American League map gathered to watch when Berra, Ford, and Skowron came to town. The local writers decamped in front of the Yankees' dugout, where Casey Stengel surveyed his audience to make sure the important columnists were present before beginning the day's soliloquy. But more than any other Yankee, it was Mantle the people came to see—in person. The Yankees appeared often on televised Games of the Week, and those broadcasts had burnished Mantle's image and stardom. He was three years removed from his Triple Crown season, when he laid claim to being the best player in the game—a contentious point, given the annual exemplary performances of, among others, Willie Mays, Henry Aaron, and Stan Musial. But just as Mantle had begun to realize his great potential, he had also shown small signs of slipping, inevitable given how prone he was to injury. Still, more than any other player in the game, Mantle at bat represented the drama of possibility, especially when he caught a ball flush, driving it farther than anyone else.

Home, however, was a different matter. At home in New York he was booed. Children squirted ink on his shirts when he did not sign autographs. A thirteen-year-old girl once punched and slapped him and grabbed at his hair as he emerged from a taxi. Grown men came out early to heckle him during batting practice—"Here comes the all-American out" and "Mantle, you couldn't play on the Bushwicks." It had been this way since 1952, his first season in center field, where he had displaced Joe DiMaggio, a sin. That he played hurt, always hurt, always taped from ankle to hip, did not much matter. The army had classified him 4-F; he'd had osteomyelitis as a teenager and almost lost his leg. Yet, it still galled the veterans that unlike almost all of his teammates, he'd never served—let alone seen action, as Bauer and Berra had, during the war.

He was strong and fast—no one was ever faster from home to first— and so it stood to reason that he was supposed to be great, always. Indeed, from his first spring training in 1951, Stengel had seen more than greatness in Mantle. He saw in him the rough contours of the man he would sculpt into the greatest player the game had ever known. Stengel's mentor, John McGraw, had had his chance with Mel Ott, who would go on to set the National League record for home runs. But as great a slugger as the undersized Ott became, Mantle, bigger, stronger, faster, could be far greater. A monument to Stengel. So long as he listened. Mantle had been a very good and occasionally spectacular player in his first four full seasons in New York, an All-Star who could be relied upon to hit .300 and perhaps thirty home runs, some of them so long they took the breath away. Then came 1956. That season Mantle became the player everyone had assumed he was destined to be.

He hit .353 in 1956, with 52 home runs and 130 runs batted in. He was living what was by all appearances a charmed life—a suite in the St. Moritz that he shared with Billy Martin and where Ford sometimes slept if it was too late to drive home to his wife and children on Long Island. Mantle, too, had a family, a wife and two sons whom he seldom saw. The writers knew about all the women who came and went in the morning, seldom to be seen a second time. But they made no mention of it, even though Mantle had done little to endear himself with the beat reporters, especially after, say, a three-strikeout performance when it was wise to allow him a wide berth. He took strikeouts, any outs really, as if they confirmed all the harsh things that were said about him.

Early on, he had carried his black moods home, as his wife, Merlyn, told *Look* magazine. "The children have learned to leave him alone. He sits glued to a chair, watching TV, a dark cloud around his head," she said. "I'm not as well-disciplined as the kids. I get mad and turn the set off." Mercifully, the family now spent the season in Dallas. Mantle still punched walls and kicked water coolers and took so badly to children hounding him for autographs that on a spring visit to San Juan he pushed to the ground a boy who'd come sprinting across the tarmac, paper in hand. "Don't worry, kid," Ford told the boy as he helped him up, "he's like that." The writers were by now familiar with his pattern— a dozen shots before dinner, after which the real drinking began. He typically slept off his benders before day games on the training room table. But he wouldn't sit out a game.

His teammates adored him for that and more, especially his willingness to play through excruciating pain without excuses. Mantle could be a crude lout to outsiders, but unlike the icy DiMaggio he was no snob with his teammates, veteran or no. If they winced, as Leonard Shecter wrote, at the site of a naked Berra scratching himself as he surveyed the food on the training table, they delighted in Mantle's company; he always insisted on picking up the tab. He was a joy in the clubhouse— funny, good with a quip, a terrific storyteller, never cruel to the new men. He was polite to their wives and gracious with their children, and his teammates did not think it their place to suggest that perhaps he'd had a few too many beers before he'd even left the clubhouse after a game. He did not mock the teetotalers; when one of them, Bobby Richardson, was seen trying to speak with him about the virtues of cleaner living, Maury Allen of the *Post* noted that Mantle listened and nodded and feigned agreement until Richardson was done and Mantle was free to head to Toots Shor's.

His 1958 holdout had brought a rebuke by Stengel, who had by now decided that Mantle would never be what he wanted him to be—the greatest. Stengel had taught Mantle how to run down line drives by looking over his shoulder, and to throw like an outfielder, not like a shortstop, the position he'd played when he first came up. Stengel had tried to teach him many more things, but Mantle did not pay attention. In truth, Mantle was uninterested in studying the finer points of the game. His play reflected his great physical gifts, no more. He was not inclined toward endless discussions of hitting, like Ted Williams, who tended to talk more than listen because he had studied so long and so hard. Nor did he give himself over to Stengel, as Berra had, so that he might master the intricacies of the game. Berra, too, had been a Stengel discovery, the funny-looking and -sounding catcher no one took seriously until Stengel arrived. "Mr. Berra," Stengel would say, "my assistant manager." Mantle was the disappointment. "Mantle should work out in center field," Stengel carped that January, after an appearance at the baseball writers' dinner. "He's missing balls over his head. Needs some practice on that. He don't seem to know which way to turn. Turns both ways and some of those balls gets over him."

In the end, Mantle got his raise in 1958, and when he reported, Stengel went on to craft a platitude that deftly managed to underscore his enduring frustration and his own importance as a baseball educator. Trying to distance himself from the suggestion that he thought Mantle was wanting defensively, Stengel said, "Mantle ain't a bad center fielder although he's got some things to learn." If his words were intended to remind Mantle of his place—a cog, an important one but a cog nonetheless, in Stengel's machine—he could have just as well saved his breath. Mantle may have needed the Yankees, but he did not need them as dearly as his teammates did, who depended for their livelihoods on remaining in the good graces of Stengel and Weiss. The team was now paying Mantle $75,000—on par with Mays, but less than Williams and Musial. But he more than made up the difference with the endorsement money his celebrity now bought him. Of the many athletes now appearing as television pitchmen, none were more prominent than Mantle.

In 1956, when the Yankees had paid him $30,000, Mantle had made an additional $70,000 from all the appearances arranged by his agent, Frank Scott. Scott had been the Yankees' traveling secretary until 1950, when Weiss decided he was too close to the players and fired him. Scott was looking for work when on a visit to Berra's home in New Jersey, Berra's wife, Carmen, noticed that he wasn't wearing a watch. She excused herself and returned to the bedroom with twenty watches from which he could choose. The watches, she explained, were payments for personal appearances. Berra, who would later become an astute man with money, hadn't thought to ask for cash. Scott had his first client, and the age of the sports agent was born. In time, Scott's list of the suddenly grateful swelled to eighty and included a good many Yankees, as well as Musial, Aaron, Gil Hodges, the football star Frank Gifford, and the retired Joe DiMaggio. But Mantle was Scott's ticket to the big money.

Mantle had been an exceptionally easy mark when he first got to town. He had lost $1,000 buying shares in a nonexistent Oklahoma insurance company and signed away half the rights to his earnings outside of his Yankees checks to a "personal representative" named Allan Savitt, who later sued him, unsuccessfully, for $250,000. Scott, who by now already represented several Yankees, asked to be introduced to Mantle, who wanted to know only how much money Scott could get him. Scott offered no promises and asked only for 10 percent on all deals. Wary of again running afoul of George Weiss, he declined to negotiate Yankees contracts.

Still, there was money to be made, particularly on television and especially with Mantle. Scott had gotten a sense of his client's earning potential in 1953, when the first of his memoirs, *The Mickey Mantle Story*, was published. Mantle was scheduled to appear at a Long Island bookstore, and by the time he arrived, the bookstore had boarded up the windows in the face of the anticipated crush. Police had to escort Mantle through the crowd of a thousand that had gathered to see him. Teenage girls swooned. He was getting twelve hundred fan letters a week. He appeared as a guest on *What's My Line?* and on *The Name's the Same*, in which he pretended that he wanted to be Prince Philip.

Now, four years later, Mantle pitched Batter-Up Pancakes, Karo Syrup—"I've been eating Karo syrup ever since I was knee-high to a baseball bat"—Wheaties, Viceroy cigarettes, Phillies cigars, Ainsbrooke pajamas, Lifebuoy soap, and Bowman bubble gum, a particularly sweet deal arranged by Scott, who assuaged Mantle's embarrassment at being photographed blowing a bubble in center field with a $1,500 fee to reuse the picture. Mantle peddled T-shirts, cereal, hair tonic, greeting cards, and cheese—and Scott made it known that for $5,000 he would lend his name for a year of exclusive ads for a particular product line. He made $1,000 for dancing on *The Arthur Murray Party*, but only after Scott got the producers to drop their demand that he perform the mambo. He made another $2,000 for appearing with Teresa Brewer on her 1956 recording of "I Love Mickey." Scott's big score that season was the

$15,000 that Kraft Foods had paid to sponsor *The Life of Mickey Mantle* on NBC, a dramatization that elevated the story of his upbringing into legend: named for the catcher Mickey Cochrane by his father, Mutt, a lead miner who tossed him endless tennis balls in the belief that his son's path to greatness lay in switch-hitting.

Mantle could now command $1,000 to appear on *The Perry Como Show*, but given his lack of interest in study, did not feel compelled to read the script. No matter; all he had to do was be Mickey Mantle. "Everything he says he says with a smile," said Como, "and I'd say his smile is fifty percent blush. That makes the audience a pushover." Mickey Mantle Enterprises Inc. was established in 1956—with Mantle as president, Merlyn as vice president, and Scott as secretary. Mantle the naive hayseed was a distant memory. "He likes to fondle those checks he's stacking up to take to the bank," Scott told the sportswriter Shirley Povich. "He never used to ask how much we were getting for a show. Now he likes to make those big scores."

In March 1960, Mantle was in Joplin, Missouri, when the *Times* tracked him down to ask when he might appear in Florida. He confessed to having no timetable, and that he would, in fact, be willing to accept a cut in pay, though not one as deep as Weiss wanted. "I'm waiting to see what happens," he said. "They're the bosses."

And so they were, up to a point.

The Continental League rebellion did not end in Houston and did not stop with Bob Howsam. He had come home to Denver, where he reported to his father-in-law, who had heard enough. Big Ed listened and then sat down and in his flowing hand began to write to Rickey. He was walking away.

"I have attended my last session of the Continental League," Johnson wrote. His upcoming schedule was full, and as much as he believed in the necessity of the new league, he would take no part in bringing it to life. He saluted Rickey as "Mr. Baseball." And then, carefully but unequivocally, he tore into him.

"Your complacency about Congressional action has me worried. I have been convinced for a long time that there cannot be a Continental

League unless the monopoly of player contracts held by the two major leagues is liquidated by federal law. You must accept responsibility for no action in this field."

It no longer mattered that Rickey had been to Washington to meet with Kefauver's aide, Paul Rand Dixon, to discuss the fine points of the antitrust bill. Nor did Big Ed seem to be interested in Rickey's amendment proposals and drafts. Johnson had warned him about dithering too long, and had made clear to Shea that he was displeased at the prospect of investing whatever political capital he still held only to be embarrassed in front of his old friends. "I plead with you and Bill Shea," he wrote, "to tell Senator Kefauver what you want the new bill to contain."

But Rickey was unmoved. The league met three days later, and low on its agenda was a request from Rickey that each franchise holder get in touch with his senator to shore up support on Capitol Hill. He also announced that Shea would return to Washington, just as soon as he could schedule an appointment with Paul Rand Dixon. There were other, more pressing, matters—chief among them was Rickey's call for a vote on his most audacious move yet: acquiring the Western Carolina League.

The league was a back-roads operation, with stops in the North Carolina towns of Gastonia, Shelby, Newton, Salisbury, and Hickory. It would come at little cost—$60,000 for the entire circuit, just $7,500 a club. For the moment, the quality of play did not matter nearly as much as the fact that Rickey had established a template for his league's way of doing business: the Western Carolina League would be bound not to individual clubs but to the Continental League itself. The league, in turn, would pay the salaries of its managers and for its spring training combined, in which players would be pooled and then distributed around the Continental's private minor league.

Rickey got the vote he wanted and an additional $1,247 for an ad in the *Sporting News* heralding his acquisition. And while the meeting ended without the acrimony of Houston, he did suffer a setback that underscored the growing distance between Rickey and the men who had persuaded him to be their leader. The rift was not over players but over Rickey's plan for achieving parity through television. If the Continental League owners balked at his recommendation that they surrender the right to negotiate their own television deals, then he wanted the league to keep and pool 90 percent of the money from all television contracts, national and local.

But the owners thought Rickey was asking too much in the interests of giving each of them an equal shot at fielding a winner.

They would share two-thirds. No more.

CHAPTER SEVEN

SPRING 1960

APRIL: A Path to Redemption

Casey Stengel entered the final year of his contract in a sour state of mind. He had predicted a pennant in 1959 and had suffered the humiliation that can come with overconfidence. "No sir, I'm predicting no pennant this time," he announced in January. "Because the whole league has improved and while we're also better ourselves, we'll have to do a lot better, a lot better if we hope to come back to where we belong."

He had arrived in Florida with a new right fielder in Roger Maris and a holdout in Mickey Mantle, and he was in no mood to spare his players' feelings. Shirley Povich of the *Washington Post* had caught up with him in March and found him in a particularly unforgiving mood. "Now you take where we finished last year, which was third, and maybe that makes me a dumb manager but I got a lot of help from my players in winning the pennant, so there you are, is that right?"

Stengel was not done, not even close. "I got a bank in California but it don't need my personal attention like the bowling alleys some of these fellows have got and some of them selling insurance. Maybe they been trying to make ends meet on Yankee time when they are supposed to be playing the national game for Topping and Webb and Weiss and me. So

Mr. Weiss said maybe he should cut some salaries and that is what he did and my heart ain't bleeding very hard for some of them tycoons and the others that didn't get raises."

He directed his greatest venom, as he always did, at the player who was his biggest disappointment. "Now I wish somebody would tell me what Mantle was doing with his bat, because he wasn't driving in many runs with it last year," he said. "Maybe if Mantle had been taking those better cuts last summer he wouldn't be taking that big cut this year."

For all the disdain directed at Mantle, Stengel conveniently ignored the fact that he had been a holdout himself, in the spring of 1917, after having had a terrific World Series for the Dodgers, only to discover that Charlie Ebbets had decided to cut his salary from $5,000 to $3,300. His squawking moved Ebbets to deepen the cut to $2,900 and then, when Stengel still refused to sign, to $2,700. "In my first at bat I hit a triple and pull a muscle slidin' into the bag," he told Arthur Daley of the *Times*. "I've outfoxed myself by being so slick and so smart."

Still, he did not think it worth his while to offer this as a cautionary tale to Mantle, who might have learned something from its moral: Mantle held out for ten days in 1960, accepted a cut of $7,000, and, when he finally reported, pulled a leg muscle on his first day of conditioning. Despite Mantle's injury, Stengel still insisted that he travel with the team to its game in Tampa.

"Why do you want me to go when you know I can't play?" Mantle asked him.

"I just want you to see the city," Stengel replied. He was so infuriated that he hinted, loudly, that he might have the versatile Tony Kubek play center field.

By the time the Yankees were preparing to head north, they had played twenty-two exhibition games and won only seven. Even the new man, Maris, had done little to impress. Mantle followed his charley horse by having fluid drained from his surgically repaired right knee. Stengel did not bother waiting for the regular season before locking the clubhouse door and ripping his players. They emerged looking baffled.

For fifty years, Stengel had performed almost every baseball task imaginable, save for one: failing to meet expectations. Little had been expected of him as a player and in his early years as a manager, and so when he failed in Brooklyn and Boston he did not disappoint. Even when his Yankees lost—as they had to the Indians in 1954, to the Dodgers in 1955, and to the Braves in 1957—they had still performed well, and whatever doubts existed about his wisdom were muted. But now defeat and his age—he would turn seventy in July—seemed more and more a burden, and his employers were beginning to question his approach. He seemed incapable of finding an escape or even a diversion through humor. He had not been a loser for a very long time, and the sensation seemed to drain him. The writers noticed that he was drinking more, and they would sometimes spot him in the dugout, dozing off.

Stengel was no longer managing merely for victory's sake but to save his job. Signs of management's displeasure abounded: his instructional school had been canceled the year before; Jim Turner, his friend and pitching coach, had been fired. And an heir apparent, Ralph Houk, had been anointed. Houk, a career backup catcher, had performed well as a minor-league manager. He was also a decorated Army Ranger, a distinction that earned him a nickname, "The Major." This brought him the admiration of another veteran, Dan Topping, who—much to Stengel's chagrin—was taking a greater interest in the running of his team.

Unlike Webb, whose overriding interest was the next business contact, Topping was not a man who had ever felt the tug of commerce. He had grown up rich and privileged in the exclusive town of Greenwich, Connecticut, the grandson of two grandees—John Topping, the president of Republic Steel, and Daniel Reid, the financier known as "the tin plate king." He had graduated from the Hun School in Princeton, New Jersey, and attended the University of Pennsylvania for a year, where he played football. But golf was his game, and he played it very well; he was a standout on the local amateur circuit and once finished in the quarterfinals of the British Amateur Championships. He dabbled in advertising after his brief stint in college, but he fancied the life of the sportsman. "Being in sports is the only business you can work at and enjoy yourself while working," he once said. In 1934, when he was twenty-two, he had bought a share of the Brooklyn franchise in the National Football League. He later owned the New York franchise in the short-lived All-America Football Conference, where he got to know Branch Rickey, who had a stake in the Brooklyn team.

As a young man, Topping was a handsome fellow whose name appeared in the society pages among the long list of escorts invited to debutante balls. He was twenty when he married his first wife, a socialite named Theodora Bottinger. She divorced him in Reno three years later on the grounds of cruelty. He then married a starlet, Arline Judge, and again divorced after three years. This freed him to marry Sonja Henie, the Olympic skater turned actress. They divorced six years later, after which he married yet another actress, Kay Sutton Weaver, whom he met while stationed in Hawaii during the war. He had entered the Marine Corps as a private and was discharged a major, and he was still in uniform when he bought a share of the Yankees in 1945. Topping divorced Weaver and married twice more, in 1952 and in 1957. He served on several boards and appeared at the stadium and at league meetings but otherwise had time on his hands. And so he increasingly turned his attention to his team and with growing dissatisfaction to his manager, who sensed his boss's displeasure. "As far back as the end of the 1958 season," Stengel later wrote, "the Yankees president, Dan Topping, would have liked to get rid of a lot of people including the manager."

As the team prepared for the long train ride north from Florida, Stengel contemplated the prospects and pitfalls of what he hoped would be his season of redemption: "A man can't look out of a train window all day without thinking of something useful. And maybe I'll come up with something."

The team opened the season in Boston, saddled with questions: Would Mantle's knees hold up? Would Skowron's back give out? Could Turley regain his twenty-win form of 1958, or was Stengel right in concluding that he had fallen into the fateful trap of thinking too much on the mound? Would Ford's arm hold up for a full season? Could Hector Lopez, so gifted with the bat, come close to competence in left field? Could Maris be what Hank Bauer had been, a mainstay in right? And were the young pitchers, Jim Coates and Ralph Terry, ready? Where would Kubek play on any given day? Was there still a place on the team for Gil McDougald, or was he bound to the Washington Senators, as Stengel had suggested, in exchange for pitching?

The Yankees took two out of three in Fenway Park to begin the 1960 season and returned to New York for their home opener, where they were welcomed by the largest Opening Day crowd they'd seen since 1952—thirty-five thousand people who, it was noted, did not include the mayor or Robert Moses. The joke in the press box was that Moses would have attended had he been able to find parking.

They had a decent home stand, winning three, losing two, before heading to Baltimore to face Paul Richards's Orioles, who few believed would cause them much trouble. But Baltimore took two out of three and the Yankees returned home to face Detroit in second place, two games over .500. If Stengel did not already suffer from agita, the season that was beginning to unfold would test his aging gut as never before.

New York had once enjoyed three Opening Days each April. But since the departure of the Dodgers and the Giants, the city had been reduced to only the festivities in the Bronx. Still, there was an attempt at approximating the event, an experience akin to being almost in love. Those New Yorkers still possessed by the need to make the Giants feel like a home team had only to turn their radios to WINS, where Les Keiter delivered the play-by-play. Sort of.

Keiter had not joined the team in San Francisco. Instead, he had remained in New York, and that is where his broadcasts originated. Unable to witness the action on the field, Keiter did what generations of radiomen had done: he faked it. Armed with teletype updates, a block of wood he struck to suggest the sound of a bat meeting a ball, and recordings of "excited crowd" and "regular crowd," Keiter re-created what had been lost. The loss was all the more painful this spring: the Giants were opening not in Seals Stadium, their cramped temporary ballpark, but in their new windswept stadium by the bay. There was to have been a section of turf from the Polo Grounds planted into the field at Candlestick Park, but the groundskeeper tossed it, insisting that it was riddled with weeds.

Yet in April 1960 there was reason to believe that Les Keiter's services might not be needed much longer. Branch Rickey and Bill Shea were prepared to give the city a hint not of an Opening Day as it might have been, but one that they believed was soon to come. They appeared at city hall and, with the mayor beside them, presented tactile evidence that their new league was coming to town. The proof was not only the mayor's long-desired statement of willingness to build the Flushing Meadows stadium for the Continental League, but also a scale model of the park itself.

It was a lovely thing to behold—round, symmetrical, topped by a ring of lights, and encased in a shell that made it look almost airy. It was surrounded, of course, by a vast, empty expanse where all the cars were meant to go.

Someone asked Rickey if he was excited.

"Excited?" he boomed. "Of course, I'm excited. Who wouldn't be after the mayor's solid backing of our plans?"

The assurance that he and the Continental League owners considered a condition of carrying on had come, albeit belatedly. Better still, Mayor Wagner now stood with Rickey and Shea and performed the ritual of being photographed pointing to the model. Murray Kempton, the *New York Post* columnist, noticed that Rickey paused as he looked at the toy cars in the lot. There were only twenty and Rickey suggested that perhaps more be added before the board of estimate voted to continue funding.

One of the television men asked Rickey if he thought there really would be a new league. "I see the assurance before me," he replied.

Soon it was time to go, time to head home and catch Les Keiter's broadcast. "Opening Day in New York," Kempton concluded, "is a thing of phantoms."

The board of estimate's vote to back the project would come two weeks later and might have been unanimous had it not been for opposition from, not surprisingly, the Bronx borough president. The Yankees had floated an offer to share Yankee Stadium with any National League club that wanted to come to town, but it was clear that the new ballpark was coming to Flushing Meadows, and there was nothing they could do to stop it.

Nor, for the moment, could Frick and the owners prevent the Continentals from breaking their control over virtually all of the nation's professional ballplayers—not that Frick hadn't questioned the legality of the Continental League's deal to buy the Western Carolina League, which offered a talent pool that, though modest, gave the Continentals their own exclusive source of players. And Rickey was not stopping there. He wanted every franchise to have a high-level minor-league affiliate of its own. Atlanta would buy the local Southern Association team and Houston would finally conclude its negotiations with Marty Marion to buy the Buffs. Dallas would acquire the local Double-A American Association team. New York would take Montreal, if they could settle on a price for the club with the holder of the city's territorial rights, Walter O'Malley.

The Continentals had gathered in New York for their monthly meeting, and Bob Howsam listened, warily, as Rickey plotted a strategy for taking the new league in a direction in which Howsam did not wish to go. Rickey may have been comfortable—and perhaps even enthralled—with the prospect of establishing an independent league, just as Ban Johnson had done six decades earlier. But Howsam, already committed to one renegade league with Lamar Hunt, had no intention of joining Rickey in another.

Denver, he told the others, would not be an outlaw.

There is nothing in the minutes to suggest that this act of defiance prompted Rickey to walk out, as he had in Houston, or that others joined with or against Howsam. Instead, Rickey called for a vote on a starting date. The Continentals, Howsam included, were unanimous: they would begin play in April 1961.

There was, for the moment, a far more pressing matter: Kefauver's committee was soon to begin hearings on a bill that contained two key provisions: the first would make it illegal to block the formation of a new baseball league; the second would limit each big-league team to one hundred men under contract, sixty of whom would be subject to a draft. Only forty players would be protected, the very number that Big Ed Johnson had pushed for a year earlier and which Paul Richards had recommended in *Look* magazine as the way to save the American League.

The time had come to return to Washington and convince Congress to wrest the players with whom the big leagues refused to part. And no more dissenting opinions would be tolerated. The league would present a united front, at last.

MAY: Showdown

Bob Howsam may have been prepared to walk if the Kefauver bill failed. But Bill Shea, who had been at this longer than anyone else, was prepared to declare war. But first he had to explain why Rickey had asked the Senate to take the major-league owners at their word the year before. Shea gathered the press at the Hotel Warwick a week before the new round of hearings was to begin to lay out the Continental League's battle plan. Rickey might have done it himself were he not in bed, suffering from a bronchial infection; best not to risk the health of a seventy-eight-year-old man with a bad heart who walked with the assistance of a cane. Shea and Jack Kent Cooke were prepared to detail the price of their innocence when Rickey had undercut Ed Johnson's denunciation of the owners by vouching for their good intentions before the Kefauver committee.

Shea was blunt in discussing the events of July 1959. "At that time, we were led to believe we would have the full support and cooperation of organized baseball in establishing a third major league," he said. "We found it was only lip service. Now, it is clear the only way we will get going is through the passage of the Kefauver bill."

The Continental League, Shea insisted, was no longer divided, not after enduring every dodge and roadblock employed by the owners. "Time is the thing that is hitting us in every direction," he explained. The latest stall was the astronomical indemnification fees demanded by the minor leagues; the International League wanted $850,000 for *each team* whose territory the new league invaded. By contrast, said Cooke, when the St. Louis Browns relocated to Baltimore in 1954, the charge paid to the local minor-league operator was a mere $48,000—5 percent of the current asking price.

Shea was equally blunt about the consequences if the Kefauver bill were to fail. "The Continental League would have to sit down and decide whether to quit or to have war," he said. He then paused for a moment, to sharpen the quote. "Make it, 'it's war or quit.'"

Shea would not shy away from battle. If it came, he said, the Continentals would launch raids against the big-league rosters. That, in turn,

might draw the owners into court, where they would try to invoke the
reserve clause as the guarantor of every player's contract. Shea questioned whether the owners had the guts to challenge them. "I don't
believe they'd dare sue us if we raided them," he said. "They know they
wouldn't have a leg to stand on.

"I'm so sure of that I'd handle the case for nothing," Shea added.
"Those contracts aren't worth the paper they're printed on."

Still, he wanted the owners to know that he had not given up on peace.
"I'm hoping it doesn't come to this," he told the reporters. "I'm hoping
the majors will have an about-face and agree to cooperate with us."

Three days later the owners huddled for six hours in Chicago with
Frick, Giles, and Cronin, in what was described as a "super secret meeting." When they emerged they refused to divulge what they'd discussed
other than to insist that all their decisions had been unanimous. The
sense was that they'd done no more than approve the script for Frick's
testimony before Kefauver's committee. The commissioner, however,
had already made his sentiments clear: "This measure is pernicious and
vicious, the most dangerous bill yet introduced in Congress."

Slim chance of an "about-face."

It was well past being news to hear Ford Frick warn of the dreadful
things that would befall the nation's game if Congress were to meddle
with baseball's legal sanction to do whatever it wished. Nor was there
anything particularly startling in hearing the dark accusations against
the owners by Bill Shea and Big Ed Johnson, who though retired from
active duty in the new league was still willing to return to Washington to
lambaste the owners. Some of the particulars were new: Frick insisted
that the Continental League threatened the very foundation of the
minor leagues; Shea delineated a year of the owners' delaying tactics.
But these were variations on familiar themes. The news that emerged
from the hearings came from Rickey, whose infection had run its course
but who might well have testified from a hospital gurney if necessary.

Rickey had returned to Capitol Hill portraying himself as a betrayed
romantic bearing an altogether darker message than he had delivered
the year before. He had vouched for the owners before Congress, and

they had lied to him. He singled out Frick, citing each instance in which the commissioner had sworn his allegiance to Rickey's cause and then broken his oath. "There has been such a unique and timely correlation of words, acts, and events effectively forcing continuous delay that anyone, suspicious of motive, might easily conclude that all opposition resulted from a premeditated concert of plan and procedure," Rickey told the committee. "The events that followed were, and are, harrowing to contemplate even in retrospect."

He had been wrong to have "believed the majors would clean its own house" and that "legislation was not necessary to bring about the expansion of baseball." He had been wrong about Frick's assuming the mantle of "savior" of the minor leagues, because on his watch the number of minor leagues had actually shrunk from forty-seven in 1953 to twenty-one in 1960.

"I contend, and I will pledge that the Continental League, if allowed to enter the sacred domain of baseball, will open 320 new jobs at the top. We would raise the number of major league opportunities by 50 percent," he said. "I ask you, gentlemen, what would happen to any industry in this country—and major-league baseball is a hundred-million-dollar industry—if the industry were enlarged by fifty percent? But will *we* be permitted the privilege of creating these opportunities for 320 additional major league stars? Our belief was that we would be so privileged."

They were not, because the men whom Rickey had counted as friends would not allow it. "It is not unusual in the history of government, or in business practices of humans everywhere, that the use of despotic power has not, sooner or later, been abused," he intoned.

The cost, he had concluded, was potentially catastrophic. He testified that the owners' arrogance and neglect had jeopardized baseball's historic position as America's sport. "Other sports in the United States, professionally a new one, soccer, may soon pass by the popularity of baseball," he said, "and the major league owners will then have only their dialectic consciences for consolation as they repent too late the loss of the prestige of the great national game."

He was wrong only in identifying the sport poised to eclipse his game.

The big-league owners, he went on, had devalued the game by succumbing to the temptation of money, especially from television. Indeed,

Rickey, too, had come to see what Bill Shea had learned early in his travels, a lesson that he had passed along to the Continental League's founders: expansion, to say nothing of a third league, jeopardized all the money the owners stood to make if they could keep the game limited to sixteen cities and charge all those millions of viewers to watch their games on pay television. Rickey saw baseball in all its pristine glory, but the owners—and especially the most clever and forward-looking among them, Walter O'Malley—saw the game as something altogether different: a studio sport. Nor longer would the nation's sixteen big-league ballparks merely be places to attend a game. Instead, they would become the locus of telecasts carried to every home in the country wired for pay-per-view. It was "at this very point," Rickey testified, "that most of the opposition to a third league centers."

Rickey wanted the senators to understand that the game was a noble enterprise that the Senate was in a position to deliver to an eager nation. It was even, perhaps, an answer to what ailed the nation and the world. Indeed, he might as well have been offering words to be chiseled on the walls in Cooperstown, if only space allowed.

"It is a game of great charm in the adaptation of mathematical measurements to the timing of human movement," he said, adding that "no parent worries when the boys depart with glove and ball." He drew on the saying that the Battle of Waterloo was won on the playing fields of Eton, and from the philosopher William James's observation that competitive sport was the "moral equivalent of war," to make the grandiose case for the universal expansion of baseball. "By rapidly expanding internationally, baseball, even in this dark present hour, may conceivably become a universal peacemaker among mankind," he proclaimed. "Why should anyone oppose it?"

Rickey bolstered his case with tables and charts that showed how the citizens of such onetime minor-league towns as Baltimore, Kansas City, and especially Milwaukee had embraced the big leaguers when they arrived. Why deprive the good people of Denver, Dallas, and Houston?

"The commissioner is saying at this very moment to every Congressman, 'if you pass this bill it will kill baseball,'" Rickey said. "Actually, the major league owners need to be saved from themselves."

<<<<<

Del Webb was playing at a charity golf event near Los Angeles several days later when a reporter stopped him to ask about the possibility of a National League team coming to New York to share Yankee Stadium.

"If it proves the best thing for baseball we wouldn't object," Webb replied. "The more I think about it the more I think New York can support two teams. We hold the territorial rights; it's up to us." So much for Frick's declaration of New York as an "open city."

But the more Webb considered the question, the more he doubted the wisdom of standing against a second team for New York. Times had changed, and circumstances had altered tastes. "It's possible New Yorkers are forgetting baseball," he said. "They're bound to lose interest, with only seventy-seven home games now compared to the two hundred thirty-one they used to have with three teams. Last July 4 there was no double header in New York for the first time in decades. Another team might be the best thing for baseball."

Webb, however, had other troubles on his mind. He had not only been denied the Chavez Ravine contract, but since March he had been compelled to conduct his baseball affairs without his most reliable ally: Arnold Johnson. During spring training the Athletics' owner had fallen ill on a drive through West Palm Beach with his wife and children. He had pulled to the curb before being struck by a massive cerebral hemorrhage, which killed him. He was fifty-three years old, and what dreams he may have had—or at least suggested—of one day bequeathing the club to his son now ended. His widow remarried quickly and put the club up for sale. There had been speculation in Los Angeles of the Athletics moving to California. But now the betting was on Kansas City putting together a group of buyers who would keep the team in town. The legacy of Johnson's dubious alliance with the Yankees lingered until late May, when the two teams completed their sixteenth transaction since 1954, bringing to sixty-one the number of players who'd changed sides, some of them twice. The Yankees reclaimed Bob Cerv, an outfielder with power whom they had sold to the Athletics in 1956, in exchange for the seldom-used third baseman Andy Carey. Cerv's return to the Bronx brought to eleven the number of former Kansas City players on the New York roster—Roger Maris, Art Ditmar, Ralph Terry, Hector Lopez, and Ryne Duren among them. Kansas City had eight former Yankees, and none was a star.

Meanwhile, Kefauver's committee was in recess when Wheelock Whitney, a leader of the Minneapolis group, got encouraging news. One of his senators, Hubert Humphrey, had written to apprise him of the bill's prospects.

"I have discussed this legislation with the committee members and I am given to understand that our Majority Leader, Senator Johnson, is in support of the measure as well as Senator Eastland, who is chairman of the full Judiciary Committee," Humphrey wrote. "This would seem to indicate that there is a pretty good chance to passage of the bill—at least here in the Senate."

The old man might yet pull this one off.

JUNE: Reversal of Fortune

Lamar Hunt did not need the NFL to make a gift of its lesser players in order for his new football league to take flight. He had an advantage the Continentals did not enjoy: his newcomers were young men who were familiar, or at the least had attended colleges that made them seem familiar; their names and photographs had appeared in the big-city newspapers. This was not the case for the lowest-level minor leaguers and Caribbean imports whom Rickey was prepared to field if the owners could not be forced to loosen their rosters. Hunt and his people were preparing to go into business with a new crop of amateur football players who were free to sign with whomever they liked. In the spring of 1960, none was more avidly sought than Louisiana State's All-American halfback, Billy Cannon.

The Los Angeles Rams had won the rights to Cannon in the NFL's draft in November 1959, and the team was so eager to have him under contract that the team's general manager, Pete Rozelle, had signed him within forty-eight hours of their first phone conversation. Cannon received a $10,000 bonus and $500 to cover expenses, but he did not cash the checks, fearful that doing so might jeopardize his eligibility to play in the Sugar Bowl. On New Year's Day, Ole Miss shut out the Tigers, and Cannon's lustrous college football career ended with him under contract with not one professional team, but two. Just before Christmas, Bud Adams, who owned the AFL's Houston franchise, had also signed Cannon—for $110,000. Cannon wanted to play for Adams, but the NFL took him to court. Leading the fight for the NFL was its new commissioner, the very same Pete Rozelle, who had recently been elected to succeed Bert Bell.

The NFL had tried mightily to stop Lamar Hunt's new league. George Halas had tempted Hunt and Adams with franchises only to have them reject his invitation because it would have meant abandoning Bob Howsam. In January, the NFL had peeled off one of Hunt's founding franchises in Minnesota, only to watch as Hunt, with a surfeit of applicants, was left to choose a replacement between Atlanta and Oakland; even Halas's town, Chicago, wanted in. The NFL had placed a new team in Dallas—*take that, Lamar*—only to discover that the Justice Department was taking depositions to determine whether to heed the AFL's call to investigate possible NFL violations of the antitrust laws.

The upstarts had the stadiums in their cities and had conducted their own college draft, signing four hundred players. And they had a television contract, too—$10.6 million for five years with ABC. The money would be split evenly—each team would get $225,000 a season, in keeping with the AFL's formula for competitive balance. Hunt would later say that he had not come upon the idea on his own. He first heard of it when he was permitted to sit in on a meeting of the Continental League and listen as Branch Rickey explained his vision for achieving parity.

The AFL also found a sponsor in Gillette, which had decided to drop its support of NBC's Friday Night Fights for a football and baseball deal with ABC. The contract had the potential of being a boon to the network and the league. ABC was then such a distant third to CBS and NBC that it did not have its own sports division. Instead, it subcontracted its broadcasts to Sports Program Inc., whose founder, Edgar Scherick, had been a pioneer sports broadcaster at CBS. Scherick, in turn, had hired a young producer named Roone Arledge to oversee ABC's growing college football programming and its AFL coverage. Arledge, who like Hunt was not yet thirty years old, surrounded himself with like-minded young men who did not subscribe to the traditional belief that the best way to televise a football game was simply to point a camera at the field. Arledge would now have his chance to try his hand televising the professionals, among them Billy Cannon.

A week after the AFL announced its TV deal, a federal judge in Los Angeles ruled that Cannon's contract with the Rams was invalid. He was free to play for Houston. The judge was especially critical of Rozelle, ruling that he had taken advantage of Cannon's innocence and naivete, calling the player "a provincial lad untutored and unwise in the ways of the business world." But Cannon was shrewd enough to know not to cash Rozelle's checks. The AFL had its first star. But Hunt kept the pressure on. The same week as the Cannon ruling, the AFL filed a ten-million-dollar lawsuit against the NFL, charging it with conspiring to monopolize professional football. The AFL accused the NFL of threatening to blacklist coaches and players who jumped, trying to stall stadium deals, and announcing plans to expand into cities with AFL teams. The suit alleged that this was part of a larger pattern dating to 1949, when the NFL succeeded in putting the fledgling All-America Football Conference out of business. But that league's demise was hastened because, unlike Hunt's people, its owners proved susceptible to temptation: the NFL ended the upstarts' threat by simply absorbing three franchises—the Cleveland Browns, the Baltimore Colts, and the San Francisco 49ers.

"There is no question in my mind that the National Football League's actions will be sustained," said Rozelle, "and the AFL charges will be proved baseless."

The case was not expected to be heard for a year. Meanwhile, the AFL announced that it would begin play on September 11, 1960, with two Sunday broadcasts—one for the West Coast, and one for the East. The Buffalo Bills would open the season against the New York Titans; on Thanksgiving Day, Lamar Hunt's Dallas Texans would play the Titans in New York before a national television audience.

<<<<<

Kenneth Keating had taken pains to assure Rickey and Shea that they had no better friend on Capitol Hill. He had offended Ford Frick on their behalf, offering to serve as an intermediary between the Continentals and the big leagues. Keating had also landed an appointment on the Judiciary Committee and had offered to cosponsor Kefauver's bill, if the Continentals would show him copies of their proposals in advance. He was available when needed, if only to listen and advise. "I would very much like to receive from you a 'progress report' as to how things stand now and what the prospects of the future are," he wrote to Rickey in March.

But the sense among the Continentals was that Keating's expressions of friendship were false and his requests for documents a ruse to leak the information to the owners. Still, Keating was in a difficult position: as a senator he could no longer be obvious in his loyalty to the owners. If he was going to do their bidding, as he had done when he was still in the House, he would have to do it subtly, so that the voters of New York could never accuse him of undermining the state's attempt to add a big-league team and maybe two.

Kefauver had been absent from the initial debate over his bill; he was back in Tennessee, campaigning for reelection. Presiding in his place was Philip Hart of Michigan, a quiet man whose commitment to civil rights legislation would one day earn him the honorary title of "the conscience of the Senate." Hart, however, had married into a big-league connection: his wife was the daughter of the former owner of the Detroit Tigers, Walter Briggs Sr., whose son and successor, Spike, had been Hart's college roommate. Hart, in fact, had worked for the team when his wife's family still owned it. The panel was now prepared to send the bill to the full Judiciary Committee, but only after some tinkering by Hart: rather than imposing a one-hundred-player limit and leaving sixty eligible for a draft, the amended bill would limit the draft only to those minor leaguers with four years of service.

Time was vanishing quickly for the Continentals if they were to begin play in 1961 as a third major league. Rickey, with little room to maneuver and in need of recognition and whatever players he could squeeze from the majors, announced that the change was acceptable. It was, he said, "calculated to cut the legs from under any opposition the majors still have to the bill." The majors, who had every reason to be pleased—they could protect their farm systems and discard only those men who in four years hadn't made it to the big club—were anything but happy and had embarked on a letter-writing campaign to senators on the committee. Even so, the amended bill landed in the Judiciary Committee, and within days the committee's ranking Republican, Everett Dirksen, moved to send it on to the full Senate for a vote, with every reason for the Continentals to be confident of Hubert Humphrey's prediction of passage.

It was at this point that Kenneth Keating raised his hand and showed his true colors. The matter, he told his colleagues, was too important for a hasty vote. He asked for a week of further study, a privilege his colleagues could not deny him.

"The week's delay has hurt us terribly," said Rickey. Congress was moving to adjournment and if the bill wasn't passed before then, the Continentals faced the prospect of a year's delay in starting play or opening in 1961 as outlaws. "Another week's delay," Rickey added, "would be ruinous."

Rickey nonetheless believed the chances of prevailing were strong. "Opposition of organized baseball understandably will go all out this week to defeat bill in Committee," he wrote in a telegram to the Continental League's owners. "If we can hold our present strength, bill will be sent to Senate for final consideration. Don't overlook a single bet to strengthen support of every Senator you can properly approach in the next few days using your best combination of courage and discretion."

He might also have advised caution, in deed and word, a quality that now deserted him at the most inopportune time. As he spoke to the press about his willingness to accept the diluted measure, Rickey was asked what might happen if the vote was delayed much longer. "Should that come to pass we would not operate under the same restrictions that the major leagues have placed upon themselves," he replied. "We would be free to sign American Legion and high school athletes."

This was just the opening that Frick and the owners had been waiting for. Rickey, in the least charitable but politically expedient reading of his words, was talking about signing *mere boys*, amateurs. The commissioner fired off a telegram to the Judiciary Committee. It was bad enough, he wrote, that the bill would deny the big leagues the chance to benefit from the growth of its minor leaguers, whom the Continentals would be able to draft. But now Rickey was talking of violating rules that were meant to "protect the amateur status of young players under organized baseball's program of cooperation with high school and American Legion ball built over the last 40 years." The big leagues, of course, had a long tradition of signing high school students as soon as they had graduated. Rickey, in Frick's view, was suggesting taking them when they were still, in a sporting sense, being swaddled.

Rickey was compelled to respond, a waste of time and momentum in a cause that had appeared to be going his way. "The last-minute wire, calculated to frighten United States Senators, and terrorize the American Legion and High School baseball groups into registering a stream of protests, charged that the Continental League planned indiscriminate signings of teen-age baseball players, regardless of education or amateur affiliation," he wrote. "The charge is not only a deliberate falsehood but a new 'low' for the administrative office of our so-called national pastime in order to block progressive legislation."

His opponents tried to press their momentary advantage. Once again, the minor leagues took up the cause of their major-league patrons, wiring the senators to alert them to the catastrophe that awaited them if the measure passed. But the Continentals battled back. Shea himself went after Keating, and he did not feign politeness.

"No one in public life has expressed himself more in favor of our objectives than you," he telegrammed his senator. "And no one of your stature has done less than you have to help us when and where it counted most. When the opportunity came for you to give our Empire State—yours and mine—two more major league teams by voting the all-sports bill to the senate floor, you alone stood in its path." The stall Keating had engineered, Shea went on, "gave Commissioner Ford Frick opportunity to launch an avalanche of phony telegrams." And as for the week of "further study" he had wanted, Shea asked, "Why, Senator, did you fail to appear with a report of your study when your committee reconvened?"

Why? Because Keating's presence, politically speaking, was unnecessary. This time, it was his colleague, Nebraska's Roman Hruska, who insisted that the committee cease its debate while the full Senate was in session. Senatorial courtesy mandated that his request be granted.

Rickey's "ruinous" second week of delay had begun.

CHAPTER EIGHT

SUMMER 1960

JULY: Last Chances

The Yankees stumbled through the spring, winning barely more often than they lost as they slipped from fourth to third and back again. The league champion White Sox were in first, trailed by Cleveland and Paul Richards's surprising Orioles: three teams to jump if the Yankees were to make a run for the pennant.

Stengel jiggered his lineup, though not with the frequency and audacity that he had displayed in the past. He settled on sending Maris to right field every day, and Hector Lopez, for the most part, to left. Mantle remained in center, where he was greeted with a daily cascade of boos. He was not hitting, for average or for power; he hit only four home runs in the season's first six weeks. Stengel, in a rebuke to Mantle's customary status as a run producer, moved him up to second in the batting order, having calculated that he could at least help the team by drawing walks and letting the other fellows drive him in. Mantle batting second—a singles hitter's spot for the brawniest fellow in the lineup.

Mantle broke a zero-for-twenty skid on the Saturday of Memorial Day weekend by homering as the Yankees beat Washington at the stadium. But Stengel missed it. He had taken ill and was confined to his apartment at the Essex House. Ralph Houk took his place. The team won on Sunday, too, with Houk again filling in for Stengel, who had now been diagnosed with a viral infection. In the days that followed, Stengel remained indoors while Houk adhered to his wishes and kept Mantle in the second spot, though occasionally letting him hit third. But the boon to Mantle's self-esteem brought little extended benefit; the team listed. Stengel, meanwhile, took a turn for the worse and when the infection did not abate he was admitted to Lenox Hill Hospital. According to the actuarial tables, he had now surpassed the average life span of the American male, and his doctors were taking no chances.

Stengel wasn't missing much save for the drama surrounding his slumping star. At the close of the Memorial Day doubleheader, Mantle hauled in a fly ball for the final out and was heading to the dugout when he found himself surrounded by young people who had vaulted the fence and wanted a piece of him. They took his cap and were grabbing at his uniform. Mantle ran, but the crowd kept up. He lowered his head and put out an arm to force his way to the sanctuary of the dugout when he was hit on the side of the face. He made it to the clubhouse with a jaw so sore that icepacks did not ease the pain. X-rays were negative, and the blow was diagnosed as a sprain. But the Yankees' switchboard began lighting up with calls from angry parents who insisted that Mantle had been rough with their kids. Mantle apologized if he had caused any pain—"I wouldn't think of taking a swing at a kid," he said, adding that he had, in fact, been "scared." The Yankees, too, issued an apology for any bruised feelings or limbs, although the team did hasten to characterize the mob as "completely uncontrollable."

The recurring verb in the press accounts was of Mantle's being "mauled," an image of a besieged star that moved Bob Addie of the *Washington Post* to offer his sympathies for the burden of simply being Mickey Mantle. Addie recalled a moment two years earlier when he met Mantle at a fund-raising event for treating Hodgkin's disease, the illness that had killed Mantle's father and uncles: "We got off in a corner and the super-star became only a confused and unhappy young man. 'Where does it all lead to?' he asked. 'Where am I going? Where do I end? I'm on a merry-go-round that never stops. I wish I could get off.'" But Mantle was back in the lineup for the Yankees' next game in Baltimore, the first of three straight losses to the Orioles.

Stengel finally emerged from the hospital and flexed his biceps for the photographers. He had been out for almost two weeks, and his doctors advised against managing immediately. Still, he thought he might head out to the stadium "just to look around and say hello. Edna won't let me hang around too long." He spent an extra day recuperating at home before finally returning to the dugout on June 7, 1960. He arrived four hours early for his first game back.

"I'm feelin' better but I gotta take some pills," he said. The team was back in fourth place, four and a half games behind Baltimore, which had slipped into first. The White Sox, who had fallen to third, were in town and Stengel did not need an update before settling on a lineup; he'd been keeping up. "I don't have to talk to nobody, because I still see pretty good," he said. "Because I saw more things on television than I ever saw before in my life. The seventh, eighth and ninth innings has been a series of numerous things and it looks like the tournament is over but it ain't."

He wanted Elston Howard behind the plate. Berra would sit. "They tell me Mr. Berra is hittin' everythin' and maybe he has a bad arm which you don't know about until I tell you now," Stengel said, cryptically.

The Yankees took the first game against Chicago. They won the next day and the next and did not lose until they'd won seven in a row. They lost one in Kansas City and then took the next six. They arrived in Detroit on June 20 not only a first-place team, but a swaggering one, having just swept the White Sox at Comiskey Park, celebrating Father's Day with a 12–5 pounding that featured Maris's nineteenth home run and Mantle's fourteenth, his eighth in the last twenty games. The sweep left the White Sox mired in fifth place, a bit of revenge for 1959 that delighted Berra. "They're dead," he said.

As the Yankees arrived in Washington for the July 4 holiday weekend, they had won twenty-three of twenty-nine games, but Stengel was anything but gracious in victory. "Now you see that makes me a genius all over again," he told Shirley Povich. "Last month I was pretty dumb and stupid when my good ballplayers weren't hitting. I don't know how

I got so smart overnight. I musta learned a lot of baseball in that hospital from those nurses. Maybe we ought to sign the nurses instead of bonus boys.

"Between them nurses, who taught me all that baseball, and Roger Maris and Mantle and Skowron, who been getting all them hits for me, I was never such a smart manager. I don't know how I ever win them nine pennants. Maybe I was just lucky."

The Yankees lost to the Senators on July 4 and lost again the next day. They now led second-place Cleveland by only a game, and the third-place Orioles by two—not nearly enough of a margin for comfort for an aging and recently ailing manager whose contract would expire in October.

Of all the mail that landed at the Fifth Avenue offices of the Continental League in the first week of July, none brought Branch Rickey more encouraging news than the letter from Paul Rand Dixon. Dixon was Senator Kefauver's top aide, a position in which he'd had an extended tutelage on the new league and on the ways the majors had worked to kill it. Dixon was a friend of the Continentals, and though he did not have a vote in determining the new league's fate, his views mattered, for what he told his boss and for the advice he was now offering Branch Rickey in the wake of what had taken place in the Senate.

Thanks to Senator Keating, the Kefauver bill had endured two weeks of delay before arriving on the Senate floor. It had not landed well. The Judiciary Committee had sent it along for a vote without a recommendation, an ominous sign; each committee member instead offered his own view. Keating had kind words to say about the measure he had worked so deftly to defeat, calling it a "shot in the arm" for the new league. He then advised his colleagues to "proceed with caution" on what he regarded as a flawed piece of legislation.

The committee had debated and rejected additional amendments by Philip Hart and by Alexander Wiley of Wisconsin, the home of the Braves. But because the panel could not come up with wording that pleased a voting majority, it had elected to let the full Senate hash things out. This was a boon to the bill's opponents, who had merely to tweak the measure enough to make it sufficiently palatable to be approved while still making sure that it offered no assistance to the upstarts. That job fell to Wiley.

His tactic, legislatively speaking, was a thing of simple beauty. He proposed that rather than consider baseball separately from football, basketball, and hockey, the Senate should bundle all four sports together in granting them limited exemption from federal antitrust laws. The limitations would, much to the owners' delight, extend to such matters as television, franchise rights, and the control of players. It was a seemingly equitable resolution, given the historic advantage that baseball enjoyed over its less-shielded competitors, but one that in reality placed all the established team owners at a decided advantage: the bill would give them control over who played their games, how those games were watched, and who could field a team. Wiley went on to say that if his colleagues approved his proposal, his next step would be to introduce another amendment, this one eliminating the player draft that Big Ed Johnson had pushed Rickey to accept as the key to wresting some of the several thousand players whose contracts the big-league owners now controlled.

The vote on Wiley's first proposal was a narrow one, and it did not help that the bill's author, Estes Kefauver, was still in Tennessee, campaigning. The final tally was a victory for Wiley and by extension the owners: 45–41 in favor of lumping together all four sports. The vote did not divide the senators along traditional party lines; rather, the amendment's foes came almost exclusively from states without big-league teams, Democrats and Republicans alike. The vote opened the way for Wiley's second amendment. Knowing that its passage would doom the new league by removing the one lever for extracting players, the Continentals' allies hastily introduced their own legislative gambit, calling on the Senate to send the bill back to the Judiciary Committee for further review. Their proposal passed overwhelmingly; the bill was alive, but just barely.

The Continentals, however, were all but out of time if they wanted to begin play in 1961. Given the looming Senate recess and the committee's timetable, the measure was unlikely to be raised again in the current session. If it were not, it would have to await the arrival of a new Congress in 1961, where the rules required that it would have to be introduced all over again. Opening Day 1961 was all but dead if the Continentals held to their desire to debut as a member of the big leagues.

Then again, they could do as they pleased if, like Lamar Hunt's AFL—and Ban Johnson's American League—they simply set out on their own.

Which was precisely what Paul Rand Dixon was now suggesting in his long letter to Rickey, which he had sent a few days after the bill's near-death experience in the Senate.

"I think the Continental League is now in the best position possible for publicly announcing that it intends to start operations whether it is accepted by baseball or not," he wrote. His views, he cautioned Rickey, were his own. He then went on to explain that the Continentals had acted in "good faith." They had sought the big-league owners' assistance, and only after being spurned had they "turned to Congress and having been turned down there."

But by going it alone, Dixon argued, the Continentals would owe the minors nothing—not the millions of dollars being demanded—for invading their turf. Instead, he insisted, the new league could spend that money luring away big leaguers whose contracts no court would honor because of the legally suspect reserve clause. Dixon recommended that the Continentals draw up contracts without a reserve clause, for multiple years if they chose. The law, he assured Rickey, would be on their side: "This would mean players who jumped into your league could not be enjoined from playing."

Dixon had come to believe that "much more is at stake than the mere acceptance of the Continental League into organized baseball. What is at stake is a pot of gold at the end of the rainbow." He, too, had seen the darker purpose of the owners' opposition that Bill Shea had discovered two years earlier. The opposition to expansion—in any form, new teams or new league—was not about diluting the quality of play or the fate of the minor leagues or the majors' unwillingness to share their castoffs. "One does not have to have much vision to foresee that in the not too distant future pay-T.V. will be a reality."

It would happen, he continued, in one of two ways: with telecasts beamed through existing telephone lines and extending no further than a state's boundaries—"think of the market that could be tapped within the confines of the State of New York," he noted—or, far more lucratively, by beaming those signals to much wider areas, across state lines. "I believe that the big league owners visualize the development of pay-T.V. on an interstate basis," Dixon wrote. "If they are successful in getting approval by the federal Congress for such programming, they need not ever expand big league baseball beyond where it is today. They have sixteen ballparks now from which baseball games could be televised into every home in America." Sixteen television studios.

"Regardless of which plan might be followed, the owners of big league baseball franchises are going to reap a bonanza," he went on. "For this reason, if I were a member of the Continental League, I would start in business immediately. Every day of delay is going to make it harder."

For the moment, however, pay television remained a distant dream. No big-league city was wired, not even Los Angeles or San Francisco, which Matty Fox had boasted of connecting to his Skiatron network three years earlier when he had testified before Emanuel Celler's committee. Skiatron, in fact, had run afoul of the U.S. Securities and Exchange Commission, which in January ruled that it had violated SEC rules and ordered it to stop selling stock. Horace Stoneham, for one, had begun losing faith and patience in the promise of pay television. Unlike Walter O'Malley, who allowed broadcasts of the eleven Dodgers games in San Francisco, Stoneham had refused to permit any free broadcasts of Giants games since arriving in San Francisco. But in March he agreed to allow ABC to carry thirteen of his team's games on its fledgling Game of the Week broadcasts for a reported $400,000—far less money than Matty Fox had once talked about. O'Malley, however, did not join with Stoneham and ABC. Instead, he held firm to his belief that one day people would pay to watch his team on television—a belief shared by Paul Rand Dixon.

Rickey had been vague about his plans in the immediate wake of the Senate vote. "I don't want to start outside the canopy of organized baseball," he said. "If forced to, I just don't know."

But now he knew.

The Continental League was to meet in New York on July 20, which gave Rickey two days to prepare the brief for independence he would present to the league owners. Time and events, however, were now working against him as he set down his thoughts:

"As I dictate this on Monday, July 18, the National League is meeting in Chicago to discuss expansion. It is my information that the National League will come out of that meeting with the appointment of a committee to cooperate with the American League in investigating and recommending a joint course of action leading to a solution of the expansion problem, and the N.L. will probably discuss itself as hopeful that such expansion can be brought about for the season of 1961."

This, he continued, will be a con. "The N.L. will not extend to expand internally and they will not expand internally in 1961 or any other time." Instead, they will do what the American League had done in the fall of 1959 and offer the lure of expansion as a way to undermine the Continental League. It was, he conceded, already working.

"Several of our clubs have now been notified that this expansion is likely to occur and have been encouraged to believe that they all— each, in turn, will be able to secure an added franchise in either the American or National League," Rickey wrote. There was talk—"it could even be called assurance to several of our cities"—that the Athletics would relocate, perhaps to Minneapolis or Dallas or Houston. He had learned that a group of businessmen from Dallas had visited Kansas City and that Marty Marion was eager to bring the Athletics to Houston. Rickey admitted that the move "might actually happen" and that it would be the quickest way for one of their group to join the big leagues; "that severance with the Continental League would be understandable." And tolerable, he went on, so long as New York remained in the league.

But Rickey saw perils in the big leagues' siren song, dangers far more troubling than all the familiar arguments about the competitive and financial risks adding a team or two posed for the game: "It is likely that at the end of the first year the plan would be abandoned and there would be an immediate return to eight clubs."

The owners will deceive you, he was telling his people. Just as they deceived me.

"They are now playing their strongest hand," he wrote of the prospect of being among the cities chosen for the possible expansion. "To what extent this propaganda is having effect I really do not know. But to whatever extent is has effect serves the full purpose of delaying the operation of our League."

But the Continentals, he insisted, still had a hand of their own to play: they could simply begin play. That is, if everyone was willing to follow his lead, just as the American Leaguers had followed Ban Johnson, sixty years before. Rickey, however, had reason to believe they would not. The big leagues, he wrote, "have been told, so they state, most reliably that at least two clubs in the Continental League will under no circumstances, be a party to any league that undertakes to organize independent of organized baseball." He knew that Bob Howsam was opposed to going outlaw. But who was the other?

He went on: "And now, a member of the National League speaks very confidently in saying that at least three clubs in the Continental League will never consent to operate without the full permission of Mr. Frick." So be it, so long, he added, as "the New York club were not to be included as one of those who would not go independently."

New York, as always, was the key, for the Continentals and for the majors. It was the "trump card," he concluded, and this would be how the owners would play it: "If the Continental League continues to be a threat in the field of existence, organized baseball will undertake to come into New York to Flushing Meadows. It is fully expected that Cincinnati or Philadelphia, or heaven knows what franchise, will be offered to New York—falsely, indeed, but with the sound of reality."

He now knew there would be no help from Congress. Even if the amended Kefauver bill somehow passed, it had been too diluted to be of use. There was only one path, and he was not alone in advocating it: "It is obvious to both Celler and Dixon, and it is obvious to me, that the Continental League will never come into existence with the consent of organized baseball."

Independence was the only path for the league—as long as its members remained resolute and united.

It was past six o'clock when a telegram arrived at the league office. It was addressed to Rickey and had come from Chicago.

"National League voted unanimously to implement expansion via

Continental League or increased membership. Invite you to meet National League Committee at your convenience. Please advise time and place."

It was signed by the committee members: Lou Perini, John Galbreath, Philadelphia's Bob Carpenter, and the chairman, Walter O'Malley.

The National League did not keep the news to itself. Warren Giles was assigned to send a message to the press, advising them of his league's initiative, so that the still restive members of Congress might know and perhaps not act against them. Bill Shea offered the Continentals' response and said what Rickey wanted to hear. "The Continental League is still the only way New York is going to get a second major league club," he said. The Continentals, he added, would accept the invitation to meet. "They still have all the marbles and they still control the game but remember this, we have the only people interested in bringing major league baseball to New York."

The owners, however, had Shea at a strategic disadvantage: he had begun his campaign in 1957 with a simple mandate—to get a new team for his town—and had never forgotten what Mayor Wagner had dispatched him to do. He said as much in his angry letter to Keating—"My sole interest in baseball is in obtaining a second major league team for my city." And though Shea had thrown in with Rickey and had stood by him in defending the Continental League and his vision, he was no longer the only one representing the interests of New York. There were the money people, like Joan Whitney Payson, and the people behind the money people, like M. Donald Grant. Grant had risen from his position as a night clerk at the Commodore Hotel to becoming Payson's broker and, more important, her escort. The two had been on the board of the New York Giants, and Grant had held out against the team's move to San Francisco. Still, it was his role as Payson's representative that had given Grant a presence and a voice that the press now sought out.

"We're sticking together," Grant announced. But then, almost immediately, he added, "If they want to take the four of us now and the other four in a reasonable time, I personally would be interested. Of course, I speak only for myself."

Which, as Rickey had come to suspect, was not entirely true.

<<<<<

The Continentals gathered at the Warwick Hotel on July 20, two days
after the National League's expansion announcement. They were no
longer the same group of founders who had stood together in announcing the league's birth in November 1958. They'd been joined by new
men such as M. Donald Grant and Houston's Roy Hofheinz, who was
outsized even by Texas proportions. Hofheinz was a political operator of
legendary skill, a judge—the title he preferred—and former mayor, who
had made important friends, among them Lyndon Johnson and the
spectacularly wealthy oil man Bob Smith. Smith, in fact, had become a
business partner, and the two had accumulated a good deal of Houston
real estate. Hofheinz was interested less in baseball than in where the
game might be played. He was intrigued with the idea of building a
great, domed, air-conditioned stadium in his city. Cullinan and Kirksey
had courted him for his muscle and for his connection to Smith, with
whom he owned parcels of land where the proposed stadium might rise.

The meeting began in the late afternoon, and the proposed agenda
was quickly abandoned so that the Continentals could decide what to do
about the National League's overture. First to be resolved was the matter of the minor leagues and the money they demanded to surrender
their territories. This was crucial if the league was still intent on going
to Chicago to seek recognition from the owners; indemnifying the
minors was the last but most vexing hurdle the owners had demanded as
the price of admission as a third major league. Rickey, Jack Kent Cooke,
and Wheelock Whitney had devised a formula for a settlement, which
had been forwarded to the minor-league executives, who had yet to
reply. Bob Howsam groused that the league's failure to strike a deal
months earlier was bound to cost everyone a lot of money. Rickey
beseeched the members to band together, and with that they broke for
dinner. It was going to be a late night.

Shea emerged to assure the waiting newsmen that the Continentals remained united. "I can tell you this much, we have no thought of
disbanding," he said. "We're going to break our necks trying to satisfy
every possible demand made of us by the majors in the hope of obtaining recognition from organized baseball as a valid third major league."

Someone asked whether the owners of the league's New York franchise might accept an invitation to join the National League.

"That's impossible. We agreed long ago not to defect," Shea replied. "I don't believe the National League will come here. Anyway, we have a moral obligation to the Continental League people. I'd rather resign than double-cross them."

Dinner lasted just over an hour. When the Continentals again closed the door to their conference room, Wheelock Whitney took the floor to deliver bad news. Minneapolis, he announced, had had "a complete reversal of opinion." The city, he explained, now believed that the promises of major-league expansion were genuine and no longer saw its baseball future in the Continental League.

Grant was next to speak. He was not prepared to bolt, but he did have a proposal, one that he had already hinted at to the press. If the big leagues approached them with an offer to take in four Continental League cities "immediately" and the other four at "some future time"— perhaps a year—he said he would be "interested." Such a deal, he went on, would mean "complete victory" for the Continental League. "We would have accomplished our purpose," he said—they would have forced the big leagues to expand. Still, he added, "the majors would have to take all eight of our cities."

The minutes do not show whether the members voted on Grant's proposal, or even whether it was greeted with enthusiasm or skepticism. Rickey spoke next, but only to say that he would insist that all eight clubs be represented at the Chicago meeting with the National League expansion committee. They would go to Chicago together. They would come seeking recognition for the league, not a deal to dismember it in exchange for vague promises. That was the plan.

"I regard this meeting as the greatest opportunity we have ever had to defeat opposition to a third major league," Rickey wrote to Hofheinz several days later. He had pushed to have Hofheinz included in the Continental League's delegation and wanted to share his thinking. "It may be that the invitation to us is insincere and only a gesture of courtesy," Rickey continued. "However, I regard the invitation as a fact-finding effort, sincerely on the part of the National League at least to accept the Continental League, if that should seem the lesser of two evils. But, now every club faces a definite commitment in favor of expansion, however defined, and there are several National League clubs who, in their hearts, so to speak, are opposed to internal expansion." O'Malley wanted a nine-team National League. Phil Wrigley wanted twelve teams, divided into two divisions. There might yet be room for the Continentals to wriggle themselves a place in the majors as an equal. "Therefore," he concluded, "Chicago is our chance."

Still, it was a curious note for him to write, given that only days earlier Rickey had written to warn the Continental League owners against counting on recognition from the majors, because he believed it would never come. He was now reconciled to losing Minneapolis—he would surely be able to find a replacement city. More troubling was M. Donald Grant's proposal to split the league in half, claiming that it would be a victory for the majors to use the Continentals to achieve the sort of expansion that Rickey insisted was doomed to fail. Rickey's optimism about what awaited him in Chicago seemed misplaced, naive.

Until Dan Daniel emerged two days later with a new prophecy.

Daniel had been the Continental League's most persistent critic, delivering the most discouraging news. But now he used his forum in the *Sporting News* to bring the welcome tidings:

"A series of meetings here on July 20 and 21 appeared to set the Continental League on the right track, and seemed to assure its achieving membership in Organized Baseball."

The new league had found a way to satisfy the minors, and that had satisfied Daniel. Even so, he still scolded the Continentals for having taken their troubles to Washington and for lobbying for "the very bad Kefauver bill." Only when the owners proposed expansion—as he had predicted they would, and should, a year earlier—were the Continentals "stirred into talking turkey." They had come up with the money, and now, Daniel wrote, the "outlook . . . was vastly improved."

Daniel did not go so far as to predict that the majors would accept them. "It may yet be that internal expansion will be the solution," he wrote. "But at the moment, the chances of the Continental League are assumed to be more hopeful than ever before."

Chances of what, precisely, he did not say.

AUGUST: Kindred Spirits

It was steamy in Chicago, ninety degrees and humid. Rickey booked a two-bedroom suite for himself and Shea and singles and doubles for everyone else at the Conrad Hilton Hotel, where the meeting was scheduled for two o'clock on the afternoon of August 2. The American League's representatives would attend as guests, Del Webb among them. The National League had invited the Continentals to talk, which meant there was no question as to whose show this would be.

"O'Malley will be the strong man of this meeting," Shea told the *Chicago Tribune*. "We think that O'Malley would like to be hailed for leading the way for the return of a second club to New York." The Continental League, Shea reasoned, could accomplish that while still keeping Los Angeles as O'Malley's exclusive preserve, safe from invasion by an American League that badly wanted an outpost on the West Coast, if only it could decide which team to send. "The Continental League owners come to Chicago with their hats in their hands," Shea said. "We know we have no control over what is to happen."

This was made clear the moment everyone took their seats in the Imperial Suite, and O'Malley called the meeting to order.

Rickey had hoped to speak. He had come with a nine-page brief that argued for his league's admission to the majors and the error of adding a team or two that would perform poorly on the field and at the gate. But O'Malley was not prepared to give him the time or the stage.

"Gentlemen," he began, "I am against the soft-soap. We are here to make serious decisions. Let us lay our cards on the table and face the facts without animosity and with a desire for the best things for baseball and this country." The owners had made their demands of the Continentals. And now, he added, "there is a tremendous baseball unrest all over the U.S." In fact, Continental League cities were asking for American League franchises—witness Minneapolis's plan to defect.

"There is only one move open. We must compromise. We will take four of your cities and later add the rest."

Just as M. Donald Grant had suggested.

The Continentals asked for a recess to consider the offer. They crowded into a back room and shut the door. There was no haggling, no dissent, no negotiation. Only a great cheer.

Rickey had seen it coming, and yet he could do nothing to keep his people from abandoning the league the instant the chance came of having a big-league club—if not now then later, provided the owners were true to their word. He had wanted to do what Ban Johnson had done: keep his league together and revolutionize the game. But he was not Ban Johnson. He was not forty years old and vital but seventy-nine and saddled with a weak heart. The recognition of the limitations of age and health would sting for years. "He would never have accepted the promises of the American and National Leagues in Chicago," Rickey would later write of Johnson. "I doubt if he would have accepted the invitation to meet with them."

Rickey had been of great use to the Continentals; they could have asked for no better front man. He had devised the plan. He had believed in the cause.

His cause.

Not theirs.

"We'll miss you, Mr. Rickey," someone said.

"Don't worry about me," he replied.

The vote to accept the deal was unanimous, even though O'Malley and his committee would not name the cities they were prepared to take immediately or when the other four would get their teams. Rickey withdrew the Continental League's bid for recognition. A reporter asked him if this meant that the league was dead.

"Obviously," he replied.

Bill Shea was thrilled. "We accomplished the job I started," he said, "and I believe my city will be one of the first to get a team. It's been a lot of work, but I set out to get a team for New York three years ago and this is it."

Rickey threw his arms around him. "I may never see you again," the older man said. "You did a great job."

In the press briefing that followed, Rickey was uncharacteristically brief and gloomy. He said kind things about the owners and about the Continentals, too, calling them "the finest group of gentlemen I have ever worked with."

But when someone asked about his plans, given that he was suddenly without a job, he replied without his usual ebullience about what lay ahead.

"I do not know or care about the future," he said.

The postmortems followed the next day, and no writer was kinder to Rickey than Jimmy Cannon, who wrote as if Rickey's return to importance had brought back reminders of a better time. "The baseball people ridiculed him," he wrote of Shea, whose persistence he praised, "but they were shaken when he hired Branch Rickey. They know all about Rickey and they hold no affection for him. He was too smart for them.

"They told themselves he was too old to put together eight 25-man squads on a field. But they never really believed what they said, because this is a guy you can never ignore."

In the end, Cannon wrote, the owners revealed themselves to be fearful men—*cowardly* was the word he used—and especially fearful of men more powerful than themselves on Capitol Hill. So they ran, from the Continentals and from Congress. "They ran as far as they could," Cannon concluded, "and yesterday in Chicago they pulled up." And when they did it was to offer a deal to men who were very much like themselves.

It took no time at all for speculation to begin as to which cities would be among the lucky first four. New York, it was generally conceded, seemed a sure thing. Houston and Minneapolis appeared likely winners, with Toronto or Dallas close behind. Atlanta, Denver, and Buffalo seemed destined for the second round.

Mayor Wagner praised Shea for his services to the city. Ford Frick proclaimed himself delighted. "I have always been in favor of expansion," the commissioner said. "The move is a step in the right direction. I cannot comment further until I have the full details."

Or perhaps until the Yankees weighed in.

Del Webb had been at the meeting and his silence suggested that the outcome pleased him. It fell then to Dan Topping to question whether the Yankees would accept a new club in town. If the National League wanted to return to New York, he was going to extract a price for the invasion of his turf.

"New York is the crux of the National League expansion plan," he announced, "and Los Angeles emphatically must figure in the coast-to-coast realignment on our side."

Los Angeles, of course, was not part of the Continental League, and so could not, in a strict reading of the deal, be part of the expansion. Unless, of course, the deal was merely a ruse by the owners to rid themselves of Rickey and Shea.

"On the surface, it would appear O'Malley is eager to keep Los Angeles exclusively a National League city," Topping added. "If this is tried, I will holler plenty and I won't stop."

The Continental League was gone. The battle of the warlords had begun.

Branch Rickey did not linger in Chicago. He flew back to New York later that day, and restless soul that he was, spent part of the flight writing a long letter to Wheelock Whitney. He liked Whitney, even though Minneapolis had twice been prepared to bolt his league. Rickey did not want Whitney feeling bad about what had happened in Chicago. Instead, he wanted him to know what awaited him, in good ways and bad, if his city was among the chosen ones.

"There is glamour, almost romance in the prospective adventure—and it is just that," he wrote. "Not at any future time do I wish you to experience the remotest sense of regret and I write you about a matter of great importance as I see it, in order to remove, as best we can, the hazard of first money loss, and second, disappointment."

If you are chosen, he continued, you must immediately begin finding players. "Your people must not trust the 'help' that may be promised or indeed provided, as coming from the majors. That will be the 'crumbs from the table.' You will be confronted with vicious competition, surely unlike any you have ever imagined. I shudder, really, when I think of what is surely in front of the 9th & 10th clubs in either major league, because and chiefly because of player weakness in the field."

So, he went on, hire a general manager who knows something of the game; there aren't many good ones. Stake an early claim to the players the majors will make available. Be prepared to lose money for three years, and hope to turn a profit in the fourth. "You must avoid somehow the probability of winning 40 of the 154 games, even in your very first year. The newness of the attraction will sustain you for a time, probably so! But the fantasy wears out rapidly with discreditable clubs."

He closed as if anticipating questions about what lay ahead for him. It had taken only a few hours for the disappointment to ebb enough to allow him to think ahead. "About me? I mean to have another fling. St. Louis was good to me. So was Brooklyn and Pittsburgh. . . . I will keep busy. In the meantime we must 'settle up' with the majors. We are not out of the woods yet."

SEPTEMBER: Indian Summer

Casey Stengel had turned seventy on July 30. Rain delayed the celebration the Yankees had planned between games of a doubleheader against Kansas City. People instead gathered in the Yankees' clubhouse. Edna Stengel cut the birthday cake and fed a slice to her husband for the photographers. Stengel winked, took a sip of the ginger ale that passed for champagne, and bemoaned all the doubleheaders coming up. "With the kind of pitching we have been getting too often of late," he said, "that is not a happy situation."

His team had not been able to shake the Orioles, and by the third week of September the Yankees found themselves in a virtual tie for first place with Baltimore. The Orioles were coming to New York for a four-game weekend series that could well decide the pennant. Stengel had decisions to make about his pitching. Whitey Ford seemed the logical choice to start the opener, but he had slumped in the past month, and there were questions about the strength in his left arm; he hadn't won a game since mid-August and had been knocked out in the first inning in his most recent start in Kansas City. Art Ditmar, on the other hand, had won five straight in June and July and had faltered only once in the past two months, narrowly losing two weeks earlier to the Orioles. The younger men, Ralph Terry and Bill Stafford, had been spectacular, but Bob Turley had not won a game since July. For their part, the Orioles had four of the best young pitchers in the league.

The writers understood that for all his reviewing of the data and consulting with his coaches, Stengel managed by feel and instinct. His instinct told him Ford in the opener. His ace rewarded him with a victory, holding Baltimore scoreless until two men were out in the ninth. Stengel went with Turley in the second game, and though he would end up using four relievers, won again. He was planning to start Ditmar in the first game of the Sunday doubleheader and Terry, who'd been his best pitcher down the stretch, in the nightcap. But rain was forecast and Stengel was prepared to switch them to ensure that Terry would have his start. Ditmar was home in New Jersey when the skies cleared and the trainer called to tell him to hurry to the ballpark; he'd be pitching the first game after all. Ditmar won the first game and in the second Terry took a perfect game into the seventh before finishing with a two-hit shutout.

Stengel used four different lineups that weekend. He opened with Bobby Richardson batting leadoff, then dropped him to eighth for the second game. Maris batted second, then third, alternating with Mantle, who batted third in the Friday game and cleanup in the last three. Stengel sat Berra in the opener and had him catch the second and third, then sat him again in the finale. The victories were especially sweet given that Paul Richards had for years disparaged Stengel as an overrated clown. "Stengel doesn't do anything different," Richards said. "He just makes a bigger act out of it." But Richards's younger, less experienced Orioles faltered, dropping balls and failing in the clutch. The Yankees would not lose another game that season.

A few days later, John Drebinger of the *Times* wrote that Stengel was never better than he had been in that series. The praise, generous as it was, seemed an act of kindness by an old friend. The writers knew that Stengel's job was in jeopardy, and they did not want to lose him. On the Sunday that completed the sweep, they presented Stengel a trophy for his "service to baseball."

Four days later, the UPI broke a story saying that Stengel had decided to retire at the end of the season, and that Ralph Houk would replace him. There were reports of his becoming the general manager in Kansas City. Stengel was evasive. He would have nothing to say about his future until the World Series ended.

The American Football League debuted in Boston on Friday night, September 2, before twenty-one thousand people at Boston University's Nickerson Field, which stood on the site of Braves Field, which Lou Perini had abandoned for Milwaukee. Bob Howsam's Denver Broncos beat the Boston Patriots, 13–10. That same night in Dallas, Lamar Hunt's Texans completed a perfect exhibition season by defeating the Houston Oilers, 24–3 at the Cotton Bowl. Fifty-one thousand people came to watch. The Oilers played again on Sunday against the Oakland Raiders in the second of the two AFL games that ABC broadcast that day. The first game originated in New York, where on a rainy afternoon the Titans defeated the Buffalo Bills before a crowd of just under ten thousand at the Polo Grounds. The game had been a defensive snore until an NFL castoff, Al Dorow, took over at quarterback for the Titans. With Don Maynard, a flanker who'd been cut by the Giants, as a target, Dorow put on such a good show of running and passing in the mud that it moved Dave Brady of the *Washington Post* to pose the question, "How good is the new American Football League? Good enough."

ABC, seizing upon the freedom that came with being a last-place network, drew on the innovations that Roone Arledge had introduced in its college football coverage. The idea was to envision the game not merely as an athletic contest but as a weekly event—a show. There were microphones along the sidelines, so that that viewers could hear the sounds of the game, and small cameras that captured close-ups of the players. One of Arledge's protégés, Jim Spence, would later recall that it was important for viewers to feel as if they had been transported to the arena, so they could hear the sound that came when a running back and a linebacker collided, and when the quarterback called the signals. There were interviews on the sidelines and cameras in the locker rooms; during halftime the network showed taped highlights and the announcers offered analysis of the big plays of the first half. Curt Gowdy did the play-by-play but the true spark came from Paul Christman, who provided the color commentary.

Christman, who'd starred at quarterback for Missouri and later played for the Green Bay Packers, was witty, sardonic, and wise about the game. He was not given to hero worship, and that alone made him different, and fun, which was, in the end, the point. So central was ABC's role in the success of the new league that Spence recalled one game in Dallas in which the referee signaled the start of play during a commercial. The producer, Jack Lubell, tore off his headset, ran onto the field, and screamed at the referee, "You don't kick off 'til we tell you." The ball was rekicked.

Meanwhile, a federal judge refused the NFL's request to throw out the AFL's ten-million-dollar lawsuit. The NFL was not disposed to being cooperative or friendly, not for the moment, and not, apparently, in the future.

"The two leagues will never be merged," announced Pete Rozelle. "As for claims that we'll meet at some time in the near future in a 'world series' of pro football, that just won't be."

CHAPTER NINE

OCTOBER 1960

Game One

The New York Yankees flew into Pittsburgh on the afternoon of October 3 with every reason to be confident that this would be their final road trip of the season. They were American League champions once again, their tenth pennant in the past twelve years. They had finished the season with a flourish, winning their last fifteen games—a powerful statement to the rest of the league that 1959 had been an aberration. Still, if things were to be put right there was a final task: dispatching the National League champion Pittsburgh Pirates—preferably in four or five games, to avoid a return trip to Pittsburgh—and completing the team's, and especially its manager's, season of redemption.

They had clinched the pennant the week before in Boston and then retreated to the visitors' clubhouse with barely a hoot or a shout. They dressed, returned to their hotel, and retired to a private banquet room for champagne and steaks. The hotel provided a television so the players could watch a football game. What palpable joy the Yankees displayed was limited to the new men and the veterans who had come to New York from losing teams and who had never before experienced the pleasure of victory that the stars had all but come to expect.

The oddsmakers liked their chances. They made the Yankees 13–10 favorites to take the series, an edge that, it seemed, had as much to do with history as with the team's closing surge. The Yankees had last come to Pittsburgh for the 1927 World Series. Baseball lore had it—and the writers, looking for an early story line, repeated it endlessly—that as the Pirates watched Babe Ruth and Lou Gehrig swat batting-practice home runs to the distant reaches of Forbes Field their self-esteem sank so low that they were as good as beaten before the first pitch was thrown. The Yankees swept them in four games, and Pittsburgh had not been back to the World Series since.

Ghosts and legends not withstanding, the 1960 Pirates were seen as a team at a historical and presumably emotional disadvantage. In truth, the two teams' records were all but identical—ninety-seven wins for the Yankees, ninety-five for Pittsburgh. There was, however, one striking difference, and that was power: the Yankees collectively hit 193 home runs while the Pirates had hit only 120. Mantle had homered 40 times that season and Maris 39. No Pirate had more than 23 home runs, and that by Dick Stuart, the self-satisfied first baseman who might have played more often if his fielding were not so atrocious.

The Pirates were a team of relatively little-known men who played in a city that, in the generation since its last pennant, had slipped to the periphery of baseball significance. In the thirty-three years since 1927, the Pirates had finished second just six times, and worse still, in the fourteen years since the end of World War II, they had finished last or next to last nine times. Branch Rickey ran the club for five of those woeful seasons, but the better side of his legacy was now visible in the Pirates lineup: Dick Groat, the shortstop who had just won the National League batting championship; Bill Mazeroski, who played second base as well as anyone in the game; Bill Virdon, the marvelous center fielder Rickey had plucked from the Cardinals; Elroy Face, whom he had snatched from the Dodgers and who had become the best reliever in the game; and the young Puerto Rican right fielder, Roberto Clemente, whom Rickey had also taken from the Dodgers. Clemente had batted .314 in 1960 and had blossomed into one of the best players in the league.

The Pirates were otherwise a team that suited their city neatly. Many of the players were young men from places like Wheeling, West Virginia;

Medway, Ohio; Lafayette, Indiana; and Pennsylvania towns like Wilkins-
burg, Roulette, and Chester, home of their manager, Danny Murtaugh.
The players whom Rickey's successor, Joe L. Brown, had acquired from
other teams had done their share of bouncing around and, for the most
part, never truly excelled until he brought them to Pittsburgh. They
were men who had been overlooked, and in some cases, all but forgotten, much like the city itself.

With the Pirates' emergence as contenders in 1960, baseball was
once again exercising its pull on a generation of Pirates fans whose connection to better times was limited to the stories their fathers and grand-
fathers had told them about Honus Wagner, Pie Traynor, and the
Waner brothers, Paul and Lloyd. When the Pirates had come back to
town from Milwaukee after they clinched the pennant, more than one
hundred thousand people—a sixth of the city's population—turned out
for an impromptu rally downtown, where the lights in the city's office
buildings were switched on to spell out what had become the city's ral-
lying cry: "Beat 'Em Bucs."

The players' arrival was delayed by their own clubhouse party. They
had lost that day in Milwaukee but had clinched the pennant when the
Cubs beat the second-place St. Louis Cardinals in Chicago. The Pirates
trudged to their lockers not at all sure of how, or whether, to celebrate.
But then Gino Cimoli, who had played on pennant winners in Brooklyn
and who was not shy in his opinions, bellowed, "Somebody dead?" With
that, the corks popped, the players tore into the food and drink, put on
silly hats and celebrated with such delight that the party continued
through the showers and dressing and then onto the team bus, where
Don Hoak, the third baseman known as "Tiger," tried to pull off the
shoe of pitcher Vernon Law. Law, a deacon in the Church of Jesus
Christ of Latter-Day Saints, had tied his shoes well and, as the rare sober
man among his teammates, could not get Hoak to desist. A week later,
his sprained ankle had yet to heal.

It was eleven o'clock before the Pirates made it back into Pittsburgh
and the downtown rally. On the highway from the airport, drivers had
pulled over to let the team bus pass, and one volunteer fire company
sounded the alarm as hundreds cheered. The Pirates kissed their wives,
who'd been presented with orchids, and climbed into the convertibles

that had lined up to carry them along the parade route. People stood ten deep to see them. Grown men and women put on pirate costumes and black eye patches and walked alongside the cars. A hearse slipped into the procession, the words *Bury the Yanks* scrawled along its side. Confetti flew from the hotel windows into the night sky. Little Leaguers were out in number, even on a school night. The crowd thickened at the end of the parade route, and people pressed around the cars. Leonard Shecter of the *New York Post*, in town to witness an event unimaginable in his city, spotted Clem Labine, the relief pitcher who had come to the Pirates in mid-August to bolster the bullpen. Labine had been a star with the 1955 world champion Brooklyn Dodgers and so knew something about celebrations for fans who felt themselves forever denied.

"Ever see anything like this?" Shecter asked.

Labine, sweating in the night air, whistled and said, "Not like this, dad. Even Brooklyn was never like this."

If Casey Stengel knew who his opening game starting pitcher would be, he was not saying. This was odd, less for his coyness than for the idea that there was any question at all. Common sense would suggest that Whitey Ford would start the opener, as he had in each of the past four World Series the Yankees had played. Ford had been a Yankee since 1950 and had started twelve series games, winning five, losing four. In the years since the retirement of Allie Reynolds and Ed Lopat and the banishment of Vic Raschi, Ford had established himself as the Yankees' ace. He was thirty-one years old, stocky and blond, and he carried himself with a confidence—some would say cockiness—that could put his less assured teammates at ease.

It was taken as a matter of faith that a manager started his best pitcher in Game One, so that he might be able to start him two more times, including a seventh game, if it were necessary. Danny Murtaugh had already announced, to the surprise of no one, that Vernon Law would open the series for the Pirates, sprained ankle or no. But Stengel was considering his options.

Perhaps if Stengel were a sentimental man his choice for his Game One starter would have been easy. But for Stengel, the past existed only in the stories he told and not how a man used to perform for him. Whitey Ford had been with him for ten years and had seldom disappointed. He had pitched well even when he lost, rarely giving up more than a run at a time. But Ford had slipped a bit in 1960, winning twelve, losing nine, with an earned run average of 3.08, a good season by any measure but below Ford's standards. Art Ditmar, on the other hand, had been marginally better—fifteen and nine, with an earned run average of 3.06. Ditmar, who had come to the Yankees from Kansas City—where else?—in 1954, had appeared in only two World Series games, both times in relief: four innings, four hits, no runs, no decisions.

Ditmar threw a sinker ball, and most of his outs came via the grounder. He had a tendency to give up home runs—the fate of the sinker that doesn't sink. He'd surrendered twenty-five in 1960. Forbes Field was large; a fly ball would have a tougher time going out. Its infield, however, had the consistency of a rock garden, hard and rough, a bad hop waiting to happen. The Yankees infielders had said as much after their workout the day before the opener; they would be busy, if a bit unsettled, if Ditmar did his work well, making the Pirates hit the ball on the ground. "You can't feel certain about the bounce," said Clete Boyer, the young, gifted third baseman.

If this concerned Stengel, it did not appear to sway his thinking. Besides, he liked to pitch Ford at Yankee Stadium, where he had always been tough to beat; he was six and three in the Bronx that season. But then Ditmar had been even stronger at home, winning nine and losing only twice. In the end, Stengel went with his gut. And his gut told him that Ford was not his man.

Ford knew it even before the season ended, when Stengel sent him in to pitch two innings in Boston in the final game. He later called the decision "the only time I ever got mad at Casey." His teammates were baffled. Those who knew Stengel best should not have been surprised.

In Stengel's ordering of the universe, there was no place for the emotional boost that a commanding presence like Ford could bring to his team, no room for the confidence that his presence on the mound might mean. Ford was a cog, like everyone else. It was Stengel who mattered, not Ford, not anyone else. The Yankees were his team and he knew best.

And so Ditmar would start Game One and Bob Turley would start Game Two. Ford would start Game Three at Yankee Stadium.

Stengel would have Whitey Ford pitch in two games, at most, not three.

Forbes Field was crowded early for batting practice, but not with familiar faces. The park had long been one of the rowdiest in the league, or rather had been so until August, when the city had decided that it would no longer tolerate fans bringing their own beer to the games; Pennsylvania law prohibited the sale of alcohol at ballparks, but fans had been free to lug in as much as they could carry and presumably drink. Still, even without the suds, Forbes Field was a noisy place, and grew ever more raucous as the Pirates inched closer to the pennant. But as the tall and rangy Vernon Law threw his warm-up pitches, the crowd that settled into their seats was decidedly tonier than usual—white gloves for the women, jackets and ties for men. Pittsburgh society had turned out for the opener, and the *Post-Gazette* sent a reporter to the stands as if it were covering a debutante ball: *Mr. and Mrs. Samuel B. Casey were luncheon guests at the home of Mr. and Mrs. Samuel B. Casey Jr. before going to the game.* The hot dog peddlers, making a hasty assessment of the crowd's revenue potential, raised their prices from a nickel to thirty cents.

Downtown Pittsburgh felt like a ghost town as people hurried into bars or electronics stores to watch the game on television. Men and women who had slept outside the ballpark the night before hoping to get tickets took their places in the standing-room section. And then all sense of decorum was punctured when a parachutist appeared, sailing high over the ballpark under a pink chute. He skirted the park, instead coming to rest on the roof of a nearby building. When the police came to take him away, he explained that the leap had been the price he paid for betting that the Pirates would not win the pennant.

Vernon Law took the mound and looked in at Tony Kubek, who greeted him with a bad-hop single off the third-base bag. But Kubek was quickly gone, erased on Hector Lopez's double play, which left the bases empty for Roger Maris. Law threw a ball and a strike and then tried to come inside and missed. Maris drove the ball into the upper deck in right field, a flash of power that reminded the nervous Pittsburgh faith-ful of what had happened the last time the Yankees came to town.

New York was leading 1–0 when the moment came for Art Ditmar to show that Stengel had made a wise choice in his starter. He opened with a walk to Bill Virdon, who was followed by Dick Groat. Groat had hit .325 that season, winning the batting championship on the last weekend of the season, even though he'd lost a month with a broken wrist. He and Virdon were roommates; they were both quiet men, and this made it easy for them to understand each other. Or so it appeared until Virdon took his lead off first and tried, for the life of him, to figure out the mes-sage Groat was trying to send.

Unlike Stengel, Danny Murtaugh gave his trusted players the lati-tude to choose when to steal or hit-and-run. Groat and Virdon had their own signs for the hit-and-run—Groat would touch his cap, then his leg, then his shirt—which they changed with the inning, to guard against theft. With the signs came brush-off signs, signals to ignore the sign just given. Now Groat began flashing signs to Virdon. And in his nervous-ness in playing in his first World Series, Groat lost track. He could not remember whether he had given Virdon the sign to be ready to run because he would be swinging, or whether he had told him to hold his ground.

Virdon was sure the hit-and-run was on. He waited until Groat took a pitch. And then he took off for second. Groat did not swing. Instead, he watched and thought, "Oh my God, I screwed up in my first World Series."

The percentages were not in Virdon's favor. He had stolen only eight bases all season. The Pirates, in fact, were the worst base stealers in the league, having stolen only thirty-four as a team, sixteen fewer than the league leader Maury Wills of the Los Angeles Dodgers had stolen on his own. The Yankees knew this, of course; each team had scouted the other well. The greater threat, they concluded, was the hit-and-run, because Groat handled the bat deftly.

But that is not how it appeared to Yogi Berra. What he saw taking place before him was nothing more complex than Bill Virdon trying to steal second. Berra was up and throwing and, too late, saw that he was without a target. Neither the shortstop, Tony Kubek, nor the second baseman, Bobby Richardson, was waiting at second for his throw. It was the hit-and-run that had worried them, and the best defense for a hit and run is for the infielders to hold their positions. And that is what they did.

Berra's throw sailed into the outfield. Virdon rounded second and by the time Kubek retrieved the ball, he was on third. Groat finally did swing on Ditmar's next pitch, which he lined to right for a double, driving in Virdon, tying the score, and putting himself in scoring position with nobody out.

Stengel made a brief visit to the mound. Bob Skinner then stepped up to bat and hit a bouncer past Richardson, scoring Groat. Dick Stuart, who tended to hit the ball in the air when he hit it at all, flied out to Maris in right. One out, one on, and Roberto Clemente coming to bat.

If prudence was a virtue, it held no appeal for Bob Skinner, whose mere twelve stolen bases had led the Pirates. He took off for second, a gangly man racing to beat Berra's throw. He might have saved the exertion, because Berra, whose arm was not what it had been in his best years, watched his throw sail high past the bag. Kubek was there to cover, and snared it before it could reach the outfield. Skinner's stay on second was brief. Ditmar succeeded in getting Clemente to hit the ball on the ground. But the ball bounced up the middle, scoring Skinner.

Art Ditmar had thrown only seventeen pitches, but Stengel had seen enough. He returned to the mound, took the ball, and handed it to Jim Coates, who came in from the bullpen. Coates retired Smoky Burgess and Don Hoak, but the Pirates had handed Law a 3–1 lead.

He did not appear ready to protect it. Berra, happy to be out from behind the plate, singled to center, and Bill Skowron followed with a base hit to right. The moment had come for Clete Boyer's first World Series at bat.

Boyer was twenty-three years old, yet another gift from Kansas City. A marvelous fielder, he had supplanted Gil McDougald at third. His hitting, however, was modest—a .242 average enhanced by the occasional home run; he had hit twelve that season. He had brought to the game all the relatives for whom he could find tickets; the competition was fierce. Boyer was one of twelve children, and his older brother, Ken, played third base for the Cardinals. He was about to leave the on-deck circle when he heard Stengel call to him. "I thought he wanted to tell me something, as he often does—to take a shot to right field, or what they were going to pitch me or something like that," he later told the writers. "He never did say anything to me."

Instead, Stengel spoke to Dale Long. He told him to get a bat.

Long was a late-season pickup from San Francisco, an experienced man with power; in 1956, playing for the Pirates, he set a record for homering in eight straight games. Stengel had two men on base and a two-run deficit and no intention of leaving matters in the hands of Clete Boyer, who could not quite fathom what was happening to him.

Neither could some of his teammates. They knew Stengel was never averse to substitutions in the early innings. But Boyer had yet to have a turn at bat, and now he was gone. It was an especially discomfiting feeling for the younger players, among them Jim Coates, who sat in the dugout, preparing to pitch the bottom of the second and wondering whether he, too, might yet suffer a humiliating fate himself. Boyer, after all, had been reassured by Stengel during the season that his glove would keep him in the lineup. "He's telling you, I don't think you can do the job for me," Coates would say years later. "He overreacted." And a ballplayer, Coates added, will lose faith in his manager when he senses the manager has lost faith in his players.

Boyer retreated to the tunnel under the stands and wept. "I wanted to die," he said later that day. "I wanted to crawl all the way home. I know I've been going bad. But how bad must I be if I can't even bat once? In the second inning? If that's what he thinks, all right—but how can I go on after that?"

In the press box, the writers who knew Stengel best and longest were equally perplexed. The logic of the move—the lefty Long over the right-handed Boyer against the righty Law—was beside the point. Maury Allen of the *New York Post*, for one, had spent enough time that season at Stengel's side to understand that Stengel did not want merely to defeat the Pirates; he wanted to sweep them, to beat them so convincingly that Topping and Webb would have no choice but to bring him back. Years later, Allen would recall the embarrassment he and his colleagues felt for Boyer and the sense that Stengel's vanity and desperation were getting the better of him. "The old man," he thought, "has lost it."

Murtaugh, too, was contemplating an early move, fearful that his sore-ankled ace was not on his game. Clem Labine and Fred Green started warming up in the Pirates' bullpen. But Dale Long would be Law's responsibility.

He fulfilled it by inducing Long to fly out to Clemente. Still, the Yankees had only one man out and Richardson at bat. He, too, drove the ball to the outfield, this time to left, where Skinner was waiting. Meanwhile, at second base, Berra was watching the flight of the ball and did not believe that Skinner would catch it; never a fast runner, Berra wanted to make sure he scored. He strayed off the bag, his first mistake. The second was being wrong about Skinner's bead on the ball. Even his headlong slide back into the bag could not save him from the embarrassment of being doubled off, effectively ending the big inning that Stengel had wasted his best-fielding third baseman to achieve.

The Yankees cut the Pittsburgh lead to 3–2 with a run in the fourth. But the Pirates scored two runs in the bottom of the inning on a home run by Mazeroski and another run in the seventh. The Yankees threatened in the top of the ninth when Elston Howard hit a home run to cut the Pirates' lead to two. Tony Kubek then singled, but Hector Lopez followed by grounding into a double play, killing the rally and giving the Pirates the early series lead.

In the clubhouse, Berra did not hide his irritation about the failure to cover second base on Virdon's first-inning steal. "On a steal it's my job to throw to the bag," he said. "You'll have to ask someone else what happened after that." The official scorers had tagged Berra with an error on the play, but Kubek insisted that they place the blame on himself. Richardson, too, tried to accept responsibility—"Either of us could have gotten it, but we thought the other had it."

Art Ditmar was displeased with the outcome, though not necessarily with his own performance. "I made only seventeen pitches and I felt fine," he said. "I wanted them to hit grounders. They did, but don't tell me they're that good that they can hit them where nobody is all the time." As for Clete Boyer, he did not shy away from taking reporters through the emotional stations of his long afternoon. "I don't know what to think, what to say. I'm still flabbergasted. Maybe I'm not the best hitter in the world, but I didn't think I was that bad," he said. "I just don't know and I can't figure it out."

For his part, Casey Stengel was not much moved by Boyer's tale of hurt and humiliation. He was in a foul mood. "They outpitched us, all right," he said. "In a good pitched game we could have won. I was disappointed in some of our players." When the subject turned to Boyer he did not obfuscate or talk in circles. Rather, he posed a series of testy rhetorical questions.

"For crying out loud, doesn't he know he's in a World Series now? Why should he be in a state of shock? Wouldn't I be in a state of shock if he went up there and struck out on me? I've been playing him all year, haven't I? I put his name down in the starting lineup today—I didn't hate him then, did I? What is he in there for, defense, right? The man I put in there has hit home runs for me as a pinch hitter. I thought I could get right back in the game. I'd have been delighted if he hit safely but he didn't. How do I know I'll have men on base in the ninth? What are pinch hitters for?"

Meanwhile, in the Pirates' clubhouse, Dick Groat had no patience for the received wisdom that the Pirates were doomed to be slaughtered. "We're not a bunch of kids," he said. "All we heard was that the Yankees have the power and we're supposed to fold up and die. I don't see why *we* have to fold up."

Game Two

Rain began falling overnight and the showers continued into the morning, raising the possibility that Game Two might have to be called.

At the press headquarters at the Hilton, a story emerged—one that would surely send reverberations back east. The source was Warren Giles, who chose this moment to share his thoughts about expansion. The National League president had never much cared for New York and had not been troubled in 1957 when his league abandoned the city. "Who needs New York?" he had said, dismissively. Giles had been the general manager of the Cincinnati Reds for fifteen years before becoming league president in 1951, and he immediately relocated the National

League's offices from New York to Cincinnati. He had never subscribed to the notion that New York was entitled to a replacement for the two teams it had lost.

"There are two schools of thought regarding New York," he said before Game Two. "There are some who believe getting such a big city as New York back would bring added prestige to the National League. We would then be truly represented from one coast to the other.

"There are others who are equally insistent that we should turn to cities which have not had any previous experience with the major leagues."

Then came the news that Bill Shea did not want to hear. "No city is assured of a franchise although there are some which have made more progress than others." He did not list them or handicap favorites.

Giles's words went out on the wires but soon were lost as the skies over Pittsburgh began to clear. Talk of expansion was temporarily halted as the fans in the Forbes Field bleachers folded their umbrellas. Bob Friend was pitching for the Pirates and, unlike Vernon Law, he had no aches or pains. In fact, Friend was feeling as good as he had all season.

The first two innings passed uneventfully. Friend surrendered two runs in the third but started the fourth by fanning Skowron and Howard, and was an out away from escaping untouched when he surrendered a single to Richardson. Burgess then committed the injustice of allowing a passed ball, which enabled Richardson to take second. Mercifully, the next batter was the opposing pitcher, Bob Turley. Friend had already struck out four and presumably would dispatch Turley with fastballs. Instead, he decided to throw a curve. Perhaps, he would later say, he was feeling a little too confident in facing so poor a hitter as Bob Turley, who in fifty-five at bats that season had garnered only four base hits. The pitch that left Friend's hand approached the plate high, and that is where it stayed. Turley swung and for only the fifth time that season connected. His single drove in Richardson. And while Friend retired Kubek, he took his seat in the dugout down not by two runs, but by three.

Turley, meanwhile, was having problems with his own curveball, and the Pirates began to take advantage. Gino Cimoli led off the bottom of the fourth with a single to right. Burgess made amends for his passed ball by following with another single, advancing Cimoli to third. Don Hoak then doubled off the wall in right, scoring Cimoli and bringing

Mazeroski to bat with runners on second and third and no one out. Stengel paid a visit to the mound, where he advised Turley to get his pitches down in the strike zone. Turley stuck with his curve to retire Mazeroski on a liner to third. Bob Friend was next to hit and his presence in the on-deck circle left Danny Murtaugh with a difficult decision. The Pirates were a base hit away from tying the score. But Friend was an even weaker batter than Turley: six hits and thirty-one strikeouts in eighty-eight at bats that season. Had Mazeroski's liner fallen for a hit, Murtaugh later said, he would have surely kept Friend in the game. But there was no assurance he would have another chance to strike. Besides, Murtaugh's bullpen had served him well down the stretch and that, he decided, is where he would put his faith. Friend had pitched well but now his day was done. Murtaugh called on Gene Baker to hit in Friend's place. Fred Green, a lefthander, would pitch the fifth.

A fly ball would score a run, but Baker popped out. It was now left to Bill Virdon to salvage the inning. He grounded to second. Turley had escaped without surrendering the tying run. Fred Green came on to pitch the fifth and, from Murtaugh's perspective, take some of the sting out of his choice. The Pittsburgh manager had reason to be optimistic: only once all year had Green surrendered more than two runs in an outing.

He opened the frame by walking McDougald on four pitches. He was luckier with Roger Maris, who bounced to first. Rocky Nelson began what held the promise of a double play by throwing to Groat covering second, forcing McDougald. But Groat's return throw was late, and Maris stood at first with Mantle coming to bat.

Mantle had been longing to face a lefty. For weeks he had been struggling to hit from the left side of the plate; the ball, he said, seemed to be on him so quickly. Now he stood in on the right side, grateful for the chance to redeem himself after a strikeout in the first. He drove Green's offering deep over the wall in center field, scoring Maris ahead of him and putting the Yankees up 5–1.

Elston Howard led off the sixth with a triple that left Virdon sprawling in his attempt to make a catch against the wall in center. Richardson followed by doubling him home. The margin now stood at 6–1, and Murtaugh had seen enough. Or so he thought. The long afternoon that began unfolding with Bob Friend's hanging curveball was, in fact, just beginning, much to the displeasure of the aging man in the fedora sitting glumly behind the Yankees' dugout.

Branch Rickey had returned to Pittsburgh, where he had begun the unhappy retirement from which Bill Shea had rescued him almost three years earlier. The Pirates were his team, but only in the most attenuated way. Joe Brown had taken the core of young men Rickey had left behind and crafted a winner. Still, the Pirates, in recognition of the work he had done, did him the courtesy of a good seat, albeit on the visitors' side of the field.

He had spent part of September at his family's "camp" on Dickerson Island, in Ontario, a location so remote that his secretary had to forward the telegrams that still came to the office via the mail boat. One came from Walter O'Malley, who had completed drafting the National League's expansion plan and wanted to share it with Rickey, when he was next in Los Angeles.

Rickey had little to do when he returned to New York. There was the matter of returning the fifty-thousand-dollar deposits to the clubs that would not be among the first four admitted to the big leagues. And there was the Western Carolina League, whose players would no longer be needed. One of the new secretaries, Judy Wilpon, would later recall how lost the old man seemed around the office.

Craig Cullinan wrote to let Rickey know that he, too, would be in Pittsburgh for the series. Cullinan had suddenly become a very popular man; both leagues were intrigued by the possibilities of a city growing as rapidly as Houston. Cullinan would make time for a meeting to attend to the final dissolution of the Continental League. He and Kirksey had been early and eager acolytes, until Rickey sensed that Cullinan wanted to ease him out.

"Turning to another subject," Cullinan now wrote, "I know you know with what thoroughly mixed emotions I considered the events at the August 2d meeting in Chicago. While I lean to the belief, now that the dust has settled, that perhaps the decisions reached in Chicago are for the best, I want you to know what a wrench it gave me to cast my vote for dissolving the project on which you had lavished so much time and care. Had the Continental League owners been more strongly united, things might have turned out differently."

The major leagues, he went on, seemed inclined to help with players, but Rickey's help in choosing the right men would be most welcome. Cullinan hoped that the old man would not "deprive" the lucky four of his guidance.

He closed with another request, this one, it seemed, for absolution.

"I hope," he wrote, "that I may accurately continue to consider myself one of Mr. Rickey's boys."

Game Three

Of all the many words to describe Casey Stengel, phlegmatic was never among them. He was as ebullient in victory as he was gloomy in defeat. His team had botched Game One, and he could not escape the accusations of his hand playing a role in the defeat, especially the decision not to start Whitey Ford. But now, as the team prepared to return home, he was once again the buoyant Stengel, his team having humiliated the Pirates, 16–3, in Game Two. The game was so lopsided that the one bit of drama that remained after the Yankees effectively ended things with seven runs in the sixth was deciding whether Mickey Mantle's second home run of the day was the longest anyone had ever seen hit at Forbes Field. Mantle himself was immune to celebration. "What in hell do two homers mean," he asked, "when the team scores 16 runs?"

Stengel, however, was happy to celebrate, for his team and for himself. "I feel as young as that fella over there," he said, gesturing at Mantle. "It was a lucky day when I quit studying to be a left-handed dentist and went into baseball." Now he had nothing but kind things to say about his center fielder, a rarity, especially when it came at his own expense. "Now there's a lot of readers your paper had, so don't make any mistakes in your column," he told David Condon of the *Chicago Tribune*. "Don't tell 'em about my silk undershirt, as the one you saw me put on is the one I generally wear to the bank directors meetings. Don't write about me being a genius, as I made a mistake today—I should have taken out Turley in the seventh to save him for some later pitching. You can write about Mantle, how he does that all on one leg."

The clubhouse attendant approached and Stengel sensed that, given the nature of the Pirates' defeat, the series might end with three more crushing Yankees victories in New York. Stengel might not return to leave a tip for the fellow who picked up the towels and packed his bags.

"You think we might not get back, huh?" Stengel asked. "Now don't you worry none. If we don't get back here, I've got your name and address. I'll do right by everybody. Got my own bank, ya know."

But the attendant had reason for his concern, as did Danny Murtaugh. Bob Friend had consoled himself with the thought that the rout had been an aberration. "Maybe it can work in our favor," he said. "I mean you can't expect them to score a lot of runs again."

They did not score sixteen in Game Three at Yankee Stadium. Just ten. Ford, starting at last, shut the Pirates out on four hits. "We Still Can't Believe It," wailed the front-page headline in the *Pittsburgh Post-Gazette;* "Bucs Are Better Than That!"

But even the several thousand Pirates faithful who had traveled east were having their doubts. They had every reason to expect Ford to have a good day and were not necessarily surprised to see Mantle's four hits, including yet another home run. But there was no explaining Bobby Richardson. The Yankees' second baseman fielded well, and generally that was enough to satisfy Stengel. By the time he came to bat in the bottom of the first, the bases were loaded and the Yankees led 3–0. The Pirates' starter, Vinegar Bend Mizell, was already gone, and in his place stood Clem Labine, who had been the best reliever in the game when he pitched for Brooklyn. But the Dodgers had since let him go, and so had Detroit before Brown picked him up for late-season help in the bullpen. He was fighting the flu but would not admit it.

Richardson had been ordered to bunt, the thought being that, given his meager contributions at the plate, he still could sacrifice a run home and leave things to the beefy fellows. But the attempts failed. Labine ran the count full and Richardson had no choice but to swing away. He hoped he would not hit into a double play.

His grand slam was only the seventh in series play and effectively ended things in the first, leaving one spectator, Indian prime minister Jawaharlal Nehru, with little to commend his first baseball game. Yankee Stadium was once again a full and happy place; New York now led the series two games to one, and the oddsmakers boosted the Yankees' chances of winning to 5–1.

As for Richardson, who cemented his moment of stardom by driving in two more runs, he confessed that he hadn't been as excited since 1956, when his minor-league manager, Ralph Houk, gave him ten days off to get married. His teammates were generous with their praise, considering that he had never before been singled out for so much attention. They talked about his religious faith, his ability to take some ribbing, and his having excused himself from the team's pennant-clinching party in Boston to speak at a church banquet.

"He made me look good, didn't he?" said Stengel.

So did Ford—so good that Stengel, who usually treated his left-hander gingerly, and who regretted not pulling Turley early in the Game Two rout, had nonetheless allowed Ford to pitch a full nine.

Game Four

It was Sunday, which meant that, in observance of a New York State law prohibiting play when church was an option, game time was set for 2:05 p.m. Still, this would not give Vernon Law time to attend services at the local Mormon church and get to the stadium in time for batting practice. Law had come to New York with his wife, Venita, and their five children, whose first names all began with the letter V. Rather than chance a late arrival, the Law family gathered for prayer in their hotel room. The *Pittsburgh Post-Gazette* had asked Law and several of his teammates to offer their thoughts under their own, ghosted bylines. Law took the occasion to explain that he was not one to pray for a win. Not that anyone would have blamed him, given that the Pirates had now been humiliated twice and were still stuck in the Bronx. Even so, Law did not believe such a prayer was seemly. "We prayed that no one on either side would get hurt and that everyone would do as well as possible," he wrote. "We did not pray for victory because that would be a selfish prayer."

Others in the Pittsburgh contingent, however, may have thought their prayers for rain—an extra day for Law to rest his aching ankle—would be answered. The skies over New York threatened and rain was forecast, along with temperatures in the sixties. But by game time, the clouds merely threatened and Stengel, taking a gamble on youth, sent Ralph Terry to the mound to see if he could put the Pirates at an impossible disadvantage. The Yankees were talking four in a row, and what better way for Stengel to shorten the odds of Topping's firing him than to take the series with two more routs?

Terry was all but perfect through the first four, striking out five and walking one. Skowron had staked him to a 1–0 lead on his fourth inning homer, but there was reason to believe that the Yankees' lead should have been far wider. They had had an early chance at Law and muffed it. Bob Cerv had led off the first with a single, and Kubek had doubled him to third. Maris flied out, but Mantle was up with two in scoring position and only one out. Berra would follow.

Baseball logic suggested that with one out and men on second and third it is not necessarily unwise to walk the most dangerous hitter in the lineup, assuming the risk of loading the bases for the chance of a double play. The logic was strained, however, when the batter to follow was Yogi Berra; no one, not even Mantle, had been better in big games—Berra held the record with sixty-four World Series hits. Murtaugh was, strictly speaking, playing it by the book by giving four wide ones to Mickey Mantle. Except that the book did not include a disclaimer should the next batter be an aging but still lethal clutch hitter. Murtaugh had exposed his team to the threat of an inning of catastrophic proportions.

Berra was a legendary bad-ball hitter; it was generally understood that the only pitch at which he would not swing was the one that went behind him. Everything else constituted his comfort zone. Law hitched at his trousers and fiddled with the resin bag and did himself a great favor by getting two quick strikes. He could now avoid the danger of throwing anything in the strike zone. He came back with a pitch low and away. Berra lunged at the ball, hitting it off the end of the bat. The Pirates' third baseman, Don Hoak, handled the ball deftly, stepped on the bag, and threw across the diamond, barely catching Berra. The rally was over before it started, and the Yankees had allowed the Deacon to wriggle away, a failure to act they would soon regret.

Terry's good fortune lasted into the fifth, and might have gone longer had the fates, once again, not put Law in the Yankees' path. Gino Cimoli led off with a single. Smoky Burgess, a doughy man saddled with bleeding ulcers, followed with a weak bouncer to first. Skowron was on the ball quickly; the prudent move would have been to take the sure out at first; Burgess was so slow he would have been out even if he had been riding a motorcycle to the bag. But the Moose was thinking about getting two and threw to Kubek at second, hoping to catch the lead runner. Cimoli, however, arrived before the ball and even with Burgess running, Kubek had no play at first. Two were on, none were out. Hoak came to bat, prepared to give himself up to move both men into scoring position. But he botched the bunt, popping it to second. Mazeroski was no more useful, popping out to first. Two out and the pitcher up, a reprieve in the making for Terry and Skowron.

Law was not without talent at the plate—which is to say that he was a decided upgrade from the likes of Bob Friend and Bob Turley. He had hit only .181 for the season, but now he doubled down the left-field line, scoring Cimoli. Bill Virdon's single scored Burgess and Law, and the Pirates were up 3–1.

The Pirates threatened again in the seventh, and once again Law found himself in the middle of things. Hoak led off with a single, and Mazeroski sacrificed him to second. Law's single to left completed Terry's day. With runners on first and third, Stengel summoned Bobby Shantz, who quickly dispatched Virdon and Groat.

All the baserunning was now taking a toll on Law's ankle. In the bottom of the seventh, Skowron led off for the Yankees with a double. McDougald singled but Skowron held at third, wisely choosing not to test Clemente's arm in right. He was rewarded for his prudence by scoring on Richardson's grounder. The Pirates now led by only a run and when pinch hitter Johnny Blanchard singled, Murtaugh called on Elroy Face.

Crucial moments had presented themselves to Stengel in the first and in the fifth, and each time he had been undone by Law. But the Deacon was gone, and though Face had been terrific all season long, Stengel had reason for hope the moment Cerv lit into his third pitch. The ball carried high and far and seemed destined to reach the outfield fence, and perhaps clear it. Virdon, who had robbed Berra in Game One, took off for the deepest recesses of Yankee Stadium. He was back quickly on the ball but needed to reach to feel for the fence. He began his jump early and hit the fence as he made the catch. He doubled over as he fell to the ground, ball in hand. The inning ended when Kubek, the next batter, grounded back to Face.

The Yankees would not threaten again. Maris, Mantle, and Berra went without a peep in the eighth, leaving them collectively hitless for the afternoon. The ninth passed uneventfully. By a score of 3–2, Pittsburgh had survived, barely. No matter who won on Monday, the teams would return to Forbes Field for a sixth game and perhaps a seventh. Casey Stengel, who had seen his opportunities to put the series away vanish, would be able to make good on his promise of a tip to the clubhouse attendant.

Game Five

Del Webb called his American League expansion committee to a secret meeting after Game Four and again the following morning. Their National League counterparts, under Walter O'Malley's direction, were scheduled to meet in a week to choose their new cities, and Webb and his people had reason for concern. Despite Warren Giles's rumination before Game Two, New York now appeared poised to be invited back into the National League. The American Leaguers would have to move quickly if they hoped to grab Houston, generally regarded as the second most lucrative prize among the Continental League cities.

As it happened, George Kirksey, who was in town for the World

Series, had run into Webb in the lobby of the Waldorf-Astoria. Webb wanted to know his intentions. "I thought for a minute he was going to invite us to join the American League," Kirksey later recalled, "but he had no definite information on what the American League was going to do." Kirksey went on to observe that while he favored admission to the American League—given the prospect of the Yankees coming to town—Craig Cullinan leaned toward the National League. In fact, Kirksey had paid a call on Walter O'Malley to tell him that Houston was prepared to commit to the National League, if the league would commit to him.

O'Malley, he said, looked at him for "what seemed like hours" before he finally replied, "All right."

Casey Stengel, meanwhile, was again suffering from an acute bout of ambivalence in choosing his starting pitcher for Game Five. He had gone to sleep on Sunday night having settled on Bill Stafford. Stafford, who had recently turned twenty-one, had won three times and lost only once since graduating to the big club in August. Stengel was so impressed with his pitching that he did not spare the praise when he invited the writers to share his thinking. "I ain't afraid to start that kid," he said. "Green pea. Keeps the ball low. Lotsa nerve. Keeps the ball low. Don't get scared. Good fast ball. Keeps the ball low. Cool customer which I ain't afraid to start but we'll see which way the thing rolls." Stafford, then, would be his man. Or was until Monday morning, when Stengel woke up thinking Art Ditmar.

He had staked so much on Ditmar in Game One when he chose him over Ford, defying conventional wisdom and the secret wishes of his players. Ditmar may have failed him, but he had pitched well at the Stadium, and the Yankees were not up a game, which, Stengel later explained, would have favored young Stafford. Instead they were tied at two games apiece, which meant that Stengel would go with experience over the promise of youth.

The skies were clear at game time. The temperature rose to a comfortable seventy-two degrees. Yet, the Monday afternoon crowd of sixty-two thousand was smaller than that of the day before—and more than seven thousand fewer than the number who had come to see Game Three. This would soon prove to be a mercy to those who stayed away and thus were spared the sight of Stengel's mortification.

Ditmar dispatched the Pirates without a blemish in the first. But in the second he was undone by his third baseman, Gil McDougald, whom Stengel had been starting ever since he had thrown over Clete Boyer in Game One. Dick Stuart had led off the inning with a single but was forced out at second by Gino Cimoli. Smoky Burgess followed by doubling down the right-field line, moving Cimoli to third and putting Don Hoak in a position to drive in two. But Hoak grounded to Kubek at short. Both runners had taken off, Cimoli toward home and Burgess to third. Kubek saw that Burgess would be the easier target and so he turned and threw to McDougald.

McDougald had been Stengel's ideal of a useful ballplayer; he could play almost anywhere in the field and hit anywhere in the lineup—and he had done so very well ever since his Rookie of the Year season in 1951. Burgess should have been a dead duck at third, but McDougald, anxious to make the tag, rushed the play and dropped the ball. The throw was true, he later said; the fault was his alone.

One run was in and the Pirates had runners at the corners. Mazeroski was up next, and this time all McDougald could do was watch Mazeroski's high bouncer sail over his head down the left-field line for a double. Now Pittsburgh led 3–0 as Stengel climbed the dugout steps, too late to make amends for his early morning change of heart about Ditmar and Stafford.

The Yankees nicked Pittsburgh's aging starter, Harvey Haddix, for runs in the second and third, but otherwise he was steadfast. Pittsburgh, which had scored again in the top of the third, led 4–2 when Murtaugh came to fetch the tiring Haddix with two on and a man out in the home seventh. Once again, he summoned Elroy Face, who made quick work of McDougald and Maris. Face surrendered just a walk in the eighth, and he was perfect in the ninth after the Pirates had scored again—his third save in three tries. Pittsburgh, which had been awaiting interment forty-eight hours earlier, had carried the day 5–2 and now stood a win away from a most improbable championship.

In the clubhouse, Stengel would not rip his starter. Nor would he take a hit for choosing him. "There was nothing wrong with starting Ditmar or with his pitching," he said. "They were bouncing balls through the holes and over heads and our fielders didn't field too good behind him, either."

Someone asked if it was fair to describe the Yankees plight as "desperate."

"You can call it that if you like," replied Stengel. "I won't. But I can count, you know."

That night ten thousand people descended upon Pittsburgh's airport to welcome the Pirates home, even though the police chief had warned them to stay away. And in Glendale, California, vandals burned the letters P-I-T-T into the lawn in front of Casey Stengel's home.

A sign, like stigmata, of his suffering. And perhaps an omen, too.

Game Six

Casey Stengel had played and managed in 4,565 major-league baseball games. If this was to be his last, the writers wanted to mark the occasion. The night before, thirty-eight of them had gathered to draft the resolution they were now prepared to present to Stengel. They approached the dugout, for once, not to listen. Stengel took the document and began to read: "We, the members of the Baseball Writers' Association . . . do hereby petition Charles Dillon (Casey) Stengel to renounce any and all plans for retirement, to return as manager of the New York Yankees and to remain as long as good health and enjoyment of the work permits."

He did not rush to speak. The writers could see that his eyes were welling up with tears. "Well," he said at last, "this is a wonderful thing. It's nice to know . . ." He stopped himself and waited a while until he was prepared to go on.

The tributes had begun appearing the day before. The *Times* scoured its morgue and unearthed the story of his last great moment as a player:

thirty-seven years ago to the day, when his home run gave the Giants a two games to one lead over the Yankees in the 1923 World Series. He was thirty-three years old—"excess baggage," went the game story, "with bad legs and a wornout body. But Casey still had the batting eye and he could sock the ball." His homer was the day's only run. "As he jogged around the bases his big frame waddled from side to side like a bear. There was a suggestion of swagger about it, and as he came triumphantly down the third base line success went to Stengel's head and he thumbed his nose at Sam Jones, the Yankee pitcher. Still, the crowd forgave that, and then paid tribute, not of a vast, cataclysmic roar, but of a half-stunned inarticulate rumble."

Perhaps the most honest and heartfelt words now came from an old antagonist, Leonard Shecter of the *Post*, whom Stengel had berated in the clubhouse in the midst of the 1959 tailspin. Yet Shecter, like all the rest, was grateful for Stengel's time, quotes, and company. The old man, he began, had been driving the beat fellows to distraction, hinting at starting Ford in the opener before going with Ditmar, and then on Monday, ditching Stafford for the benighted Ditmar. "What does all this mean?" he asked, rhetorically. "That Stengel is a mean old man who has little left after living 70 years on this earth that he can think of nothing better to do than confuse the newspaper industry? Not a bit. Stengel is the most enchanting man we have ever had the good fortune to encounter." Stengel, he went on, was a man of parts, "a lovable curmudgeon" and "spellbinding raconteur" but "also mean, nasty, selfish and egotistic," which, in the end, left Shecter to conclude that "if he was any other way, he couldn't be so damn charming."

If this was to be the final game of his final season, Shecter did not believe that Stengel wished it so. "We can't help but think," he wrote, "that Stengel doesn't want to go."

Casey Stengel had met with his players before the team's off-day workout at Forbes Field. He had gathered them in the clubhouse to bid farewell; he might not have another chance. "By the time I get through talking with you fellers after a game my players are back in their hotels," he told the writers. "I told my players they had a good year, except for the last two games."

But he still had a game to prepare for and decisions to make. If this was to be a farewell performance, he was not inclined to disappoint. "It could be Turley or Ford," he announced, "and it could even be both of them."

Both?

"I can't pick the man on enthusiasm alone. He's got to have the skills to go with it. Now, should it be Turley with five days' rest or Ford with three? The man has pitched for me for ten years and he's pitched good for me and I know if I ask him he'll pitch with one day's rest. He's an amazing man to have around. And if I started either one, then switched to the other one and everyone would be asking who's gonna be my pitcher on Thursday and I would have to say Stafford and, oh yes, Mantle is hurt and I told him not to do any running today in the workout, but I expect him to play tomorrow." He paused for breath. "I've got to build up my defense. Who's gonna be in my outfield and who's gonna be in my infield? What about the catcher? I'm not saying. Now, if you ask me position by position, you'd know, but I ain't gonna say."

The writers listened as he made a case for playing a man only to argue against it. And when he was done, they returned to their hotel, and there, on the bulletin board, they found a note from Walter O'Malley. Houston, it proclaimed, had joined New York in formally applying to join the National League. "The Houston announcement," read the memo, "should bring the problem of expansion to a head. This is one city that has strong consideration by the committee. The Houston people still have some problems to work out but I am sure they will qualify."

Just as he had agreed with Craig Cullinan.

"Now I hope the Continental people in New York will meet with the Yankee management and discuss the possibility of a National League franchise in New York," O'Malley's note went on. "This would complete the expansion program of the National League."

The response from the Yankees came the following day. Del Webb announced that the American League had received eighteen applications for its two expansion slots, which meant that the commitment to the Continental League clubs was fraying. He would not handicap the likely winners. The early line, however, liked Dallas–Fort Worth and

Minneapolis–St. Paul. Webb said nothing about Los Angeles, and nor, for the moment, did anyone else. Jack Kent Cooke, meanwhile, had written to Ford Frick, seeking a Toronto franchise in the American League.

Stengel was so pleased with the petition that he showed it to the out-of-town writers, who were chiefly concerned with the identity of his starter. Murtaugh was again turning to Bob Friend, whose hanging curveball had unleashed the furies in Game Two. Stengel did not have the luxury of thinking of a seventh game. He would go with his winner, Ford, on three days' rest. Tomorrow, after all, might never come.

Elston Howard would catch; Berra would play left. McDougald was out at third, and in his place was Clete Boyer, who led off the game by grounding back to Friend, an inauspicious start. Kubek and Maris went quickly, and it did Stengel's heart no good when Virdon opened the bottom of the first with a single. Dick Groat, however, offered the best possible salve by grounding into a double play, which left the bases empty when Clemente singled. Ford then struck out Dick Stuart to spare his manager further discomfort.

The Yankees appeared poised for big things in the top of the second when Berra walked, Skowron singled, and Howard reached first after being hit on the hand. But the errant pitch was a costly one, breaking Howard's pinkie and ending his series. Still, the bases were loaded for Richardson, the Game Two hero. His fly ball, however, was too shallow to allow Berra to tag. Ford, however, salvaged the inning by singling home the run and giving himself a 1–0 lead.

Stengel's reprieve began in top of the third and happened with the sudden ferocity for which his teams were known and feared. Friend hit Kubek. Maris doubled him to third. Mantle singled them both home. Berra singled Mantle to third. And just like that, Friend was gone. The Yankees, however, had not completed their work. Mantle scored on Skowron's fly ball to center. Johnny Blanchard, in for the injured Howard, singled Berra to second. And once again, Bobby Richardson came to bat. His triple scored two and stretched the Yankee lead to 6–0.

Richardson tripled in the seventh, too, once again making a victim of Clem Labine as he drove in his twelfth run of the series, a record. When he scored on Ford's bunt, the Yankees had extended their lead to ten, which they padded with another two runs by the time Pittsburgh's Hal Smith grounded into a game-ending double play.

In the clubhouse, Ford insisted he was not as sharp as he had been in Game Three; he had given up seven hits and Stengel had felt compelled to visit the mound in the fifth inning when the Pirates had two men on with no one out. "He wanted me to slow down, mainly. He wanted time for the pitchers in the bullpen to warm up and he wanted me to work slower," Ford said. "You see the men warming up and you think if you hurry up and get them out, he might not take you out of the game. But you're wrong."

Stengel kept him in for the fifth and made no changes even when the game was all but won. He let Ford complete his shutout. He had pitched wonderfully when, in truth, it was least needed. Ford would be in the bullpen for Game Seven, although, he said, he would not play the hero, offering to pitch when he felt he had nothing. Five innings of work, he would later say, finished a man for pitching the following day.

He had not quite forgiven Stengel for holding him out of the opener, although, he would later say, "You couldn't get mad at Casey very long." They had been together for ten years and Ford was familiar with Stengel's ways, like the knowing wink that followed the scolding. Two weeks earlier, he had gushed about Stengel to Leonard Koppett of the *Post*. "I love that old man," Ford had said. "Some of the fellows give him a hard time now and then and you can get awfully mad at him sometimes but I just love him. He knows so much and he fights so hard. I'm glad we won this for his sake."

With Game Six won, Stengel now worked his way through the clubhouse crowd and extended a hand to Ford. He had survived, for a day at least, and was not feeling cautious about the men he knew wanted him out. "You done a very good job for your owners," he told Ford. "They'll receive a little money now."

"What do you mean?" Ford asked.

"You done it for them," Stengel replied. "You made it go seven games and they made a lot of money."

Stengel smiled at Ford. "But you didn't get it, did you?" he said. "All you got is a lot of bushwah."

He had applied the needle. But Stengel was otherwise in no mood to gloat or preen. Instead he wanted to give credit where he felt it was due.

"He saved me," he said of his ace, "that's all."

Game Seven

He would start Bob Turley over Bill Stafford. He would send Yogi Berra to left field. Johnny Blanchard would catch. He would play Clete Boyer at third; all the rest would remain the same, for the moment. Casey Stengel would hand his lineup card to the home-plate umpire, return to the dugout, and assume his accustomed viewing stance, leaning on the leg he perched on the top step. Then he would do as he had done thirteen hundred times in Brooklyn and Boston and nineteen hundred times in New York and all the many times in Toledo, Kansas City, Milwaukee, and Oakland: he would wait to see if his players could prove his decisions were wise.

Pittsburgh was unseasonably warm, and unlike New York, where seats at the Stadium had gone wanting, the overnight crowd still gathered outside Forbes Field for tickets. They filed in and took their seats after writing their names and addresses on the sheet outside the box office, so that they would not lose touch with one another when the series ended, sometime that afternoon.

Stengel's pitchers, starters and relievers alike, crowded into the bullpen, knowing he would not wait to call on them the moment Turley stumbled.

The moment came quickly. Murtaugh's starter, Vernon Law, the winner of Games One and Four, worked an uneventful first. But with two out in the bottom of the inning, Turley ran the count full on Bob Skinner before losing him to a base on balls. Rocky Nelson stepped in. Nelson was a legend, though of minor-league proportions; he was thirty-five years old, a veteran of parts of eight major-league seasons distinguished by his inability to replicate the remarkable numbers he had amassed in the minors—234 home runs, three Most Valuable Player awards, and a .319 batting average.

Nelson's batting stance suggested the boxing pose of John L. Sullivan, hands held close to his face and his right foot at an unorthodox ninety-degree angle to the left. It had not served him especially well in his stops with the Cardinals, Pirates, White Sox, Dodgers, and Indians. Joe Brown had picked him up in 1959 as a backup first baseman to Dick Stuart, whose vanity was matched by fielding so poor there was little to be gained and much to be lost by playing him when he wasn't hitting. In the series, Stuart had three hits in twenty times at bat, all the evidence Murtaugh needed to start Nelson in Game Seven. Turley ran the count on Nelson to two balls and a strike, the last a call that displeased Nelson so much he squawked to the umpire. Turley's next pitch arrived high in the strike zone, the one place Stengel had warned his pitchers to avoid. Nelson met it flush, driving it over the wall in right, sending Skinner home ahead of him. Rocky Nelson had been playing baseball professionally for eighteen years and had never hit a bigger home run. Pittsburgh led 2–0.

Smoky Burgess's single leading off the second ended Turley's day. Stengel summoned Stafford, handed him the ball, and returned to the dugout, careful, as always, to avoid stepping on the foul line; his luck had so far been bad enough. Stafford began his afternoon by walking Hoak on four pitches, and then he allowed the bunting Mazeroski to outrace his throw to first, loading the bases. Stengel's superstitious tick, however, appeared to work when Law, so good with the bat in Game Four, grounded back to Stafford who threw to Blanchard who then threw to first to complete the double play. Two were on and two were out for Bill Virdon, whose hitting had so far been eclipsed by his fielding. His single, however, drove in Hoak and Mazeroski. Stengel was now down by four, and it was only the second inning.

Skowron brought him a run closer when he homered to lead off the fifth. Pittsburgh had been unable to press its advantage against Bobby Shantz, whom Stengel had sent in to relieve Stafford in the third and who had so far retired the nine men he had faced. Murtaugh, meanwhile, had ordered Face to begin warming up. Law's ankle still throbbed and Murtaugh, seeing how he favored it, worried that if he pushed the Deacon

much longer he risked lasting injury. But Law retired the next three batters without incident, and when he came to bat in the bottom of the fifth
narrowly missed a homer of his own.

His undoing came in the sixth. Richardson led off with a single, and
when Law walked Kubek, Murtaugh decided he could go no further. He
had Harvey Haddix warm up, too, but had said before the game that he
would not hesitate to call on Face early. Murtaugh had been unusually
philosophical before the game, going so far as to quote from Kipling.
"The tumult and the shouting dies," he had said, reciting from "Reces-
sional." "The captains and the kings depart." As if on cue, Law left to a
standing ovation. In came Face, to happy applause.

It did not last. Face got Maris to foul out to Hoak, but Mantle's single
just past Groat's mitt scored Richardson, with Kubek moving to third.
Yogi Berra stood in. He fouled off Face's first pitch and then drove the
second over the wall in right. In the all-too-familiar blink of an eye, the
Yankees had gone ahead, 5–4. What could be better, Red Smith wrote
that day, than for the pivotal moment in Stengel's last game to feature
Berra as the agent of his vindication—"how sweet that it should be a gift
from Yogi, the only Yankee who was a Yankee when Casey arrived in
New York, the only one who has shared his triumph and disaster since
1949."

But the sentiment was premature; the game would not be settled
here. Casey Stengel's longest afternoon was just beginning.

Shantz preserved the illusion of normalcy through the sixth and seventh, retiring every man he faced save one. But even Smoky Burgess's
leadoff single in the seventh went for naught when Hoak lined to Berra
and Mazeroski hit into a double play. The base hit, however, was not
meaningless; only when the game was done would its true significance be
understood. Because Burgess was a liability on the base paths, Murtaugh
had replaced him with a pinch runner, Joe Christopher, and in the top of
the eighth with a new catcher, Hal Smith. It was an unremarkable change
of personnel that would set in motion a chain of events that no one could
have foreseen, not even the wizened man in the visiting dugout who
stood six outs from a championship.

In the top of the eighth, Face dispatched Maris and Mantle but lost
Berra to a base on balls. Skowron then sent a bouncer toward third that

Hoak fielded. The play, however, unfolded too slowly for Hoak to force Berra at second or to get Skowron at first, and the Yankees had two on for Johnny Blanchard. His single scored Berra. Then Boyer, showing Stengel that he could be as able with a bat as he was with a glove, doubled Skowron home. New York led 7–4, and Forbes Field grew quiet as the game headed toward a conclusion so predictable it felt preordained: the Yankees were going to win, as they always did.

Gino Cimoli pinch-hit for Face to open the home eighth and singled to right. Virdon took a strike on the outside corner and then committed the worst possible offense by sending a double-play ball straight to Kubek at short.

Years later, Kubek, a thoughtful and perceptive man, would be pressed to recall ever witnessing—let alone fielding—a bad hop like the one that now took flight toward him. No one could. Because this hop was headed not for his glove—as he intended—or for his chest, which would have been a bad though not unheard-of event, but straight for the small and therefore easy-to-miss target of his Adam's apple.

The ball caught Kubek flush on the neck. He was down quickly and could feel his mouth filling with blood. He grabbed his throat. He could not talk. His windpipe was swelling but he felt no pain. Richardson rushed to him, followed by Blanchard, the trainers, Mantle, and Stengel.

Kubek, who left the field to a round of applause, was on his way to the hospital; with Cimoli at second and Virdon at first, Joe DeMaestri came in to play shortstop for the Yankees.

"The bad hop," Mel Allen told his audience on NBC, "gives the Pirates a new lease on life."

Shantz now faced Groat, the National League batting champion who had had a decent, though hardly spectacular, series at the plate. Shantz's first pitch came inside and nicked the corner for a strike, a call with which Groat took issue. Shantz came inside again, further this time and Groat jumped back to avoid being hit. His third pitch was again inside, but this one caught too much of the plate and Groat was on it. His grounder skipped past Clete Boyer, scoring Cimoli and cutting the Yankees' lead to two.

Stengel had squeezed all he could from Shantz and wanted Jim Coates to face Bob Skinner, a counterintuitive move: Skinner, like Shantz, was a lefty, and the advantage would presumably be with the pitcher. But convention, in Stengel's approach, existed only to be defied. He wanted a ground ball and Coates, he would later say, "had his sinker and his slider ready." So in he came.

Skinner squared and bunted. Boyer threw him out, but not before the runners advanced. Coates now had one man down but runners on second and third and another lefty to face in Rocky Nelson. Coates subscribed to the belief that no home run was to be left unpunished. He was not about to hit Nelson and put a second runner on base. But he was not averse, now or ever, to letting a man experience the menacing rush of a fastball under the chin. Nelson jumped back as the pitch approached and almost lost his balance. Coates decided to come inside again, but this time Nelson was prepared. His fly ball to Maris, however, was too shallow to score Virdon. There were two outs for the next batter, Roberto Clemente.

The Yankees had decided that Clemente could be bullied with pitches that threatened to hit him and that he, like Berra, had such an expansive view of the strike zone that he could be induced to swing at most anything. So while Coates's sensibilities might have suggested at least one pitch at the skull, he chose to work Clemente away. Clemente fouled off Coates's first pitch and the second and broke his bat on the third. The bat boy brought him a replacement, but Clemente declined the offer and instead retreated to the dugout to find something more to his liking. He did not choose propitiously.

His bouncer bled toward first, a rally killer. Skowron was on it quickly and, ball in hand, rose and turned to throw to first and end the inning. But no one was there.

It should have been Coates; it did not take a spring semester in Stengel's academy to know that when the first baseman fields a ball, the pitcher covers the bag. Coates, however, had other ideas; "I thought," he would say years later, "I could get the ball." If Skowron yelled, "I got it," he went on, he never heard him over the din. "Maybe I should have gone to the bag." He broke late, and Clemente was there before him. Virdon scored. The Yankees now led 7–6, and Coates returned to the mound to face Hal Smith, the backup catcher who had replaced Smoky Burgess.

The Yankees had originally signed Smith and had run him through their farm clubs before sending him to Baltimore in 1955. He stayed for a year before moving to Kansas City, where he played well enough to draw the interest of Joe Brown, who needed a catcher who could hit and spell Burgess. In 1960, Smith had hit .295 with eleven home runs in the seventy-seven games he played, a good man with a bat though not one to inspire fear in an opposing pitcher. Coates's first pitch was a called strike. Smith wailed and missed at the next one, a high fastball. Coates came back higher still for ball one. Smith liked Coates's fourth offering but changed his mind and checked his swing. Still, Coates would later say, "Two and two, it's my count. Not his." It was time, as he put it, to change Smith's "eye level" by throwing something lower in the strike zone. Coates's pitch crossed the plate across from Smith's belt and as it did he swung. The bat, Smith would later say, did not vibrate in his hands, a sensation that occurred only in those rare moments when a bat meets a ball perfectly. "Doggone it," Smith told himself, "that's great."

Berra watched the ball sail over the wall in left. As Smith reached second, he could see the fans cheering for him. "Oh man," he told himself, "what have I done?"

Clemente was waiting at home to lift him in the air. The Pirates now led 9–7 and needed only three outs in the ninth to make their comeback complete. The task would fall to Bob Friend.

To this point, Casey Stengel had made only three managerial decisions since play began. He had replaced Turley with Stafford, who had surrendered two runs. He had then brought in Shantz, who might have escaped untouched were it not for Kubek's unfortunate encounter with Virdon's bouncer. Stengel had broken with standard practice by bringing in Coates to face a lefty and had paid the price with Coates's failure to cover first on Clemente's dribbler. Stengel made his fourth pitching change in the eighth, after Smith's home run. Stengel trudged back to the mound to fetch Coates and waited there long enough to hand the ball to Ralph Terry.

Terry was not, strictly speaking, a reliever, but like every Yankees pitcher he was expected to be available. Stengel had not been sure of what use to make of him but wanted him ready just the same. Terry had warmed up with Stafford and then with Shantz and then a third time with Coates, only to sit each time. He would be up five times before Stengel finally called for him. His arm was a little tired, and as his warm-up pitches sailed high he understood that he had grown too accustomed to the smaller and lower mound in the bullpen. His first batter of the afternoon was Don Hoak, who lifted a fly ball to Berra in left field to end the eighth inning. An out, but a disconcerting one, on a pitch too high for comfort.

The Yankees came to bat in the ninth to face Bob Friend, the Game Six starter they had treated so roughly the day before—five hits and five runs. But now Friend sought the ultimate redemption, to be the man on the mound at the last out of the World Series.

"Bob, keep the ball down to this guy," Hal Smith told Friend as Bobby Richardson stepped in.

"I know it," he replied.

Richardson took a pitch for a strike and then blooped a single to left, his eleventh hit of the series.

Stengel sent in Dale Long to pinch-hit for Joe DeMaestri. And he sent word to the bullpen to have Ford begin throwing.

Long fouled off Friend's first pitch and drove the second to right for a single. Danny Murtaugh came to the mound.

"Let's bring Haddix in," he said. Friend surrendered the ball.

"Good year," said Murtaugh, meaning it.

Mel Allen introduced Harvey Haddix by reminding viewers of the Pittsburgh pitcher's singular, heartbreaking achievement: in May 1959 he had thrown twelve perfect innings in a game against Milwaukee, only to lose in the thirteenth.

Haddix started Maris with a ball, low and away, before getting him to pop up to Smith for the first out. Maris flung his bat and Mantle stepped in.

Mantle already had two hits on the day and had driven in a run. He took Haddix's first pitch for a ball, low and away. He sent the second to right, a single that scored Richardson and sent Long to third, cutting the Pirates' lead to one. Berra was up, and only after Haddix tried to get him to chase a ball low and away did Stengel send in McDougald to run for Long.

Berra let Haddix's second pitch go for ball two but could not resist the third. His shot down the line came quickly to Rocky Nelson at first, who was hugging the line to keep Mantle close to the bag.

Nelson had played 351 major-league games at first base, and while not known for his defense, generally fielded his position without incident. He did not make mistakes, but nor was he regarded as an asset in the field, and perhaps that is the most generous way of explaining what he now chose to do. Nelson fielded Berra's shot deftly. And then he stepped on first. A prudent play but not a bold one. The better play, the game ender, would have been to throw to second to retire Mantle, and be ready to take the return throw that would complete the double play. But by stepping on first, Nelson had retired Berra, precluding the possibility of forcing Mantle. He would have to be tagged out.

Mantle knew this. He also knew that he had made a dreadful mistake. He had drifted too far off the bag and now stood in limbo as he faced Nelson, who had the ball and the game in his hands and the chance to make good.

For a moment the two men looked at each other. And then Mantle dove for the bag. Nelson was a moment late in applying the tag. Mantle was safe. McDougald had scored from third. The game was tied at nine.

Skowron had the chance to put New York ahead. But his grounder to Groat forced Mantle at second.

Forbes Field had been noisy with anticipation when the inning began and had roared with Friend's first strike against Richardson. But the succession of Yankees base hits had so stilled the crowd that the public address announcer's voice soon sounded like a clarion against the quiet. Friend had departed to a sprinkling of boos, and Haddix had been welcomed with hopeful applause. People screamed at Berra's shot to Nelson and moaned when Mantle evaded Nelson's tag. Skowron's groundout was accompanied not with cheers but with what sounded like a collective sigh.

Now, as Bill Mazeroski stood in to lead off the bottom of the ninth, the stadium fell silent.

In the Pirates' dugout, Dick Groat took his helmet and bat; he was scheduled to bat fourth in the inning. Dick Stuart waited on deck to pinch-hit for Haddix. Vernon Law stood in the tunnel between the dugout and clubhouse. Clem Labine, still feeling fluish, was in the trainer's room. In his box, Joe Brown, the general manager, turned the point of his pencil toward the field. Brown used the pencil to keep score and also to see if it might somehow jinx the visiting team by turning the point away when they batted.

Ralph Terry completed his warm-up pitches and still could not seem to get the ball to stay down. He had, by his own admission, been lucky on the fly ball that retired Hoak in the eighth; the pitch, he would later say, had nothing on it.

His first pitch to Mazeroski sailed high for a ball. Blanchard walked halfway out to the mound and yelled, "Fire it in there."

And so he did.

Labine could hear the crowd and raced from the trainer's room to the field. Law had been closer and was already on the first dugout step as he saw Berra move back on the ball in left field only to stop and watch as it sailed over the fence. Mazeroski began his leaping run around the bases, pinwheeling his arm, a group of fans already in pursuit as he rounded third.

Ralph Terry did not linger on the mound. He walked through the dugout into the clubhouse, and when he saw the attendant he asked for a beer. He had wanted a Schlitz but the attendant gave him a local brew. He wanted to talk to Stengel. He was grateful to Stengel for seeing good things in him and for offering early, wise advice: "This is a serious business. This is a serious job. I want you to take it seriously." He found Stengel in his office, his uniform shirt off.

"What's up, kid?" Stengel asked. "How were you trying to pitch him?"

"I couldn't get the ball where I wanted, Casey," Terry replied.

"As long as you pitch you're not going to get the ball where you wanted," said Stengel. "Forget it, kid."

Absolution.

Stengel kept the clubhouse door locked for fifteen minutes, and when the writers at last came in they found him smoking a cigarette and drinking a beer.

They wanted to know his thoughts about the game. But more important, they wanted to know whether he had decided that this would be his last one.

"I won't say anything about the future," he told them. "I'm going to decide what I'm going to do later in October. I've got a lot of things to find out first."

The writers, spotting Dan Topping, tried him, too, but without success. "I won't talk about it now," he said and not warmly.

It was all but impossible to squeeze through the door and into the bedlam of the Pittsburgh clubhouse. Mazeroski admitted that he had guessed on the pitch. His teammates poured a good deal of champagne on one another's heads and consumed a good deal more. It was a loud and happy place. One by one, the players, their manager, their general manager, and even the mayor paraded to the microphone where Pirates announcer Bob Prince asked them to describe their feelings to a "coast-to-coast" television audience. Everyone said they were very happy, and that things were great and "unbelievable." Their effervescent joy offered a convincing argument for the narrative strength of tragedy over comedy.

Stengel and his men dressed and boarded their bus. As they pulled away from the ballpark, the streets were becoming all but impassable. The crowd had surged onto the field, chasing Mazeroski home, and when he ducked into the clubhouse, they set to work grabbing the bases and fighting to pry up home plate, which was finally wrested away by Alex DeMao, a tavern keeper. Boys wrestled behind home, and people in the cheap seats threw paper onto the field. Church bells pealed and air-raid sirens wailed as people ran out onto the streets. Men and women raced to the roofs of office buildings, where they began to drink and toss paper onto the streets. Within a half hour, downtown Pittsburgh was so crowded with people and confetti that trolley cars could no longer pass. The bars filled up so quickly that for the first time in anyone's memory, doormen were posted outside to keep the crowds at bay. The police issued an alert advising people to avoid downtown, but no one paid any mind. Office girls snake-danced through the streets, and the confetti was so deep it looked as if there had been a blizzard. Though the police detail was doubled, there was no stopping the tens of thousands of people who would not leave the city center as night began to fall.

Ralph Terry tried to get drunk on the plane back ride home. He drank double bourbons but to no effect; the adrenaline was still rushing and he still felt sober by the time the team arrived back in New York.

Whitey Ford had been unable to bring himself to talk to Stengel on the flight—so much for not being able to stay angry at Casey very long. "The way I was pitching," he wrote years later, "I know I would have beaten them three times and we would have been world champs again." Mantle, too, blamed Stengel for what he later called "the worst disappointment of my baseball career." He and his teammates were convinced that theirs was the better team and that the loss had been an avoidable fluke. "The truth is," Mantle later wrote, "Casey blew it by not using Whitey Ford in the opener."

Stengel had tinkered with his pitching, with his lineup, and with his substitutions, just as he always had. But too little of his plotting had succeeded, and for this he was punished, again and again, by having to witness the failures his choices had wrought. He had gambled with Ditmar in the opener and then watched what Ford accomplished with such command in Game Three. He gambled again with Ditmar over Stafford in Game Five, and then watched Stafford follow him with five shutout innings. He had humiliated Clete Boyer before he could even bat in Game One, and for his decision to pinch-hit Dale Long he was subjected to the dispiriting sight of Long's useless fly ball. But then Boyer played because of his glove, not his bat; yet, when Stengel finally decided to play him again he tripled in Game Six and doubled home a run in Game Seven. Every move was now open to question: Why did Stengel wait a pitch before dispatching McDougald to run for Long in the ninth inning of Game Seven? Why, by his own admission, didn't he pull Turley early in the Game Two rout, so he could save him for another day? Had he ordered Ralph Terry to warm up a few too many times in Game Seven?

All of which led to one question: had Stengel really blown the series by his decisions, or did the failure lie with the players he selected at key moments? The problem for Stengel was not one of execution—Murtaugh had made his share of questionable choices, too—but of forgetting that a manager's role was, in the end, limited by the performance of the men on the field and by factors that only the heavens controlled. How else to explain the bad hop that bloodied Tony Kubek's windpipe? But Casey Stengel had always managed his Yankees in the belief that his great intelligence and vast experience could overcome the vagaries and mysteries of the game. It was as if he could not tolerate simply letting his men play their game. But it had been and would always be *their* game, and there was just so much even a daring and clever fellow like Stengel could do to make it his. He had tried, this time perhaps too hard. And for his troubles he had lost at the very moment when winning was the only way he might somehow save his job.

And Then . . .

On the day after the series ended, Mayor Robert Wagner wired Walter O'Malley and the members of his expansion committee, offering an official reminder of New York's interest in restoring National League baseball to the city. "Our stadium project is past the drawing board stage in that the final plan and specifications will be ready for bidding by December 1, 1960," he wrote. "Your early indication that a franchise will be granted to New York would permit us to expedite our construction program." He recommended that if the committee had additional questions, it should contact Bill Shea.

Wagner had no reason to worry. On the morning of Monday, October 17, 1960, three years and nine days after O'Malley had announced that he was leaving Brooklyn and set in motion the chain of events that would compel the mayor to send Shea out in search of a team, which would lead a frustrated Shea to Branch Rickey, which would convince Shea of the wisdom of starting a third major league, which would draw the interest of cities across the country, which would raise the threat of congressional action, a reluctant O'Malley had finally decided to end his league's resistance to expansion and grant franchises to two cities, Houston and New York.

Warren Giles, as titular head of the league, made the announcement. "To all intents and purposes we are now a ten-team league," he said, "with operations beginning in 1962." The American League would meet the following week, amid rumors that it might renege on the deal that had been agreed upon in August in Chicago and would take no Continental League clubs. The American League—really, the Yankees—wanted Los Angeles as the price for the National League's return to New York. Walter O'Malley was not going to stop them, although he did not think it wise to rush. "I don't think it would be smart of them to move to Los Angeles right now, although I would not oppose it," he said. "I believe eventually they will come to the coast, but there are other fine cities which would make finer major league franchises."

The birth of the teams that would become the New York Mets and the Houston Colt .45s, however, was overshadowed almost immediately by more sensational news. The following morning, the Yankees summoned the press to the Savoy Hotel, down the block from their Fifth Avenue offices. The hotel's Salon Bleu was filled to capacity when Dan Topping and George Weiss walked in with Casey Stengel. The Yankees' manager wore a gray suit and a gray-and-white striped tie. He was not smiling. Topping, a statement in hand, put on his half-moon reading glasses.

"Two years ago," he began, "Stengel quite reluctantly signed a new two-year contract to manage the Yankees, with the understanding that after the first year he could retire if he desired to do so."

Which, as Stengel might have said, he did not desire.

"At that time, it was a question of his retirement from baseball and devoting more time to his personal affairs." But times had changed, Topping explained, and in the interim the Yankees had embarked on "a program for the eventual replacement of Casey. Naturally, this has been a difficult job." The program imposed a mandatory retirement age of sixty-five. Stengel was seventy, his contract was up, and it was now apparent that Topping would continue to speak of Stengel's tenure in the past tense. The Yankees, he concluded, would pay him $160,000 from the club's profit-sharing plan.

"Do you mean he's through?" asked a reporter.

Topping did not reply. Instead, he yielded the floor to Stengel, who did not appear at all at ease. He fidgeted with his tie and jacket and thrust his hands into his coat pockets. His rumble began slowly.

"Mr. Webb and Mr. Topping have started a program for the Yankees. They want to put in a youth program as an advanced way of keeping the club going," he said. "They needed a solution as to when to discharge a man on account of age. They have paid me off in full and told me my services are not desired any longer by this club. I told them if this was their idea not to worry about Mr. Stengel, he can take care of himself."

He had departed from the script. He, Topping, and Webb had met several days earlier, and the owners had walked away convinced that Stengel had agreed to retire. That, at least, was the plan. But now Stengel was warming to his familiar task.

"Casey," someone asked, "were you fired?"

"No," he shouted. "I wasn't fired. I was paid up in full." He was not laughing, although everyone else was. "Write anything you want. Quit, fired, whatever you please. I don't care."

Still, he wanted it understood—and he could be quite clear when the occasion warranted—that this had not been his choice. "Two or three days ago I don't know what was in the owners' minds," he said. "On meeting Topping and Webb I saw their plan and I said to them: if that's the way it is why go into my demands?

"I wanted to stay managing. At the end of the season I said to him"—he meant Topping—"'I know what your plans are and I know you want me out.'"

George Weiss remained silent. He was now sixty-six years old himself, and the writers understood that he was not long for his job, now that the club was Topping's. "Mr. Webb," said Stengel, "is now letting Mr. Topping run the club." The change had come gradually and in a manner Stengel had not appreciated. He had been hearing the criticism from above since 1958, though never directly. "I got a lot of it, which reached me through you writers and other people," he said, "and what it added up to was I didn't know beans about managing."

Webb was in Los Angeles, and when a reporter tracked him down he did not dispute Stengel on the division of labor. "Topping is the baseball man," he said. "I'm in the construction business but I'm co-owner of the club." Still, he was troubled by the suggestion that the parting had been something less than acceptable to Stengel. "He and Dan Topping and I mutually agreed that Stengel would retire," he said. After all, he went on, he was worried about the toll that age was taking on Stengel, for whom he offered the glowing tributes typically heard when the gold watch is being presented. "We all get to the age where we can't continue our jobs," he said. "In our construction firm the retirement age is 65. Stengel is past 70. Casey had a sick spell last season and at his age he might find the strain of managing too great for him. We felt we couldn't afford to get into a position of losing our manager through illness in the middle of the season."

But Stengel would have none of it. Age, he insisted, did not stop a man from doing his work. "Depends," he said, "on what a man can do."

The reporters wanted to know about his future.

"That's pretty personal," he told them. "However, Mrs. Stengel is my wife and she possibly would like me to get some money someplace else."

The questions came to an end and Stengel announced, "I'm gonna get a drink. Where's a drink?" He sat for a while with a group of reporters and told his stories until it was time for lunch with Topping and the other men with whom he had worked. "I'm taking a jet home, and I'm charging it to the club," he said. "A man gets his transportation paid for even if they don't want him anymore."

The press rallied to Stengel, and it was not surprising that the most trenchant interpretation of his dismissal came from the guardian of tradition, Dan Daniel. "Casey Stengel," he wrote, "was let go as manager of the Yankees today because he is 70."

Jimmy Cannon wrote an open letter to Joan Whitney Payson, beseeching her to hire Stengel to manage her new National League team—he suggested naming them "the New Yorkers."

"I am not asking you to engage Casey for sentimental purposes," he wrote. "Most of your players will be obscure kids or used-up old timers. Casey's the most famous man in baseball. He's the only box office manager in the game."

The other columnists took their shots at Topping, reminding those readers who might have forgotten of his privileged childhood and succession of wives. "By the fortunate circumstances of birth and inheritance Topping has never been fired," wrote Milton Gross in the *Post*, seizing upon the populist undercurrent of the story, which was, in truth, the tale of one millionaire firing another. "Reportedly he has been unsuccessful, vocationally and domestically, but the only penalty he has had to pay has been money, which happens to be the one thing Topping has to worry about least.

"Obviously Topping, who has had six wives, thinks he finally has become mature enough at 48 to run his baseball empire and thought Stengel no longer could do it without his overseer's hand."

But as Gross was soon to discover, this was Topping's moment, and in ways not limited to who would run his club.

The American League, which had been the quicker of the two circuits in placing impediments in the path of the Continentals, had moved glacially in staking its claims to the best of the new territories. It had lost Houston, even as its people insisted that they were far happier with the prospect of adding Minneapolis–St. Paul and Dallas–Fort Worth, which promised to build a stadium in Arlington, midway between the two cities. But losing Houston had been a blow, and as the American Leaguers prepared to gather in New York there was a growing sense that the league was contemplating such bold maneuvers as moving the Athletics from Kansas City to Los Angeles, and perhaps shifting the Cleveland Indians, too. The meeting was believed to be so riddled with complexity that it was expected to last two days.

But at the end of the first day, Joe Cronin emerged to announce that not only was his league expanding to ten teams but that it would not wait until 1962 to get started. Their new teams would begin play in April 1961, just six months away. But first Calvin Griffith had at long last been granted his wish of moving the Washington Senators to Minnesota. The league, well aware of how sensitive the nation's elected representatives had been at the prospect of losing the club they thought of as their own, moved quickly to place an expansion team in the nation's capital. The new club would be called the Washington Senators (the old Senators were now to be known as the Minnesota Twins) and would play in Griffith Stadium while the District of Columbia completed work on the new modern ballpark that Griffith had hoped might be built for him. For his troubles, however, Griffith would collect rent from the new club, whose owners were not yet known but would not, it was quite certain, come from the ranks of the Continental League.

Nor would the new owners in the league's second new outpost: Los Angeles, the city that Topping had insisted upon taking if the National League invaded New York. There was talk that the franchise might go to Hank Greenberg, the Hall of Fame player who was now Bill Veeck's partner in Chicago, or to a group headed by Kenyon Brown, a radio and television executive who had recently sold his 20 percent stake in the Detroit Tigers for one million dollars. In a sad irony, Mark Scott, who had approached Branch Rickey about Los Angeles joining the Continental League, had died several months earlier. A pity, because it now emerged that Los Angeles was indeed going to get a second big-league team.

"What was the use of waiting?" asked Del Webb. "We'd procrastinated too long as it was. We'd sent Hank Greenberg out to firm it up a month earlier."

Even as they talked up Dallas–Fort Worth.

"It wasn't a case of double crossing the NL," Webb continued. "But the NL saw a chance to tie up two cities, and they did it. Walter O'Malley got caught in his own trap. When his league grabbed off Houston and New York it forced us into action. We had to move fast. We had a realignment problem.

"Actually, we're in a better spot than the NL. They don't even have the ballparks. We do." He even had a manager in mind for Los Angeles, the banker from Glendale, Casey Stengel. "I'm not mad at Casey," he said. "I just hope he and Edna aren't mad at me and close my account at their bank."

The war that had begun with the owners against the Continental League had given way to a slugfest between the two established leagues for primacy in the most lucrative markets. And Webb, in his candor, made clear who the true and important combatants were. O'Malley had struck first, and he had now countered. O'Malley would be heard from again, and soon.

The big fellows were now at each other, which perhaps explained why little was made by the press of the American League's reneging on the terms agreed upon with the Continental League. One anonymous

American League official did not see the move to the West Coast as a betrayal. "Don't forget," he told the *New York Times*, "that so-called commitment was nothing more than a recommendation by the two expansion committees." So where were the Continentals going to take their beef? To the commissioner?

Still, Branch Rickey, whose name had all but vanished from the sports pages in the weeks since the death of his league, emerged, loud and furious. "The action of the American League at its recent meeting was a very great disappointment," he said. "The National League 'kept its word' and, I am sure, will continue to 'keep its word,' by selecting two additional teams from the Continental group. Surely, the American League must do likewise."

But only he and Shea—who called the American League's action "one of the lowest blows in the history of sport"—were troubled. In Minneapolis, Wheelock Whitney, whose ownership group had lost the chance for a franchise with the Senators' move, pronounced himself "elated."

"We are ready to do everything possible to help Griffith make a success of his new move," he said. And in Dallas, J. W. Bateson, whose city had gotten nothing, was still hopeful that his city might still land a club, given Cronin's hint that the American League's maneuvering was not necessarily complete. Even Emanuel Celler, perhaps the owners' harshest critic on Capitol Hill, said he was pleased. "He's been fooled because the National League has put a team in New York," said Shea. "He apparently doesn't understand yet what has happened."

Or perhaps he did.

The future was upon them all. By 1962, there would be four new teams. And for now it did not matter that the new clubs would be at a great disadvantage when they played the established teams. The very scenario that Rickey had warned against had come to pass: not a new order, where a growing population of fans could come to their ballparks assured that on any given afternoon or evening their team could beat any foe. Instead, the men who dominated the game, Walter O'Malley and Del Webb, had succeeded after three years of delay in devising a formula for getting Congress off their backs by shifting one franchise and adding four second-division novelty acts. O'Malley and Webb were wealthy and successful men, and for their cleverness they would be rewarded in the months to come with money—and in the case of Del Webb, with what he valued above all else, a new stadium to build in Anaheim, California.

And if there was still a lingering illusion about where the great game's power resided, it was put to a rest when the commissioner finally spoke. No one, it seemed, had thought it necessary to fill him in on all the changes about to come to his game.

"I haven't seen anything officially yet," said Ford Frick. "There are so many angles to consider, such as ball parks and what to do regarding players, that I cannot make any comment until I have talked to the people involved officially."

Not that this would have any bearing on the shape of things to come. The "people involved" had spoken.

▪ EPILOGUE ▪

The Continental League never played a game or fielded a team, and it vanished a year after its birth. The name itself is largely forgotten, evoking the sort of response heard at high school reunions when someone mentions a classmate whose face cannot quite be recalled. But the story, though told less and less, lived on: an upstart rival league that forced the majors to expand.

New teams did come to the American League in 1961 and to the National League in 1962, and with the addition of four new clubs in 1969, each league split into two divisions. Some of the men who had joined with Branch Rickey and Bill Shea stayed on in baseball, and when they spoke of their rebellion it was with a wink and a nod, as if to dampen any illusions that they had ever been serious about striking out on their own. "It was ridiculed as a sham," Craig Cullinan once said, "but on the contrary it was an enormous success because it ran what became the biggest bluff in the history of professional sports."

The others did not disagree, and so in the years to come the league would be remembered as little more than a spectacular ruse, a con. Cullinan may have wished to be regarded as one of "Mr. Rickey's boys," and may have been sincere in the confessional letter he sent on the eve of 1960 World Series, expressing his sorrow and his regret for the league's failure to remain united behind Rickey that August in Chicago. But as Rickey had come to suspect, the men who had enlisted in his crusade did not share his vision for the league and for the game. Rather, they were the spiritual heirs of Charlie Weeghman, who had thrown in with the Federal League so that he might win a place in the majors.

And who could blame them? To have stayed with Rickey might well have meant all the struggles, losses, headaches, and prospects of failure that came with the outlaw life. Cullinan and the others had needed Rickey; he knew everyone, and perhaps his reputation and presence would be enough to broker a deal—teams for them all under the umbrella of organized baseball. Rickey was not without his own considerable vanity, and early on he plotted as if he thought this way, too. In fact, he was so confident of his plan that he allowed himself to believe that the owners—*his friends*—would surely appreciate and accept its wisdom. Even when they turned against him and worked furiously to defeat him, he did not give up on his belief that he had devised a way to save the game. If the owners would not accept it, he would do it without them.

There is nothing in Rickey's letters or papers that remotely suggests that he regarded the Continental League as a "bluff." He thought it was real. Despite his protestations about the burdens of age, he threw himself into the job with the energy of a young man who saw a higher purpose in his work. To read his correspondence is to sense the excitement of a man who believes that he is onto something grand: he would do what only Ban Johnson had succeeded in doing—create a new and better major league. Rickey went to his grave believing that had the imperious Johnson commanded the Continentals "it would surely be in existence today as a third major league of eight clubs."

Still, by all appearances things worked out well for the Continental League cities, even though the American League reneged on the deal Rickey thought had been struck in Chicago. New York and Houston got teams, and Minneapolis–St. Paul got the Senators, who, despite their decades of futility, quickly became contenders as the Minnesota Twins. In 1965, they won the pennant. Atlanta got a team in 1966, when the Braves abandoned Milwaukee. The others would have to wait. In 1972, Dallas–Ft. Worth got the expansion Washington Senators, who had been as unsuccessful as their predecessors in the nation's capital, on the field and at the gate. The team was renamed the Texas Rangers. Toronto got the Blue Jays in 1977. It took thirty-three years for Denver to land a club, the Colorado Rockies, who debuted in 1993. Only Buffalo was left out, even as Oakland, San Diego, Montreal, Kansas City (again), Milwaukee (again), Seattle, Miami, Phoenix, Tampa–St. Petersburg, and Washington, D.C. (again) became big-league towns.

The owners may have accepted the wisdom of expansion, but they were not prepared to offer franchises without a price. Although the big leagues did not impose franchise fees on that first group of newcomers in 1960, each new club was required to pay $2.1 million for the players made available by the owners for a draft—fifteen of the forty men they would have under contract. In addition, the New York Mets and the Los Angeles Angels each paid hundreds of thousands of dollars to the Yankees and to the Dodgers in restitution for invading their towns.

Baseball extended its reach across the country, just as Rickey had wanted. But as he had predicted, the new clubs could not compete with the established teams and remained buried in the second division for most of the 1960s. One early exception was the Angels' third-place finish in 1962, their second season; they finished ninth the following year. Rickey had even predicted that a team stocked with rookies and castoffs would win no more than forty games, which was just what happened to the 1962 Mets.

Dreadful as they were, however, the Mets were among the best-drawing teams in the league. They were so popular that they drew only two hundred thousand fewer fans to their temporary home at the Polo Grounds in 1963 than the reigning world champion Yankees did in the Bronx. In 1964, the Mets moved to their new home in Flushing Meadows, to the stadium that had been so much at the center of the fortunes of the Continental League, and would outdraw the Yankees for the next twelve seasons.

The Mets' improbable World Series victory in 1969 was, for the owners, proof of their wisdom. The worst team in the history of the game now stood as champions, and what better way to enhance the tale than to place it in the context of all those dreadful seasons that came before. That same season, the Houston Astros drew 1.4 million fans to their domed ballpark—sixth best in the league, despite their having finished next to last in their division—and the Senators had their best season in memory, drawing 918,000 and finishing with a rare winning record. The transplanted Twins had another good season, drawing their customary 1.3 million and capturing the American League's Western Division championship.

Looking at those numbers, it was not unreasonable to conclude that as the decade drew to a close, all was good with the game. Despite their endless pleas of poverty, the owners were almost all doing well; almost every team was turning a profit. Those owners who had decided to sell—there were ten changes of ownership during the 1960s—discovered that the values of their franchises had grown considerably. The average sale price of $7.7 million reflected a doubling of franchise values since the 1950s, which, in turn, had doubled over the average value in the 1940s. In fact, franchise values were 70 percent higher by the 1960s than they had been fifty years earlier. Among the sellers were Del Webb and Dan Topping, who had paid $2.8 million for the Yankees in 1945 and sold the team to CBS in 1964 for $14 million. "The best deal I ever made," Webb said after he and Topping quintupled their investment.

It would soon become clear, however, that Webb and Topping had chosen a wise time to cash out. The fortunes of their team were about to decline, as would those of the game. A new sport—professional football—was gaining on baseball, doing so primarily by drawing on the very lessons that Branch Rickey had preached in vain.

The men who ran baseball, meanwhile, continued to go about their business as if nothing had changed. They remained untroubled by the enduring disparity in income and performance between rich and poor teams, especially as television money became an ever more lucrative source of each team's income—from 10 percent on average in 1950 to 28 percent by 1970. The money came nationally and locally, and while the national television contracts grew by 20 percent over the decade, this money was split evenly among the teams—a practice that began in 1965; before then, the money had been divided by game-of-the-week appearances, a formula that most benefited the Yankees, whose share in 1964 was $550,000, compared to the St. Louis Cardinals, who made only $100,000.

Baseball had never embraced the idea of sharing; for years the less pros-perous teams had been powerless to stop the richer clubs from cutting the percentage of the gate that went to the visiting team. Each club, however, could keep all its local broadcast revenue, which grew by 13 per-cent during the 1960s. This meant that while Houston earned $1.4 mil-lion from its local broadcasts in 1964, Washington took in only $300,000.

Still, one owner in particular had calculated that the money to be made in selling those local television rights paled before what he stood to make if did not let people watch his team's games for free. Walter O'Malley continued blacking out Dodgers games, home and away, except for the eleven games his club played against the Giants in San Francisco, as he continued to bank on the possibilities of pay TV. Matty Fox never did make good on his boast of wiring Los Angeles and San Francisco; Skiatron went under and Fox died in 1964. By then, however, another firm, Subscription Television Inc., had wired 2,500 homes in a four-square-mile section of West Los Angeles. The network was far smaller than what the firm had promised its shareholders, among them the Dodgers and the Giants. But the number of homes was sufficient to allow the firm to launch its first pay-per-view baseball telecast on July 17, 1964, with the Dodgers hosting the Cubs. The game cost each subscriber $1.50. It was aired in color, and five cameras followed the action. O'Malley was so pleased with the quality of the picture that he considered installing monitors around the ballpark. But the foes of pay TV—led by movie theater owners—mounted a vigorous campaign to halt the telecasts. They succeeded in placing on the ballot a referendum banning paid telecasts, and that November the measure passed.

Even with that setback, no owner profited as handsomely as did O'Malley during the 1960s. In 1962, he opened his new ballpark, and a beautiful thing it was: modern and spacious, and on summer nights it was impossible to visit Dodger Stadium and not believe that O'Malley had made a very judicious move when he abandoned Brooklyn. That season 2.8 million patrons came to the new park—a million more than had come to see the team in their last year at the Coliseum, and 1.7 million more than had come to Ebbets Field in 1957. The Dodgers would con-sistently draw close to 2.5 million fans for each of the next four seasons. O'Malley was able to re-create in Los Angeles what he had inherited from Rickey in Brooklyn—a winning team that did not necessarily win every season. O'Malley understood that a team that won every season was less of an attraction than the team that offered the *promise* of success—witness all those empty World Series seats at Yankee Stadium during Stengel's championship years. In their first five seasons at Dodger Stadium, the Dodgers won three pennants and two World Series.

Nor did O'Malley suffer too dearly from denying himself the revenue from a lucrative local television contract. As part of the deal that allowed the American League into Los Angeles, the Angels agreed to play four seasons at Dodger Stadium, where O'Malley charged an annual rent of $200,000 or 7.5 percent of their revenue, whichever was higher. He also insisted on taking all the money from parking and concessions and on charging the Angels for half the cost of landscaping, toilet paper, paper towels, and window cleaning, even though their offices had no windows. The Angels mercifully moved to their new stadium in Anaheim in 1966. That stadium's opening marked a triumphant final bow to the game for Del Webb. Having been denied the chance to build Dodger Stadium, he had won the $16 million contract to build Anaheim Stadium.

Webb's final years as a Yankees owner had been good ones on the field. The Yankees won the World Series in the first two seasons after Stengel's firing, and they followed with pennants in 1963 and 1964, tying their own record for five consecutive league championships. Yet, attendance slipped even as the team continued: 1.8 million fans came to Yankee Stadium in 1961, a figure that fell to 1.5 million in 1962 and 1.3 million in 1963 and 1964. Then the tailspin began. The team fell to sixth place in 1965 and in 1966. The stars were aging: Whitey Ford retired in 1967, and Mantle hung on through 1968, his skills so diminished that he ended the season hitting .237, with eighteen home runs and fifty-four runs batted in as a transplanted first baseman who somehow managed to drag his worn and aching body through 144 games. The farm system was no longer bursting with the best prospects, not after 1965 when the owners instituted a player draft designed to keep the wealthiest teams from hoarding the best young talent. Much as Paul Richards had warned in *Look* magazine against the perils of the Yankees' dominance, the American League was more and more deprived of its greatest box-office attraction. The Twins, Orioles, Red Sox, and Tigers became pennant winners. But with the exception of a terrific four-team pennant race that Boston won in 1967, the American League races tended to be as uneventful as those in the years when the Yankees had pulled ahead and won easily.

Attendance, as always, varied with a team's fortunes, but across both leagues a troubling pattern emerged in the 1960s: the addition of four new teams had not brought a boon in spectators. Twenty million people had attended ball games in 1960; an additional 2.5 million came to the expanded schedule of games in 1962. But attendance slipped by 1.3 million in 1963. Total attendance rose to 25.2 million in 1966 but then fell by almost a million in 1967 and by 2 million in 1968. More alarming was the average game attendance, which stood at 14,000 in 1969, lower by 2,000 than it had been in 1960.

Rickey had been right in his prediction about the fleeting impact of novelty acts on the gate. The Mets may have drawn well, but in Houston the initial excitement in having a big-league team quickly subsided, and as it did attendance dropped: the Colt .45s drew 924,000 spectators in their first season but only 700,000 in each of the next two years while the city waited for the Astrodome to be completed. The team changed its name, and in its first season playing indoors its economic fortunes improved, when it drew 2.2 million patrons to "the eighth wonder of the world." But the Astros typically finished next to last—the cellar belonged to the Mets for most of the 1960s—and did not have a winning season until 1972.

Rickey had envisioned a fundamental change in the nature of the game: the imposition of competitive balance through the sharing of money, scouting, and, as a result, talent. He had subscribed to Ban Johnson's belief that competition was relative; it did not matter whom a team played so long as the outcome was in doubt. It was not only the new clubs that suffered on the field: the perennially weaker franchises—the Chicago Cubs, the Kansas City Athletics—remained losers at the gate and in the standings, so much so that in 1962 the lowest attendance in the major leagues—609,000 for the season—was at Wrigley Field, the park that Charlie Weeghman built.

Rickey had also warned that the game risked seeing its appeal diminish as other sports caught the nation's fancy. And with the rise of Lamar Hunt's American Football League, that was precisely what happened.

The AFL did not have an easy birth. There were struggles in the early years: Hunt felt compelled to relocate his club from Dallas to Kansas City in 1963; money troubles were particularly acute for the New York Titans, whose owner, Harry Wismer, struggled to meet his payroll and sold season tickets out of his apartment. In its inaugural season of 1960, the AFL averaged 16,500 spectators a game. In 1961, however, the number rose to 18,000 and to 20,500 in 1962. In fact, attendance would rise each season, and by 1969 had soared to 29,500—nearly twice that of 1960.

The Houston Oilers—with their star running back, Billy Cannon—won the first two AFL championships, and in those first two seasons the league appeared to be facing the same sorry fate of the All-America Football Conference, whose fortunes had declined under the perennial dominance of the Cleveland Browns. But the Dallas Texans won the title in 1962 and the San Diego Chargers in 1963. In fact, the league was so well balanced that by the end of the decade, seven of the original eight AFL teams—the league would add franchises in Cincinnati and Miami in 1966—had played for the league championship; only the Denver Broncos had fallen short.

The rising popularity of the AFL did not go unnoticed by its rival. The NFL and its most passionate defenders may have derided the new league for its perceived lack of toughness—too much passing; too little defense. But Pete Rozelle, the NFL commissioner, had seen much in the AFL to emulate. Chief among these was the idea of what Rozelle would call "league think"—the understanding that all could profit if they could see beyond their own narrow interests. At the core of this belief was the idea of sharing money, an idea that Hunt had imposed upon his league and for which he refused to take credit. He first got the idea, he later said, sitting in at a meeting of the Continental League, and listening to Branch Rickey.

"I met Mr. Rickey only once (during a planning session regarding the Continental League), and I do recall hearing his idea about sharing TV revenue for the proposed Continental League," he wrote in 2001 to

Rickey's biographer, Lee Lowenfish. "I did copy this idea in relation to the start of the American Football League."

In early 1966, Hunt and Tex Schramm, the president and general manager of the NFL's Dallas Cowboys, began meeting secretly to discuss a merger of the two leagues: competition for the best players had set off a costly bidding war. Three months later, the two sides agreed to join together in 1970 to form a newly expanded NFL that would be divided into two conferences. The two leagues also agreed to play a championship game in the intervening seasons—a contest that, like the merger, Rozelle had once insisted would never happen. The NFL's Green Bay Packers won the first two Super Bowls, but the perceived disparity between the leagues evaporated in January 1969 when the AFL champion New York Jets upset the highly favored Baltimore Colts in Super Bowl III.

In 1972, the Gallup Organization asked Americans to rank their favorite sports. The question had last been posed in 1960, and the change was striking: baseball, which had been the favorite of 34 percent of the respondents in 1960, had fallen to 24 percent. Football, favored by 21 percent in 1960, had seen its popularity rise to 32 percent.

Football did enjoy advantages that baseball did not. Teams played only once a week, which enabled a visionary broadcaster like Roone Arledge to replicate with the professionals what he had done with the college game: building the anticipation of an event, and not merely a game. Professional football also imposed a blackout on home games, so those fans who wanted to see their teams had to attend in person. There were no local television contracts, only a national package, as Rickey had hoped to implement in the Continental League. And because the professionals played during the day on Sunday, a growing audience of fans began to build their days not around one game but two; by carrying a second game that did not feature the local club—and with a second game always on another network—football fans began seeing the game as a national sport and developed an interest in the fortunes of teams far from home.

Football's greatest advantage, however, lay not on the field or on the screen, but in having powerful leaders—Lamar Hunt and Pete Rozelle—to whom the owners deferred. The AFL founder had displayed his loyalty when it most mattered, refusing to abandon Bob Howsam when the NFL tried to divide the fledgling league. Rozelle, meanwhile, succeeded in guiding his league because the older men who had founded the NFL were willing to accept his vision for their collective success. Baseball, on the other hand, had chosen as its commissioners the feckless Ford Frick, who was followed by an ineffectual retired general, William Eckert, and then by Bowie Kuhn, of whom it was often said that his greatest loyalty was to his most powerful patron, Walter O'Malley. If football was run as a monarchy, then baseball was ruled by warlords, for whom power and wealth had always come at the expense of everyone else.

So baseball rumbled on. It remained what it had been since the earliest professional days: a local game built upon local followings. There may have been televised World Series and games of the week. But the essential, if unquantifiable quality that sustained the sport decade after decade, the daily conversation between friends and strangers—*Did you catch yesterday's game? Can you believe how they blew that one?*—remained focused on the daily fortunes of the home team. Change, of course, did come to baseball with the end of the reserve clause in 1974 and the advent of free agency; with the first stabs at parity through revenue sharing, and with long-overdue innovations in broadcasting.

But by the time adaptation was imposed upon the game, the momentum in popularity had swung so dramatically toward football that when Gallup next conducted a poll on fan preferences in 1981, football was the choice of 38 percent of the respondents and baseball had fallen to 16 percent. Baseball's popularity would continue to slide; by 2007 it would slip into a virtual tie in popularity with basketball, each of them trailing football by roughly 30 percentage points. By then the game had endured strikes in 1972, 1981, and 1994, the last of which forced the first cancellation of the World Series since 1904.

Could the Continental League have forestalled or even reversed the slide in baseball's fortunes? Football may have been simply too alluring. But it does not feel too great a leap to think of what might have been. The AFL, after all, was born at the same time and faced many of the same obstacles that confronted the Continentals: an established rival that did all it could to defeat it and a pool of players that, early on, were not in a position to compete with those in the NFL. Granted, the NFL did not enjoy baseball's blanket antitrust exemption, and the AFL was free to recruit from the nation's colleges. But the AFL also recognized and tapped into a source of players the NFL had long ignored: the historically black colleges—just as Rickey had believed that there existed a great pool of baseball talent to be tapped in the Caribbean.

Like the Continental League, the AFL brought professional football to cities that had no teams of their own. And even if those teams fared poorly at first, the fans who might have stayed away when the teams lost returned when, after a losing season or two, their fortunes improved. The Oakland Raiders, after all, were not playing the Green Bay Packers, not yet at least. They were playing the Boston Patriots or the Denver Broncos or the Buffalo Bills, and with the annual infusion of new and more talented men—the draft always favors the weakest teams—there was reason to believe that on any given Sunday their team could beat any other. There is also every reason to believe that, given the formula that Rickey had devised—and which Hunt was only too happy to borrow— an eight-team league playing baseball in New York and in new towns against teams of comparable ability might have enjoyed some of the same success as the American Football League.

Branch Rickey did not want to force a rival upon the major leagues; he wanted to be embraced. The owners, however, saw in Rickey's plan the very threat from which the antitrust exemption had protected them: competition. The exemption had bred lassitude and arrogance and gave them no compelling reason to change. The NFL owners may have been no more welcoming about a competitor, but Hunt gave them no choice. They would have to change. And so they did.

The abandonment of the Continental League by the men who helped found it, however, left baseball free to go about its affairs with a minimum of disruption. And to this day the game pays a price for its enduring hubris and greed: the knowledge of what might have been.

Baseball has never been more successful than it is today. Attendance is higher than it has ever been—sellouts, all but unheard of a generation ago, are common—and more teams now play for pennants than ever before, a phenomenon aided since 2005 by the imposition of a more equitable system of revenue sharing. Franchises now command an average value of $472 million; the Yankees are estimated to be worth $1.3 billion.

But football franchises are worth nearly twice as much—an average of $957 million. And there is something more: the most valuable football team, the Dallas Cowboys, is valued at $1.5 billion—twice as much as the Minnesota Vikings, who are valued at $782 million, last in the league. On the other hand, baseball's lowest-valued franchise, the Florida Marlins, are worth $256 million—one-fifth the value of the Yankees. But perhaps the greatest evidence of the wisdom of football's embrace and imposition of parity is the phenomenon of the Green Bay Packers, a publicly owned team that plays in a city with a population of just over one hundred thousand—as small a market as exists in professional sports—but has become one of sports' most storied franchises. For all the success of such "small market" clubs as the Oakland Athletics and Minnesota Twins, it is hard, if not impossible, to imagine a baseball team playing in a city roughly the size of Green Bay, Wisconsin—say Peoria, Illinois, or Lowell, Massachusetts—and enjoying the Packers' success. Not the way baseball does business.

The enduring irony of the AFL is that in return for sticking together the league's founding owners were rewarded with the very thing the Continental League owners had rushed so recklessly to seize: a place in the big league—not as bottom dwellers, but as equals.

Casey Stengel did not stay away from the game long. In 1962, he returned to the Polo Grounds, where forty years earlier he had played for John McGraw, this time to manage the Mets. There he was reunited with George Weiss, whom the Yankees had fired soon after they had let Stengel go. Together Weiss and Stengel built a dreadful club, having calculated that the fans would come if they could see familiar, if aging, faces: Gil Hodges, Richie Ashburn, Gene Woodling, Frank Thomas, Vinegar Bend Mizell, Clem Labine, and later, Duke Snider. But, as Jimmy Cannon had written in 1960 in his open letter to Joan Whitney Payson, the only manager in the game who could draw at the box office was Casey. And that he did.

Gone was any pretense of genius. Instead, he was reduced once again to playing the clown, holding court to dazzle his writers as he carped about the utter futility of his team—"Can't anybody here play this game?" he famously quipped. He was seventy-two now, and for all his talk about the possibilities that awaited the "youth of America" on the diamond, he was powerless to do much of anything with the club Weiss had put together. He managed for three and a half seasons and then, at a boozy party at Toots Shor's in July 1965, he lost his balance and fell, breaking his hip, an old man's injury. He never managed again.

Stengel was elected to the Hall of Fame in 1966; given his advanced years, the voters chose to honor him early rather than wait the required five years. He was still asked for autographs and, with his induction, always appended his signature with the words *Hall of Famer*. Still, he was gone from the game, and his last years were especially lonely; Edna slipped into senility, and when writer friends called to check in he was always grateful because, he told them, no one called anymore. He was eighty-five when he died on September 29, 1975, the day after the season ended.

Bill Shea was handsomely rewarded for bringing a new team to New York. There had been suggestions of naming the Flushing Meadows stadium for Branch Rickey, but Rickey insisted that the honor go to Shea, who became the only corporate lawyer ever to have a stadium bear his name. In time, he became perhaps the most politically well-connected attorney in town, and among the clients of his firm were the New York Mets and the New York Yankees. He also served on the board of directors of the Washington Redskins; he and Jack Kent Cooke bought a share of the team in 1961, though Shea later sold his stake.

In the years that followed his death in 1991 at the age of eighty-four, Shea Stadium, which had been heralded as the cutting edge of stadium architecture when it opened, had become an unloved anachronism, a vast, featureless bowl. Next door, in its parking lot, would rise a new stadium, which, like all the new ballparks, was designed to approximate the look and feel of those old, smaller parks that stadiums like Shea were built to replace. This was especially true of the Mets' new park, Citi Field, which sought to capture the look and sensibility of Ebbets Field—the ballpark that Walter O'Malley so desperately wanted to escape, and whose abandonment set in motion the drama that would bring Branch Rickey back to baseball, and, for a brief and heady time, the Continental League to life.

The men who followed Rickey would not stay long in baseball. Craig Cullinan and George Kirksey were pushed aside in Houston by Roy Hofheinz. Kirksey, always in search of a new scheme and a new life, moved to France, bought a Porsche, and was killed in a car accident in 1972 in the middle of the night on his way to a Grand Prix auto race. Cullinan died in 2004. Jack Kent Cooke never became a major-league owner. He left Toronto, became an American citizen, and bought the Washington Redskins, the Los Angeles Lakers, and the Los Angeles Kings. He also took an interest in the growing business of pay-per-view television and was a backer of several championship fights, most famously the first Ali-Frazier fight in 1971. He died in 1997.

By the time Shea Stadium was scheduled for demolition, only two of the Continental League's founders were still alive: Wheelock Whitney and Bob Howsam. Whitney, who owned stakes in the Twins and later in the Minnesota Vikings and Minnesota North Stars, had only happy memories of the time he spent with the Continentals, especially of his friendship with Rickey. He even kept the letter that Rickey had written to him on the flight back to New York after Whitney and the others had voted to scuttle the league.

Bob Howsam, who died in 2008, spent his final years living in the first of the retirement communities that Del Webb had built on the outskirts of Phoenix—a series of developments that brought Webb to such heights of prominence that in 1962 he was featured on the cover of *Time* magazine. Howsam had stayed with Hunt and the AFL for one season and then, having lost a quarter of a million dollars on the Denver Broncos, decided to sell. He was out of work when, in the late summer of 1964, Branch Rickey called.

Rickey, now eighty-two, was in St. Louis, the city where he had begun his career as a player and, more important, as an executive. The Cardinals' owner, August Busch, had brought Rickey back to the team's front office in 1962, not as general manager but as a consultant. The post was vaguely defined, and Rickey, incapable of suppressing his opinions and enthusiasms, quickly ran afoul of the general manager, Bing

Devine, whom he had hired out of high school twenty years earlier to work in the Cardinals' publicity office. Rickey had also alienated the press and the fans when it became known that he had written a memo asking that the team's great aging star, Stan Musial, be asked to retire. Musial was an icon and Rickey had blundered, badly.

By the time Rickey called Howsam, the team was foundering and Busch wanted Devine out. Busch asked Rickey to recommend a new general manager, and Rickey turned to Howsam. He arrived that August, and the team's fortunes quickly reversed. The Cardinals won the pennant by a game and defeated the Yankees in the World Series. But Rickey could not stop meddling, and as the team's fortunes began sliding in 1965, Busch decided that the old man had to go. He assigned the task to Howsam, who reached Rickey by phone in Florida.

"But Robert," Rickey said, hearing the news, "I had so looked forward to working with you." Howsam told him that he was considering resigning, but Rickey would not hear of it.

He was, at long last, gone from the game. He began writing his book about baseball. He still accepted speaking invitations, traveling widely and often. He suffered another heart attack in November 1965 but insisted, against his doctor's orders, on being discharged so that he could attend a Missouri-Oklahoma football game and then speak at the Missouri Sports Hall of Fame dinner. His theme was to be spiritual courage. As Rickey was about to recount a story from the Bible, he staggered and fell to the floor. "I don't believe I can continue," he said and then lost consciousness.

Branch Rickey slipped into a coma and lingered for twenty-six days before dying on December 9, 1965, just days before his eighty-fourth birthday.

Bob Howsam stayed on in St. Louis until 1967, when he moved to Cincinnati as the general manger of the Reds. He was, by his own admission, a demanding and remote boss; he did not think it his place to be his players' friend. But in Cincinnati, Howsam built a dynasty, the great Reds team of the 1970s, the Big Red Machine. He retired in 1985, admired for his skill in building a club, though by then regarded by the game's progressives as too conservative for the times.

He was seventy-five when baseball finally came to Denver in 1993—a generation after the Continental League's demise. His one regret was that his father-in-law, Big Ed Johnson, who had died in 1971, did not live to see big-league baseball come to his town. But Howsam was otherwise untroubled by the major leagues' long delay in making good on the promise it had made to the Continentals on that steamy day in Chicago in 1960, that one day all their cities would become members of the big leagues.

"I don't feel that way," he said of the way things turned out. "I don't feel that any of us felt that way."

After all, Howsam added, reflecting on his own long and distinguished career, "it all worked out so well."

▪ SOURCES ▪

The reporting in this book came primarily from personal interviews and from archival research.

Branch Rickey was an inveterate saver of paper, and his archives at the Library of Congress provided the bulk of the material on the founding and workings of the Continental League, as well as on Rickey's vision for a third major league. This material was augmented by the George Kirksey Papers at the University of Texas, the Estes Kefauver Collection at the University of Tennessee, the Kenneth B. Keating Papers at the University of Rochester, the Robert Moses Papers at the New York Public Library, and the Robert Wagner Papers at the New York City Archives.

Branch Rickey III was generous with his time in talking about his grandfather, as was Clark Griffith in talking about his father, Calvin Griffith. Patricia Shea Ryan and William Shea Jr. helped broaden my picture of their father, Bill Shea, as did Shea's friends and colleagues Milton Mollen and Kevin McGrath. Roger Noll was an invaluable resource and sounding board on understanding the economics of baseball, as were Marvin Miller and former commissioner Fay Vincent. Tom Villante helped explain the early days of sports broadcasting, especially from the perspective of Walter O'Malley, and Jim Spence offered a firsthand view of sports broadcasts at ABC under Roone Arledge. Wheelock Whitney and the late Bob Howsam were generous with their time in sharing their memories and insights about the Continental League. Judy Wilpon's memories offered a look into the league office. Joel Tarr and Bob Ruck helped broaden my understanding of Pittsburgh in 1960. Maury Allen took me into the Yankees' clubhouse, a view bolstered by the recollections of the late Jack Lang. Roy McHugh provided insights into the Pittsburgh Pirates.

I am grateful to those biographers who offered their time in deepening my understanding of their subjects: Robert Creamer on Casey Stengel; Lee Lowenfish on Branch Rickey; Mickey Herskowitz on Mickey Mantle; and Campbell Titchener on George Kirksey. In addition, my understanding of the game in the 1950s was bolstered by the baseball historians John Murdough of Cleveland, Russell Schneider of Cincinnati, David Finoli of Pittsburgh, and Andy McCue of the Society for American Baseball Research. Sally O'Leary helped put me in touch with the members of the 1960 Pittsburgh Pirates who, in turn, were so generous with their time: Joe Brown, Joe Christopher, Elroy Face, Bob Friend, Dick Groat, Vernon Law, Bob Oldis, Hal Smith, and Bill Virdon. My understanding of the team was augmented by interviews with Minnie Minoso and Jill Corey. Similarly, Jim Coates, Art Ditmar, Whitey Ford, Tony Kubek, Jerry Lumpe, Bill Skowron, and Ralph Terry fielded all my many questions about the New York Yankees.

My reporting drew me back to two wise souls who have since died: Buzzie Bavasi and Clem Labine. My work will not be the same without them.

I drew heavily on newspaper and magazine accounts and am grateful to the staff of the microforms reading room at Butler Library at Columbia University, whose collection includes articles cited from the *New York Times*, the *New York Post*, the *New York Herald Tribune*, the *New York World-Telegram*, the *New York Journal-American*, the *New York Amsterdam News*, the *Pittsburgh Courier*, and the *Milwaukee Journal*. In addition, I drew upon articles in the *Atlanta Journal-Constitution*, the *Boston Globe*, the *Chicago Tribune*, the *Los Angeles Times*, and the *Wall Street Journal*. The librarians at *Sports Illustrated*, in particular Natasha Simon, were, as always, generous with their files and their time. I am also grateful to the staff at the Pittsburgh Public Library for their assistance in my researching archival material from the *Pittsburgh Post-Gazette*. In addition, I drew upon articles from *Forbes*, the *Journal of Broadcasting and Electronic Media*, the *Journal of Sports Economics*, *Life*, *Look*, *McClure's*, the *New York Times Magazine*, the *New Yorker*, *Newsweek*, *Nine: The Journal of Baseball History and Culture*, the *Saturday Evening Post*, the *Sporting News*, *Television Magazine*, and *Time*.

The National Archives provided information about Dan Topping's contribution to Kenneth Keating's Senate campaign. The FBI provided copies of its file on Del Webb through the Freedom of Information Act.

The Web is a vast repository on all manner of baseball data, and several sites were invaluable: baseball-reference.com; baseball-almanac .com; ballpark sofbaseball.com; baseball-stats.net; bizofbaseball.com; and gallup.com.

I would like to note several particular citations. The section in chapter 2 on George Kirksey's conversation with Bob Smith comes from Campbell Titchener's *The George Kirksey Story*. The account of Casey Stengel's farewell press conference is drawn from Robert Creamer's *Stengel*. The section in chapter 9 recounting Kirksey's conversation with Del Webb about the American League possibly coming to Houston comes from Robert Reed's history of the Houston franchise, *A Six-Gun Salute*, which is also the source of Craig Cullinan's assessment of the legacy of the Continental League that appears in the epilogue.

I also relied on valuable histories, biographies, and other published accounts. A list of these sources follows.

Baldassaro, Lawrence, and Richard A. Johnson, eds. *The American Game: Baseball and Ethnicity*. Carbondale: Southern Illinois University Press, 2002.

Cannon, Jimmy. *Nobody Asked Me, But . . . : The World of Jimmy Cannon*. Edited by Jack Cannon and Tom Cannon. New York: Holt, Rinehart and Winston, 1978.

Caro, Robert A. *The Power Broker: Robert Moses and the Fall of New York*. New York: Alfred A. Knopf, 1974.

Castro, Tony. *Mickey Mantle: America's Prodigal Son*. Washington, D.C.: Brassey's, 2002.

Chandler, Happy, with Vance H. Trimble. *Heroes, Plain Folks, and*

Skunks: The Life and Times of Happy Chandler. New York: Simon and Schuster, 1989.

Creamer, Robert W. *Stengel: His Life and Times.* New York: Simon and Schuster, 1984.

Denton, Sally, and Roger Morris. *The Money and the Power: The Making of Las Vegas and Its Hold on America, 1947–2000.* New York: Alfred A. Knopf, 2001.

Falkner, David. *The Last Hero: The Life of Mickey Mantle.* New York: Simon and Schuster, 1995.

Finnerty, Margaret. *Del Webb: A Man, a Company.* Phoenix: Heritage Publishers, 1991.

Ford, Whitey, with Phil Pepe. *Slick.* New York: William Morrow, 1987.

Frick, Ford C. *Games, Asterisks, and People: Memoirs of a Lucky Fan.* New York: Crown, 1973.

Goldstein, Warren Jay. *Playing for Keeps: A History of Early Baseball.* Ithaca, N.Y.: Cornell University Press, 1989.

Golenbock, Peter. *Dynasty: The New York Yankees, 1949–1964.* Englewood Cliffs, N.J.: Prentice-Hall, 1975.

Gorman, Joseph Bruce. *Kefauver: A Political Biography.* New York: Oxford University Press, 1971.

Groat, Dick, and Bill Surface. *The World Champion Pittsburgh Pirates.* New York: Coward-McCann, 1961.

Harris, David. *The League: Inside the NFL.* New York: Bantam, 1986.

Havill, Adrian. *The Last Mogul: The Unauthorized Biography of Jack Kent Cooke.* New York: St. Martin's Press, 1992.

Hays, Samuel P., ed. *City at the Point: Essays on the Social History of Pittsburgh.* Pittsburgh: University of Pittsburgh Press, 1989.

Helyar, John. *Lords of the Realm: The Real History of Baseball.* New York: Villard Books, 1994.

Herskowitz, Mickey, with Danny Mantle and David Mantle. *Mickey Mantle: Stories and Memorabilia from a Lifetime with the Mick.* New York: Stewart, Tabori and Chang, 2006.

Holtzman, Jerome, ed. *No Cheering in the Press Box.* New York: Holt, Rinehart and Winston, 1974.

Horrigan, Jack. *The Other League: The Fabulous History of the American Football League.* Chicago: Follet Publishing Company, 1970.

Howsam, Robert Lee. *My Life in Sports*. 1999.

James, Bill. *The Bill James Guide to Baseball Managers: From 1870 to Today*. New York: Scribner, 1997.

Klatell, David A., and Norman Marcus. *Sports for Sale: Television, Money, and the Fans*. New York: Oxford University Press, 1988.

Koppett, Leonard. *Koppett's Concise History of Major League Baseball*. Philadelphia: Temple University Press, 1998.

Lowenfish, Lee. *Branch Rickey: Baseball's Ferocious Gentleman*. Lincoln: University of Nebraska Press, 2007.

Lubove, Roy, ed. *Pittsburgh*. New York: New Viewpoints, 1976.

———. *Twentieth-Century Pittsburgh: Government, Business and Environmental Change*. New York: John Wiley and Sons, 1969.

Mantle, Mickey, with Mickey Herskowitz. *All My Octobers: My Memories of Twelve World Series When the Yankees Ruled Baseball*. New York: HarperCollins, 1994.

Maraniss, David. *Clemente: The Passion and Grace of Baseball's Last Hero*. New York: Simon and Schuster, 2006.

McComb, David G. *Houston: The Bayou City*. Austin: University of Texas Press, 1969.

Nealon, C., R. Nottebart, S. Siegel, and J. Tinsley. "The Campaign for Major League Baseball in Houston." *Houston Review* 7, no. 1 (1985).

Noll, Roger G., ed. *Government and the Sports Business: Papers Prepared for a Conference of Experts, with an Introduction and Summary*. Washington, D.C.: Brookings Institution, 1974.

O'Brien, Jim. *Remembering Roberto: Clemente Recalled by Teammates, Family, Friends, and Fans*. Pittsburgh: James P. O'Brien, 1994.

O'Toole, Andrew. *Branch Rickey in Pittsburgh: Baseball's Trailblazing General Manager for the Pirates, 1950–1955*. Jefferson: McFarland and Company, 2000.

Peterson, Richard, ed. *The Pirates Reader*. Pittsburgh: University of Pittsburgh Press, 2003.

Polner, Murray. *Branch Rickey: A Biography*. New York: Atheneum, 1982.

Powers, Ron. *Supertube: The Rise of Television Sports*. New York: Coward-McCann, 1984.

Quinlan, Sterling. *Inside ABC: American Broadcasting Company's Rise to Power*. New York: Hastings House, 1979.

Quinn, Kevin G., and Paul B. Bursik. "Growing and Moving the Game: Effects of MLB Expansion and Team Relocation, 1950–2004." *Journal of Quantitative Analysis in Sports* 3, no. 2 (2007).

Quirk, James, and Rodney D. Fort. *Pay Dirt: The Business of Professional Sports*. Princeton, N.J.: Princeton University Press, 1992.

Rader, Benjamin G. *In Its Own Image: How Television Transformed Sports*. New York: Free Press, 1984.

Reed, Robert. *A Six-Gun Salute: An Illustrated History of the Houston Colt .45's*. Houston: Gulf Publishing Company, 1999.

Reiss, Steven A. "Professional Baseball and Social Mobility." *Journal of Interdisciplinary History* 11, no. 2 (Autumn 1980).

Rickey, Branch, with Robert Riger. *The American Diamond: A Documentary of the Game of Baseball*. New York: Simon and Schuster, 1965.

Ross, Charles K. *Outside the Lines: African Americans and the Integration of the National Football League*. New York: New York University Press, 1999.

Shecter, Leonard. *The Jocks*. Indianapolis: Bobbs-Merrill, 1969.

Spink, J. G. Taylor. *Judge Landis and Twenty-five Years of Baseball*. New York: Thomas Y. Crowell, 1947.

Titchener, Campbell B. *The George Kirksey Story: Bringing Major League Baseball to Houston*. Austin: Eakin Press, 1989.

Veeck, Bill, with Ed Linn. *Veeck as in Wreck: The Autobiography of Bill Veeck*. New York: Simon and Schuster, 1962.

Wade, Richard C. *The Urban Frontier: Pioneer Life in Early Pittsburgh, Cincinnati, Lexington, Louisville, and St. Louis*. Chicago: University of Chicago Press, 1964.

Wendel, Tim. *The New Face of Baseball: The One-Hundred-Year Rise and Triumph of Latinos in America's Favorite Sport*. New York: Rayo, 2003.

Zimbalist, Andrew. *Baseball and Billions: A Probing Look Inside the Big Business of Our National Pastime*. New York: Basic Books, 1992.

———. *In the Best Interests of Baseball? The Revolutionary Reign of Bud Selig*. Hoboken, N.J.: John Wiley and Sons, 2006.

———. *May the Best Team Win: Baseball Economics and Public Policy*. Washington, D.C.: Brookings Institution Press, 2003.

▪ ACKNOWLEDGMENTS ▪

I am deeply indebted to many people without whom this book would have been far less a pleasure, and infinitely more difficult to research and write.

No author could ask for a wiser and more enthusiastic editor than Paul Golob, who helped me craft the idea, and who in the ensuing many months remained an unflagging booster, an incisive critic, a fount of baseball knowledge, and a fellow sufferer through not one but two late-season collapses by the New York Mets. My friend and agent Barney Karpfinger is an author's dream: an advocate and guide who makes the writing life possible.

I was assisted in my archival research by Amelia Abreu, Nathaniel Friedman, Helen Hull, Mary M. Huth, Melanie D. G. Kaplan, Rodney A. Ross, and Jeremy Saucier. I am also grateful for the assistance of Rory Costello, David McComb, Lynne McHugh, and Bob Nottebart, as well as by Dan O'Connor of MLB Films, Courtney Urbano of the Pittsburgh Pirates, Lou Hernandez of the Chicago White Sox, and John Horne of the National Baseball Hall of Fame.

Tom Schilling and Dan Nachman offered essential insights about Denver and Mickey Mantle respectively. David Klatell and Richard Wald helped unravel the mysteries of the early days of television and sports. Miles Corwin, Sam Freedman, Mike Hoyt, Sandy Padwe, David

Remnick, Walter Shapiro, and Dan Sneider endured too much prattling on my part about Branch Rickey and Casey Stengel. I am grateful, as always, for the support of my parents, Herbert and Lorraine Shapiro, and my brother, James, and sister, Jill.

My greatest debt, now and always, is to my family—my wife, Susan Chira; my daughter, Eliza; and my son, Jake—who together fill my life with happiness that no words can fully capture.

This book, and everything else, is for them.

▪ INDEX ▪

ABOUT THE AUTHOR

MICHAEL SHAPIRO is the author of *The Last Good Season: Brooklyn, the Dodgers, and Their Final Pennant Race Together*. A professor at the Columbia School of Journalism, he is the author of five previous books, and his articles have appeared in the *New York Times, Sports Illustrated, Esquire*, the *Wall Street Journal*, and the *New Yorker*. He lives in New York City with his wife and two children.